D0058318

TAO SONG

AND

TAO DANCE

Other Books in the Soul Power Series

Tao II

Divine Transformation

Tao I

Divine Soul Mind Body Healing and Transmission System

Divine Soul Songs

The Power of Soul

Soul Communication

Soul Wisdom

TAO SONG
AND
TAO DANCE

*Sacred Sound, Movement, and Power
from the Source for Healing,
Rejuvenation, Longevity, and
Transformation of All Life*

Dr. and Master Zhi Gang Sha

ATRIA BOOKS
New York London Toronto Sydney New Delhi

Heaven's Library
Toronto

ATRIA BOOKS

A Division of Simon & Schuster, Inc.
1230 Avenue of the Americas
New York, NY 10020

Toronto, ON

Copyright © 2011 by Heaven's Library Publication Corp.

First Atria Books hardcover edition November 2011

ATRIA BOOKS and colophon are trademarks of Simon & Schuster, Inc.

Heaven's Library and Soul Power Series are trademarks of Heaven's Library Publication Corp.

For information about special discounts for bulk purchases,
please contact Simon & Schuster Special Sales at 1-866-506-1949
or business@simonandschuster.com.

The Simon & Schuster Speakers Bureau can bring authors to your live event. For more information or to book an event contact the Simon & Schuster Speakers Bureau at 1-866-248-3049 or visit our website at www.simonspeakers.com.

Manufactured in the United States of America

10   9   8   7   6   5   4   3   2   1

ISBN 978-1-4516-7312-8
ISBN 978-1-4516-7315-9 (ebook)

Contents

Soul Power Series

*T*HE PURPOSE OF life is to serve. I have committed my life to this purpose. Service is my life mission.

My total life mission is to transform the consciousness of humanity and all souls in all universes, and enlighten them, in order to create love, peace, and harmony for humanity, Mother Earth, and all universes. This mission includes three empowerments.

My first empowerment is to teach *universal service* to empower people to be unconditional universal servants. The message of universal service is:

> *I serve humanity and all universes unconditionally.*
> *You serve humanity and all universes unconditionally.*
> *Together we serve humanity and all souls in all universes unconditionally.*

My second empowerment is to teach *healing* to empower people to heal themselves and heal others. The message of healing is:

I have the power to heal myself.
You have the power to heal yourself.
Together we have the power to heal the world.

My third empowerment is to teach *the power of soul,* which includes soul secrets, wisdom, knowledge, and practical techniques, and to transmit Divine Soul Power to empower people to transform every aspect of their lives and enlighten their souls, hearts, minds, and bodies.

The message of Soul Power is:

> *I have the Soul Power to transform my consciousness*
> *and every aspect of my life and enlighten my soul,*
> *heart, mind, and body.*
> *You have the Soul Power to transform your conscious-*
> *ness and every aspect of your life and enlighten your*
> *soul, heart, mind, and body.*
> *Together we have the Soul Power to transform con-*
> *sciousness and every aspect of all life and enlighten*
> *humanity and all souls.*

To teach the power of soul is my most important empowerment. It is the key for my total life mission. The power of soul is the key for transforming physical life and spiritual life. It is the key for transforming and enlightening humanity and every soul in all universes.

The beginning of the twenty-first century is the transition period into a new era for humanity, Mother Earth, and all universes. This era is named the Soul Light Era. The Soul Light Era began on August 8, 2003. It will last fifteen thousand years. Natural disasters—including tsunamis, hurricanes, cyclones, earthquakes,

floods, tornados, hail, blizzards, fires, drought, extreme tempera-
tures, famine, and disease—political, religious, and ethnic wars,
terrorism, proliferation of nuclear weapons, economic challenges,
pollution, vanishing plant and animal species, and other such up-
heavals are part of this transition. In addition, millions of people
are suffering from depression, anxiety, fear, anger, and worry. They
suffer from pain, chronic conditions, and life-threatening illnesses.
Humanity needs help. The consciousness of humanity needs to be
transformed. The suffering of humanity needs to be removed.

The books of the Soul Power Series are brought to you by
Heaven's Library and Atria Books. They reveal soul secrets and
teach soul wisdom, soul knowledge, and practical soul techniques
for your daily life. The power of soul can heal, prevent illness,
rejuvenate, prolong life, and transform consciousness and every
aspect of life, including relationships and finances. The power of
soul is vital to serving humanity and Mother Earth during this
transition period. The power of soul will awaken and transform
the consciousness of humanity and all souls.

In the twentieth century and for centuries before, *mind over
matter* played a vital role in healing, rejuvenation, and life transformation. In the Soul Light Era, *soul over matter*—Soul Power—
will play *the* vital role to heal, rejuvenate, and transform all life.

There are countless souls on Mother Earth—souls of human
beings, souls of animals, souls of other living things, and souls of
inanimate things. *Everyone and everything has a soul.*

Every soul has its own frequency and power. Jesus had miraculous healing power. We have heard many heart-touching
stories of lives saved by Guan Yin's[1] compassion. Mother Mary's

---

1. Guan Yin is known as the Bodhisattva of Compassion and, in the West, as the Goddess of
Mercy.

love has created many heart-moving stories. All of these great souls were given Divine Soul Power to serve humanity. In all of the world's great religions and spiritual traditions, including Buddhism, Taoism, Christianity, Judaism, Hinduism, Islam, and more, there are similar accounts of great spiritual healing and blessing power.

I honor every religion and every spiritual tradition. However, I am not teaching religion. I am teaching Soul Power, which includes soul secrets, soul wisdom, soul knowledge, and practical soul techniques. Your soul has the power to heal, rejuvenate, and transform life. An animal's soul has the power to heal, rejuvenate, and transform life. The souls of the sun, the moon, an ocean, a tree, and a mountain have the power to heal, rejuvenate, and transform life. The souls of healing angels, ascended masters, holy saints, Taoist saints, Hindu saints, buddhas, and other high-level spiritual beings have great Soul Power to heal, rejuvenate, and transform life.

Every soul has its own standing. Spiritual standing, or soul standing, has countless layers. Soul Power also has layers. Not every soul can perform miracles like Jesus, Guan Yin, and Mother Mary. Soul Power depends on the soul's spiritual standing in Heaven. The higher a soul stands in Heaven, the more Soul Power that soul is given by the Divine. Jesus, Guan Yin, and Mother Mary all have a very high spiritual standing.

Who determines a soul's spiritual standing? Who gives the appropriate Soul Power to a soul? Who decides the direction for humanity, Mother Earth, and all universes? The top leader of the spiritual world is the decision maker. This top leader is the Divine. The Divine is the creator and manifester of all universes.

In the Soul Light Era, all souls will join as one and align their consciousnesses with divine consciousness. At this historic time, the Divine has decided to transmit divine soul treasures to humanity and all souls to help humanity and all souls go through Mother Earth's transition.

Let me share two personal stories with you to explain how I reached this understanding.

First, in April 2003 I held a Power Healing workshop for about one hundred people at Land of Medicine Buddha, a retreat center in Soquel, California. As I was teaching, the Divine appeared. I told the students, "The Divine is here. Could you give me a moment?" I knelt and bowed down to the floor to honor the Divine. (At age six, I was taught to bow down to my tai chi masters. At age ten, I bowed down to my qi gong masters. At age twelve, I bowed down to my kung fu masters. Being Chinese, I learned this courtesy throughout my childhood.) I explained to the students, "Please understand that this is the way I honor the Divine, my spiritual fathers, and my spiritual mothers. Now I will have a conversation with the Divine."

I began by saying silently, "Dear Divine, I am very honored you are here."

The Divine, who was in front of me above my head, replied, "Zhi Gang, I come today to pass a spiritual law to you."

I said, "I am honored to receive this spiritual law."

The Divine continued, "This spiritual law is named the Universal Law of Universal Service. It is one of the highest spiritual laws in the universe. It applies to the spiritual world and the physical world."

The Divine pointed to the Divine. "I am a universal servant." The Divine pointed to me. "You are a universal servant." The Divine swept a hand in front of the Divine. "Everyone and everything is a universal servant. A universal servant offers universal service unconditionally. Universal service includes universal love, forgiveness, peace, healing, blessing, harmony, and enlightenment. *If one offers a little service, one receives a little blessing from the universe and from me. If one offers more service, one receives more blessing. If one offers unconditional service, one receives unlimited blessing.*"

The Divine paused for a moment before continuing. "There is another kind of service, which is unpleasant service. Unpleasant service includes killing, harming, taking advantage of others, cheating, stealing, complaining, and more. If one offers a little unpleasant service, one learns little lessons from the universe and from me. If one offers more unpleasant service, one learns more lessons. If one offers huge unpleasant service, one learns huge lessons."

I asked, "What kinds of lessons could one learn?"

The Divine replied, "The lessons include sickness, accidents, injuries, financial challenges, broken relationships, emotional imbalances, mental confusion, and any kind of disorder in one's life." The Divine emphasized, "This is how the universe operates. This is one of my most important spiritual laws for all souls in the universe to follow."

After the Divine delivered this universal law, I immediately made a silent vow to the Divine:

> *Dear Divine,*
>
> *I am extremely honored to receive your Law of Universal Service. I make a vow to you, to all humanity, and to all souls in all universes that I will be an unconditional universal servant. I will give my total GOLD* [gratitude, obedience, loyalty, devotion] *to you and to serving you. I am honored to be your servant and a servant of all humanity and all souls.*

Hearing this, the Divine smiled and left.

My second story happened three months later, in July 2003, while I was holding a Soul Study workshop near Toronto. The Divine came again. I again explained to my students that the Divine had appeared, and asked them to wait a moment while I bowed down 108 times and listened to the Divine's message. On this occasion, the Divine told me, "Zhi Gang, I come today to choose you as my direct servant, vehicle, and channel."

I was deeply moved and said to the Divine, "I am honored. What does it mean to be your direct servant, vehicle, and channel?"

The Divine replied, "When you offer healing and blessing to others, call me. I will come instantly to offer my healing and blessing to them."

I was deeply touched and replied, "Thank you so much for choosing me as your direct servant."

The Divine continued, "I can offer my healing and blessing by transmitting my permanent healing and blessing treasures."

I asked, "How do you do this?"

The Divine answered, "Select a person and I will give you a demonstration."

I asked for a volunteer with serious health challenges. A man named Walter raised his hand. He stood up and explained that he had liver cancer, with a two-by-three-centimeter malignant tumor that had just been diagnosed from a biopsy.

Then I asked the Divine, "Please bless Walter. Please show me how you transmit your permanent treasures." Immediately,

I saw the Divine send a beam of light from the Divine's heart to Walter's liver. The beam shot into his liver, where it turned into a golden light ball that instantly started spinning. Walter's entire liver shone with beautiful golden light.

The Divine asked me, "Do you understand what software is?"

I was surprised by this question but replied, "I do not understand much about computers. I just know that software is a computer program. I have heard about accounting software, office software, and graphic design software."

"Yes," the Divine said. "Software is a program. Because you asked me to, I transmitted, or downloaded, my Soul Software for Liver to Walter. It is one of my permanent healing and blessing treasures. You asked me. I did the job. This is what it means for you to be my chosen direct servant, vehicle, and channel."

I was astonished. Excited, inspired, and humbled, I said to the Divine, "I am so honored to be your direct servant. How blessed I am to be chosen." Almost speechless, I asked the Divine, "Why did you choose me?"

"I chose you," said the Divine, "because you have served humanity for more than one thousand lifetimes. You have been very committed to serving my mission through all of your lifetimes. I am choosing you in this life to be my direct servant. You will transmit countless permanent healing and blessing treasures from me to humanity and all souls. This is the honor I give to you now."

I was moved to tears. I immediately bowed down 108 times again and made a silent vow:

Dear Divine,
*   I cannot bow down to you enough for the honor you have given to me. No words can express my greatest grati-*

tude. How blessed I am to be your direct servant to download your permanent healing and blessing treasures to humanity and all souls! Humanity and all souls will receive your huge blessings through my service as your direct servant. I give my total life to you and to humanity. I will accomplish your tasks. I will be a pure servant to humanity and all souls.

I bowed again. Then I asked the Divine, "How should Walter use his Soul Software?"

"Walter must spend time to practice with my Soul Software," said the Divine. "Tell him that simply to receive my Soul Software does not mean he will recover. He must practice with this treasure every day to restore his health, step by step."

I asked, "How should he practice?"

The Divine gave me this guidance: "Tell Walter to chant repeatedly: *Divine Liver Soul Software heals me. Divine Liver Soul Software heals me. Divine Liver Soul Software heals me. Divine Liver Soul Software heals me.*"

I asked, "For how long should Walter chant?"

The Divine answered, "At least two hours a day. The longer he practices, the better. If Walter does this, he could recover in three to six months."

I shared this information with Walter, who was excited and deeply moved. Walter said, "I will practice two hours or more each day."

Finally I asked the Divine, "How does the Soul Software work?"

The Divine replied, "My Soul Software is a golden healing ball that rotates and clears energy and spiritual blockages in Walter's liver."

I again bowed to the Divine 108 times. Then I stood up and offered three Soul Softwares to every participant in the workshop as divine gifts. Upon seeing this, the Divine smiled and left.

Walter immediately began to practice as directed for at least two hours every day. Two and a half months later, a CT scan and MRI showed that his liver cancer had completely disappeared. At the end of 2006 I met Walter again at a signing in Toronto for my book *Soul Mind Body Medicine*.[2] In May 2008 Walter attended one of my events at the Unity Church of Truth in Toronto. On both occasions Walter told me that there was still no sign of cancer in his liver. For nearly five years his Divine Soul Download healed his liver cancer. He was very grateful to the Divine.

This major event of being chosen as a direct divine servant happened in July 2003. As I mentioned, a new era for Mother Earth and all universes, the Soul Light Era, began on August 8, 2003. The timing may look like a coincidence but I believe there could be an underlying spiritual reason. Since July 2003 I have offered divine transmissions to humanity almost every day. I have offered more than ten divine transmissions to all souls in all universes.

I share this story with you to introduce the power of divine transmissions or Divine Soul Downloads. Now let me share the commitment that I made in *Soul Wisdom*,[3] the first book of my

2. *Soul Mind Body Medicine: A Complete Soul Healing System for Optimum Health and Vitality* (Novato, California: New World Library, 2006).
3. *Soul Wisdom: Practical Soul Treasures to Transform Your Life* (Toronto/New York: Heaven's Library/Atria Books, 2008).

Soul Power Series, and that I have renewed in every one of my books since:

From now on, I will offer Divine Soul Downloads in every book I write.

Divine Soul Downloads are permanent divine healing and blessing treasures for transforming your life. There is an ancient saying: *If you want to know if a pear is sweet, taste it.* If you want to know the power of Divine Soul Downloads, experience it.

Divine Soul Downloads carry divine frequency with divine love, forgiveness, compassion, and light. Divine frequency transforms the frequency of all life. Divine love melts all blockages, including soul, mind, and body blockages, and transforms all life. Divine forgiveness brings inner peace and inner joy. Divine compassion boosts energy, stamina, vitality, and immunity. Divine light heals, prevents sickness, rejuvenates, and prolongs life.

A Divine Soul Download is a new soul created from the heart of the Divine. The Divine Soul Download transmitted to Walter was a Soul Software. Since then, I have transmitted several other types of Divine Soul Downloads, including Divine Soul Herbs, Divine Soul Acupuncture, Divine Soul Massage, Divine Soul Operation, and Divine Soul Mind Body Transplants.

A Divine Soul Transplant is a new divine soul of an organ, a part of the body, a bodily system, cells, cell units, DNA, RNA, the tiny matter in cells, or the spaces between cells. When it is transmitted, it replaces the recipient's original soul of the organ, part of the body, system, cells, cell units, DNA, RNA, tiny matter in cells, or spaces between cells. A new divine soul can also replace the soul of a home or a business. A new divine soul can be transmitted to a pet, a mountain, a city, or a country to replace their original souls. A new divine soul can even replace the soul of Mother Earth.

A Divine Mind Transplant is also a light being created by the Divine. It carries divine consciousness to replace the original consciousness of the recipient's system, organ, part of the body, cells, cell units, DNA, RNA, tiny matter, or spaces.

A Divine Body Transplant is another light being created by the Divine. This light being carries divine energy and divine tiny matter to replace the original energy and tiny matter of the recipient's system, organ, part of the body, cells, cell units, DNA, RNA, tiny matter, or spaces.

Everyone and everything has a soul. The Divine can download any soul you can conceive of. These Divine Soul Downloads are permanent divine healing, blessing, and life transformation treasures. They can transform the lives of anyone and anything. Because the Divine created these divine soul treasures, they carry Divine Soul Power, which is the greatest Soul Power among all souls. All souls in the highest layers of Heaven will support and assist Divine Soul Downloads. Divine Soul Downloads are the crown jewel of Soul Power.

Divine Soul Downloads are divine presence. The more Divine Soul Downloads you receive, the faster your soul, heart, mind, and body will be transformed. The more Divine Soul Downloads your home or business receives and the more Divine Soul Downloads a city or country receives, the faster their souls, hearts, minds, and bodies will be transformed.

In the Soul Light Era, the evolution of humanity will be created by Divine Soul Power. Soul Power will transform humanity. Soul Power will transform animals. Soul Power will transform nature and the environment. Soul Power will assume the leading role in every field of human endeavor. Humanity will deeply understand that *the soul is the boss*.

Soul Power, including soul secrets, soul wisdom, soul knowledge, and practical soul techniques, will transform every aspect of human life. Soul Power will transform every aspect of organizations and societies. Soul Power will transform cities, countries, Mother Earth, all planets, stars, galaxies, and all universes. Divine Soul Power, including Divine Soul Downloads, will lead this transformation.

I am honored to have been chosen as a divine servant to offer Divine Soul Downloads to humanity, to relationships, to homes, to businesses, to pets, to cities, to countries, and more. In the last few years I have already transmitted countless divine souls to humanity and to all universes. I repeat to you now: *I will offer Divine Soul Downloads within each and every book of the Soul Power Series*. Clear instructions on how to receive these Divine Soul Downloads and, since 2010, Tao Soul Downloads[4] will be provided in the next section, "How to Receive the Divine and Tao Soul Downloads Offered in the Books of the Soul Power Series," as well as on the appropriate pages of each book.

I am a servant of humanity. I am a servant of the universe. I am a servant of the Divine. I am a servant of Tao. I am extremely honored to be a servant of all souls. I commit my total life and being as an unconditional universal servant.

I will continue to offer Divine and Tao Soul Downloads for my entire life. I will offer more and more Divine and Tao Soul Downloads to every soul. I will offer Divine and Tao Soul Downloads for every aspect of life for every soul.

---

4. Tao Soul Downloads are offered in the sixth and eighth books of the Soul Power Series, *Tao I: The Way of All Life* and *Tao II: The Way of Healing, Rejuvenation, Longevity, and Immortality*, as well as in this book.

I am honored to be a servant of Divine and Tao Soul Downloads.

Human beings, organizations, cities, and countries will receive more and more Divine and Tao Soul Downloads, which can transform every aspect of their lives and enlighten their souls, hearts, minds, and bodies. The Soul Light Era will shine Soul Power. The books in the Soul Power Series will spread Divine and Tao Soul Downloads, together with Soul Power—soul secrets, soul wisdom, soul knowledge, and practical soul techniques—to serve humanity, Mother Earth, and all universes. The Soul Power Series is a pure servant for humanity and all souls. The Soul Power Series is honored to be a Total GOLD[5] servant of the Divine, Tao, humanity, and all souls.

The final goal of the Soul Light Era is to join every soul as one in love, peace, and harmony. This means that the consciousness of every soul will be totally aligned with divine consciousness. There will be difficulties and challenges on the path to this final goal. Together we will overcome them. We call all souls of humanity and all souls in all universes to offer unconditional universal service, including universal love, forgiveness, peace, healing, blessing, harmony, and enlightenment. The more we offer unconditional universal service, the faster we will achieve this goal.

The Divine and Tao give their hearts to us. The Divine and Tao give their love to us. The Divine and Tao give Divine and Tao Soul Downloads to us. Our hearts meld with the Divine's and Tao's hearts. Our souls meld with the Divine's and Tao's souls. Our consciousnesses align with the Divine's and Tao's

---

5. Total GOLD means total gratitude, total obedience, total loyalty, and total devotion to the Divine and Tao.

consciousnesses. We will join hearts and souls together to create love, peace, and harmony for humanity, Mother Earth, and all universes.

> *I love my heart and soul*
> *I love all humanity*
> *Join hearts and souls together*
> *Love, peace and harmony*
> *Love, peace and harmony*

Love all humanity. Love all souls.
Thank all humanity. Thank all souls.
Thank you. Thank you. Thank you.

Zhi Gang Sha

How to Receive the Divine and Tao Soul Downloads Offered in the Books of the Soul Power Series

THE BOOKS OF the Soul Power Series are unique. For the first time in history, the Divine and Tao are downloading their soul treasures to readers as they read these books. Every book in the Soul Power Series will include Divine or Tao Soul Downloads that have been preprogrammed. When you read the appropriate paragraphs and pause for a minute, divine gifts will be transmitted to your soul.

In April 2005 the Divine told me to "leave Divine Soul Downloads to history." I thought, "A human being's life is limited. Even if I live a long, long life, I will go back to Heaven one day. How can I leave Divine Soul Downloads to history?"

In the beginning of 2008, as I was editing the paperback

edition of *Soul Wisdom*, the Divine suddenly told me: "Zhi Gang, offer my downloads within this book." The Divine said, "I will preprogram my downloads in the book. Any reader can receive them as he or she reads the special pages." At the moment the Divine gave me this direction, I understood how I could leave Divine Soul Downloads to history.

The Divine is the creator and spiritual father and mother of all souls.

Tao is the Source and creator of countless planets, stars, galaxies, and universes. Tao is The Way of all life. Tao is the universal principles and laws.

At the end of 2008 Tao chose me as a servant, vehicle, and channel to offer Tao Soul Downloads. I was extremely honored. I have offered countless Divine and Tao Soul Downloads to humanity and wan ling (all souls) in countless planets, stars, galaxies, and universes.

Preprogrammed Divine or Tao Soul Downloads are permanently stored within this book and every book in the Soul Power Series. If people read this book thousands of years from now, they will still receive the Tao Soul Downloads. As long as this book exists and is read, readers will receive the Tao Soul Downloads.

Allow me to explain further. Tao has placed a permanent blessing within certain paragraphs in this book. These blessings allow you to receive Tao Soul Downloads as permanent gifts to your soul. Because these Tao treasures reside with your soul, you can access them twenty-four hours a day—as often as you like, wherever you are—for healing, blessing, and life transformation.

It is very easy to receive the Divine and Tao Soul Downloads in the books of the Soul Power Series. After you read the special paragraphs where they are preprogrammed, close your eyes. Receive the special download. It is also easy to apply these divine and Tao treasures. After you receive a Divine or Tao Soul Download, I will immediately show you how to apply it for healing, blessing, and life transformation.

You have free will. If you are not ready to receive a Divine or Tao Soul Download, simply say *I am not ready to receive this gift.* You can then continue to read the special download paragraphs, but you will not receive the gifts they contain. The Divine and Tao do not offer Divine and Tao Soul Downloads to those who are not ready or not willing to receive the Divine's and Tao's treasures. However, the moment you are ready, you can simply go back to the relevant paragraphs and tell the Divine and Tao *I am ready.* You will then receive the stored special download when you reread the paragraphs.

The Divine and Tao have agreed to offer specific Divine and Tao Soul Downloads in these books to all readers who are willing to receive them. The Divine and Tao have unlimited treasures. However, you can receive only the ones designated in these pages. Please do not ask for different or additional gifts. It will not work.

After receiving and practicing with the Divine and Tao Soul Downloads in these books, you could experience remarkable healing results in your spiritual, mental, emotional, and physical bodies. You could receive incredible blessings for your love relationships and other relationships. You could receive financial blessings and all kinds of other blessings.

Divine and Tao Soul Downloads are unlimited. There can be a Divine or Tao Soul Download for anything that exists in the physical world. The reason for this is very simple. *Everything has a soul, mind, and body.* A house has a soul, mind, and body. The Divine and Tao can download a soul to your house that can transform its energy. The Divine and Tao can download a soul to your business that can transform your business. If you are wearing a ring, that ring has a soul. If the Divine downloads a new divine soul to your ring, you can ask the divine soul in your ring to offer divine healing and blessing.

I am honored to have been chosen as a servant of humanity, the Divine, and Tao to offer Divine and Tao Soul Downloads. For the rest of my life, I will continue to offer Divine and Tao Soul Downloads. I will offer more and more of them. I will offer Divine and Tao Soul Downloads for every aspect of every life.

I am honored to be a servant of Divine and Tao Soul Downloads.

What to Expect After You Receive Divine and Tao Soul Downloads

Divine and Tao Soul Downloads are new souls created from the heart of the Divine or the heart of Tao. When these souls are transmitted, you may feel a strong vibration. For example, you could feel warm or excited. Your body could shake a little. If you are not sensitive, you may not feel anything. Advanced spiritual beings with an open Third Eye can actually see a huge golden, rainbow, purple, or crystal light soul enter your body.

These divine and Tao souls are your yin companions[6] for life. They will stay with your soul forever. Even after your physical life ends, these divine and Tao treasures will continue to accompany your soul into your next life and all of your future lives. In these books, I will teach you how to invoke these divine and Tao souls anytime, anywhere to give you divine and Tao healing

---

6. A yang companion is a physical being, such as a family member, friend, or pet. A yin companion is a soul companion without a physical form, such as your spiritual fathers and mothers in Heaven.

or blessing in this life. You also can invoke these souls to radiate out to offer divine and Tao healing or blessing to others. These divine and Tao souls have extraordinary abilities to heal, bless, and transform. If you develop advanced spiritual abilities in your next life, you will discover that you have these divine or Tao souls with you. Then you will be able to invoke these souls in the same way in your future lifetimes to heal, bless, and transform every aspect of your life.

It is a great honor to have a divine or Tao soul downloaded to your own soul. The divine or Tao soul is a pure soul without bad karma. The divine or Tao soul carries divine and Tao healing and blessing abilities. The download does not have any side effects. You are given love and light with divine and Tao frequency. You are given divine and Tao abilities to serve yourself and others. Therefore, humanity is extremely honored that the Divine and Tao are offering Divine and Tao Soul Downloads. I am extremely honored to be a servant of the Divine, of Tao, of you, of all humanity, and of all souls to offer Divine and Tao Soul Downloads. I cannot thank the Divine and Tao enough. I cannot thank you, all humanity, and all souls enough for the opportunity to serve.

Thank you. Thank you. Thank you.

Foreword to the Soul Power Series

I HAVE ADMIRED DR. Zhi Gang Sha's work for some years now. In fact, I clearly remember the first time I heard him describe his soul healing system, Soul Mind Body Medicine. I knew immediately that I wanted to support this gifted healer and his mission, so I introduced him to my spiritual community at Agape. Ever since, it has been my joy to witness how those who apply his teachings and techniques experience increased energy, joy, harmony, and peace in their lives.

Dr. Sha's techniques awaken the healing power already present in all of us, empowering us to put our overall well-being in our own hands. His explanation of energy and message, and how they link consciousness, mind, body, and spirit, forms a dynamic information network in language that is easy to understand and, more important, to apply.

Dr. Sha's time-tested results have proven to thousands of students and readers that healing energies and messages exist within specific sounds, movements, and affirmative perceptions. Weaving in his own personal experiences, Dr. Sha's theories and practices of working directly with the life-force energy and spirit are practical, holistic, and profound. His recognition that Soul Power is most important for every aspect of life is vital to meeting the challenges of twenty-first-century living.

The worldwide representative of his renowned teacher, Dr. Zhi Chen Guo, one of the greatest qi gong masters and healers in the world, Dr. Sha is himself a master of ancient disciplines such as tai chi, qi gong, kung fu, the *I Ching*, and feng shui. He has blended the soul of his culture's natural healing methods with his training as a Western physician, and generously offers his wisdom to us through the books in his Soul Power Series. His contribution to those in the healing professions is undeniable, and the way in which he empowers his readers to understand themselves, their feelings, and the connection between their bodies, minds, and spirits is his gift to the world.

Through his Soul Power Series, Dr. Sha guides the reader into a consciousness of healing not only of body, mind, and spirit, but also of the heart. I consider his healing path to be a universal spiritual practice, a journey into genuine transformation. His professional integrity and compassionate heart are at the root of his being a servant of humankind, and my heartfelt wish for his readers is that they accept his invitation to awaken the power of the soul and realize the natural beauty of their existence.

Dr. Michael Bernard Beckwith
Founder, Agape International Spiritual Center

How to Receive Maximum Benefits from My Books

*L*IKE MANY PEOPLE worldwide, you may have read my books before. You may be reading my books for the first time. When you start to read my books, you may realize quickly that they include many practices for healing, rejuvenation, and longevity, as well as for transforming relationships and finances.

I teach the Four Power Techniques to transform all life. I will summarize each of the Four Power Techniques in one sentence:

Body Power: Where you put your hands is where you receive the benefits for healing and rejuvenation.

Soul Power: Apply Say Hello Healing and Blessing to invoke the Divine, Tao, Heaven, Mother Earth, and countless planets, stars, galaxies, and universes, as well as all kinds of spiritual fathers and mothers on Mother Earth and in all

layers of Heaven, to request their help for your healing, rejuvenation, and transformation of relationships and finances.

Mind Power: Where you put your mind, using creative visualization, is where you receive the benefits for healing, rejuvenation, and transformation of relationships and finances.

Sound Power: What you chant is what you become.

My books are unique. Each one includes many practices with chanting (Sound Power). I repeat some chants again and again in the books. The most important issue for you, dear reader, is to avoid thinking *I already know this*, and then quickly read through the text without doing the practices. That would be a big mistake. You will miss some of the most important parts of my teaching: the practices.

Imagine you are in a workshop. When the teacher leads you to meditate or chant, you have to do it. Otherwise, you will not receive the benefits from the meditation and chanting. People are familiar with the ancient Chinese martial art and teaching of kung fu. A kung fu master spends an entire lifetime to develop power. In one sentence:

Time is kung fu and kung fu is time.

You have to spend time to chant and meditate. Remember the one-sentence secret for Sound Power: *What you chant is what you become.* Therefore, when you read the practices where I am leading you to chant, please do it. Do not pass it by. The practices are the jewel of my teaching. Practice is necessary to transform and bring success to any aspect of your life, including health, relationships, finances, intelligence, and more.

There is a renowned spiritual teaching in Buddhism. Millions of people throughout history have chanted *Na Mo A Mi Tuo Fo*. They chant only this one mantra. They could chant *Na Mo A Mi Tuo Fo* for hours a day for their entire life. It is a great practice. If you are upset, chant *Na Mo A Mi Tuo Fo* (pronounced *nah maw ah mee twaw faw*). If you are sick, chant *Na Mo A Mi Tuo Fo*. If you are weak, chant *Na Mo A Mi Tuo Fo*. If you are emotional, chant *Na Mo A Mi Tuo Fo*. If you have relationship challenges, chant *Na Mo A Mi Tuo Fo*. If you have financial challenges, chant *Na Mo A Mi Tuo Fo*. To transform life takes time. You must understand this spiritual wisdom so that you will practice chanting and meditation more and more. The more you practice, the more healing and life transformation you could receive.

For success in any profession, one must study and practice again and again to gain mastery. My teaching is soul healing and soul transformation of every aspect of life. One must apply the Four Power Techniques again and again to receive the maximum benefits of soul healing and soul transformation for every aspect of your life.

If you go into the condition of *what you chant is what you become*, a wonderful healing result may come suddenly, and transformation of relationships and finances may follow. "Aha!" moments may come. "Wow!" moments may come.

I bring my workshop or retreat to you in every book. Practice each line of sacred Tao Song mantras seriously. Chant and meditate using the Four Power Techniques. Practice with me by using the DVD included with the first printing of this book or the video recordings posted on my YouTube channel, www.youtube .com/zhigangsha.

My books have another unique aspect: the Divine and Tao offer Soul Mind Body Transplants as you read. Divine and Tao Soul Mind Body Transplants are permanent healing and blessing treasures from the Divine and Tao.

These treasures carry Divine and Tao frequency and vibration, which can transform the frequency and vibration of your health, relationships, finances, intelligence, and more.

These treasures also carry Divine and Tao love, which melts all blockages and transforms all life.

These treasures carry Divine and Tao forgiveness, which brings inner joy and inner peace.

These treasures carry Divine and Tao compassion, which boosts energy, stamina, vitality, and immunity.

These treasures carry Divine and Tao light, which heals, prevents sickness, purifies and rejuvenates soul, heart, mind, and body, and transforms relationships, finances, and every aspect of life.

I summarize and emphasize the two absolutely unique aspects of my books: first, I bring my workshops and retreats to you in my books. Please practice seriously, just as though you were in a workshop with me in person. Second, as you read, you can receive permanent treasures (Soul Mind Body Transplants) from the Divine and Tao to transform your health, relationships, finances, and more.

Pay great attention to these two unique aspects in order to receive maximum benefits from this book and any of my books.

I wish you will receive maximum benefits from this book to transform every aspect of your life.

Practice. Practice. Practice.

Transform. Transform. Transform.

Enlighten. Enlighten. Enlighten.

Success. Success. Success.

List of Tao Soul Downloads

List of Figures

Foreword to Tao Song and Tao Dance

MASTER SHA IS divinely blessed and guided to heal the world and everything that is in it. From the smallest situation to the largest, he has the faithful gift of power to make things right.

Nothing in Master Sha's voice interferes. When the voice is completely free of interference, the voice simply is. His voice is incredible and carries incredible power. His vowel sounds are so clear and strong. Every sound from Master Sha's voice is so pure. This can only be because his voice is from and of the soul. Only the soul can produce sounds like that. His voice is amazing.

The Tao Song that Master Sha sings is a musical gift beyond the sound of any voice singing that you can hear every day. It holds a purity and a resonance that only he can lay claim to. His voice is beyond anything and that is what makes him the great teacher and healer. His voice is like the voice of God singing. God's voice in his body is so unique that it is definitely a healing sound.

Roberta Flack
Grammy Award–winning American songstress
and humanitarian

On Master Sha's Tao Song Singing, Teaching, and Training

MY NAME IS Helene Ziebarth. I am a professional singer, a voice teacher, and a vocal coach. My students include world-renowned opera singers.

I searched my whole life for the truth in singing and the deeper meaning. I empowered my singers always to sing better, and to sing with love and compassion. Something was missing, but I had not discovered what it was.

I found the answer when I met Master Sha in Montreal in 2008, and I had an "aha!" moment when he taught about singing from the soul.

I said, "I have been searching my whole life for the ancient singing secrets and for the secrets of healing, rejuvenation, and longevity. The solution has been given to me through Master Sha's teachings. I will never forget this moment."

After this initial meeting in 2008, I attended four more retreats with Master Sha in Atlanta, Germany, and Hawaii (twice).

I became a Divine Soul Teacher and Healer and received many divine treasures.

Master Sha's Soul Song—and now his Tao Song singing—has improved so much in the last few years. Words cannot express what has taken place. Master Sha's Tao Song singing is a very high-level professional voice. I do not hear any ego. There is a beauty in his voice that expresses the beauty of his soul, the Divine, Tao, and the universe. Master Sha sings from the Hui Yin area, which is at the bottom of the torso, between the genitals and anus. In my experience, singers who do this are very rare. Four examples that come to mind are Luciano Pavarotti, Plácido Domingo, Birgit Nilsson, and Maria Callas, four of the brightest stars in the operatic firmament.

Master Sha is not only a beautiful Tao Song singer, he is a powerful teacher to train people to sing. He uses the *divine* way to transform a person's singing by Divine Karma Cleansing and Divine Soul Mind Body Transplants. I have personally witnessed a one-time divine blessing that produced results equal to five to eight years of professional coaching.

I am astounded by Master Sha's divine way to sing and to train singers. I am very honored to be his student and to learn the divine wisdom and the divine way. Master Sha has offered a Divine Download to me to write a book.

I want to share that Master Sha's teaching is revolutionary for singers. It is the breakthrough way to empower singers to bring out their singing potential. As a vocal coach, I have used Master Sha's teaching system with professional singers. In one day—*in one session*—professional singers can experience significant transformation of their singing.

Master Sha is a divine teacher and healer. His divine way to train the general public to sing Soul Song and Tao Song and to train professional singers to transform their singing is a divine gift for humanity. I recommend every professional singer who can receive Master Sha's training to do so. This is a blessing to all: professional singers and the public.

I am very thankful for Master Sha's selflessness and generosity in sharing the ancient secrets, wisdom, knowledge, and practical techniques in order to teach people to sing and to empower professional singers. My singing has received tremendous transformation. I wish many professional singers can receive this same training and teaching.

I am very grateful. I thank you, Master Sha, for your teaching.

With love,
Helene Ziebarth

Introduction

$\mathcal{A}$UGUST 8, 2003, is a historic day that humanity should re-member forever. On that day, the Divine held a conference in Heaven and announced that the last universal era was ending and the new universal era was beginning.

Reincarnation is a universal law. Human beings reincarnate. Mother Earth reincarnates. Time reincarnates. Mother Earth's reincarnation goes through a cycle of phases or eras. Each one lasts fifteen thousand years. These eras are named:

- Shang Gu (上古, pronounced *shahng goo*—"far an-cient"). The most recent Shang Gu era lasted from about forty-five thousand years ago to about thirty thousand years ago.
- Zhong Gu (中古, pronounced *jawng goo*—"middle ancient"). The most recent Zhong Gu era lasted from about thirty thousand years ago to about fifteen thou-sand years ago.

- Xia Gu (下古, pronounced *shyah goo*—"near ancient"). The most recent Xia Gu era started about fifteen thousand years ago and ended on August 8, 2003.

On August 8, 2003, the most recent Xia Gu era ended and a new Shang Gu era started. It will again last fifteen thousand years, until about 17000 AD. Then a new Zhong Gu era will follow. It will also last fifteen thousand years. Then a new Xia Gu era will begin. This is the time reincarnation of Mother Earth.

Throughout history, every time there is a transition from one era to the next (from Shang Gu to Zhong Gu, from Zhong Gu to Xia Gu, or from Xia Gu to Shang Gu), Mother Earth goes through huge changes. These transition times are very important for Mother Earth.

Mother Earth is in such a transition period now. In the last few years, we have seen more and more natural disasters, including earthquakes, tsunamis, volcanic eruptions, hurricanes, floods, droughts, tornados, and more. Financial challenges and many other challenges are deeply affecting humanity and Mother Earth. Millions of people are suffering from all kinds of sickness in their spiritual, mental, emotional, and physical bodies. Wars, power struggles, greed—all kinds of unpleasant things are taking place all around us on Mother Earth now.

You may be wondering why humanity and Mother Earth are suffering like this. Millions of people are wondering. What are the root causes of the suffering? What can we do about the suffering? More and more people are searching for spiritual secrets, wisdom, knowledge, and practical techniques to transform the suffering of humanity and Mother Earth in order to enjoy good health, relationships, and finances.

There could be thousands of explanations for the causes of the suffering. There could be thousands of methods and techniques to transform the suffering. I would like to summarize my personal insights in a one-sentence secret:

Bad karma is the root cause of the suffering of humanity and Mother Earth.

Mother Earth is going through a special time of transition and humanity is enduring great suffering because of bad karma that has been created over thousands of years. War, killing, greed, corruption, stealing, cheating, taking advantage of others, power struggles, damaging Mother Earth, including cutting of forests, wrenching natural resources from the land and the water, testing nuclear weapons, pollution, and much more have created huge bad karma.

Karma is easy to understand. Karma is cause and effect. Humanity has harmed each other tremendously. Humanity has damaged Mother Earth almost beyond repair. These are the causes over thousands of years of recorded human history. The effects are what has been happening in front of our eyes in the last few years. These effects will continue.

According to the spiritual guidance that I have received from Heaven, Mother Earth's transition could last another ten years or more and become much heavier. We have to prepare humanity and Mother Earth to pass through this difficult time. The best way to help humanity and Mother Earth get through this difficult time is to join the hearts and souls of humanity in unconditional service, which is selfless service to others. This will empower humanity to self-clear its bad karma.

How can a person self-clear bad karma? One must offer love, forgiveness, compassion, and light to others. I have shared the divine teaching about these four qualities in previous books of my Soul Power Series.

Love melts all blockages and transforms all life.

When you experienced true love from your loved ones, from your spiritual fathers and mothers, and from the Divine and Tao, your heart was deeply moved, touched, and opened. You could have been moved and touched to tears. You could have been speechless.

True love is unconditional love. True love is pure love. True love is a golden key to unlock any door in your life, in the lives of your loved ones, and for Mother Earth and countless planets, stars, galaxies, and universes.

Forgiveness brings inner joy and inner peace.

Think about all of your relationships. Think about you and your spouse or partner, your girlfriend or boyfriend, your children and parents. Have you ever been upset in any of these relationships? Have you been irritated, angry, or jealous, or had vengeful thoughts? Think about your working relationships—with your colleagues and boss and with companies and organizations. Have you had similar blockages in any of these relationships? Think about other relationships—between companies, organizations, religions, and nations. Think about all the competition, conflict, and more in these relationships.

If unconditional forgiveness could be applied in all of these relationships, peace and harmony would occur. If forgiveness truly were to happen on any occasion and in any moment, there would be no conflict in a family, in a workplace, in a city, or in a country. There would be no conflict on Mother Earth.

Forgiveness is another golden key to transform all life by bringing inner joy and inner peace.

Compassion boosts energy, stamina, vitality, and immunity.

Compassion touches one's heart and soul deeply. To offer true compassion is to resolve conflicts easily. Compassion can remove all kinds of blockages. If one were to offer true compassion, every aspect of life could be deeply transformed. Compassion boosts energy, stamina, vitality, and immunity. Compassion is the third golden key to transform all life.

Light heals, prevents sickness, rejuvenates, and transforms every aspect of life, including relationships and finances.

Light is the fourth golden key to transform all life. A human being needs physical food to sustain and nourish physical life. A soul needs soul food to sustain and nourish soul life.

Light is soul food. Love, forgiveness, and compassion are also soul food. Light can remove all kinds of blockages to transform health, relationships, and finances.

Love, forgiveness, compassion, and light are the four golden keys to unlock any door in your life. They are four divine treasures and tools to transform all life. In this book, I will lead you in many practices to apply love, forgiveness, compassion, and light to self-clear bad karma and to transform every aspect of your life, including health, relationships, and finances.

How can humanity clear bad karma? Humanity must offer

love, forgiveness, compassion, and light to each other and to all souls. Unconditional service—selfless service—is the key for transforming the karma of humanity. There are thousands of organizations and groups on Mother Earth that teach and promote love, peace, harmony, and compassion. There are thousands of spiritual leaders who lead millions and billions of people to offer all types of unconditional service to humanity.

There are three ancient secrets for transforming bad karma:

- shen mi (身密, pronounced *shun mee*)
- kou mi (口密, pronounced *koe mee*)
- yi mi (意密, pronounced *yee mee*)

"Shen mi" means *body secret*. Many spiritual practitioners use special hand positions called mudras when they meditate. These special hand (and body) positions promote energy flow within the body to remove blockages. They open the heart and soul fully to receive love, forgiveness, compassion, and light from Heaven, Mother Earth, universes, the Divine, and Tao.

"Kou mi" means *mouth secret*. This secret is to chant mantras. There are many ancient mantras that are extremely powerful for healing, rejuvenation, purification, and cleansing bad karma.

Powerful mantras are generally created by a spiritual leader such as a buddha, saint, lama, or another kind of major spiritual father or mother. When such a leader does spiritual practice, he or she can receive a special mantra from Heaven. Mantras usually do not come with a translation into human language. Mantras are special souls and sounds that carry a special spiritual frequency and vibration, with love, forgiveness, compassion, and light.

"Yi mi" means *thinking secret*. This secret is to purify the mind. Human beings have negative mind-sets, negative beliefs, and negative attitudes, as well as ego, attachments, and more. To stop negativity and think positively, with love, forgiveness, compassion, and light, is vital for purification and clearing all types of mind blockages.

The Divine guided me to share the Four Power Techniques with humanity in all of my books.

The first power technique is Body Power, which is the ancient shen mi.

Body Power means *special hand and body positions for healing, rejuvenation, longevity, and life transformatio*n. Body Power can be summarized in one sentence:

Where you put your hands is where you receive healing, rejuvenation, and longevity.

The second power technique is Sound Power, which is the ancient kou mi.

Sound Power means *to chant mantras*. Sound Power can be summarized in one sentence:

What you chant is what you become.

The Divine and Tao have given me Divine Soul Songs and Tao Songs, which are sacred divine and Tao mantras. In *Divine Soul Songs*,[1] the fourth book in my Soul Power Series, I shared eight major Divine Soul Songs with humanity. In this book, I will share sacred Tao Songs. Tao Songs are sacred Tao mantras from the Source.

---

1. *Divine Soul Songs: Sacred Practical Treasures to Heal, Rejuvenate, and Transform You, Humanity, Mother Earth, and All Universes* (Toronto/New York: Heaven's Library/Atria Books, 2009).

The third power technique is Mind Power, which is the ancient yi mi.

Mind Power means *creative visualization*. Mind Power includes all types of meditation to make the mind peaceful and positive and to enable one to go into emptiness, which is the stillness condition.

A brain has billions of cells. For most human beings, only 10–15 percent of the brain cells are developed, which means about 85–90 percent of the brain cells are not developed. To meditate is to develop more brain cells in order to increase one's Mind Power to transform life.

Mind Power can be summarized in one sentence:

Where you concentrate in your body is where you receive healing, rejuvenation, transformation, and enlightenment.

The fourth technique is Soul Power, which is a most important divine technique that the Divine guided me to teach humanity.

Soul Power means to *say hello* through soul communication. Directly call the souls of buddhas, holy saints, healing angels, archangels, ascended masters, lamas, gurus, and all kinds of spiritual fathers and mothers to come to heal and bless you. You can also directly call the Divine and Tao to heal, rejuvenate, and bless you.

Soul Power can be summarized in one sentence:

**Souls, including the Divine and Tao,
are available if you call them.**

This book, *Tao Song and Tao Dance: Sacred Sound, Movement, and Power from the Source for Healing, Rejuvenation, Lon-*

gevity, and Transformation of All Life, reveals new sacred Tao Song mantras to help humanity self-clear bad karma and transform every aspect of life, including health, relationships, and finances.

Sacred Tao Song mantras carry Tao frequency and vibration, which can transform the frequency and vibration of all life.

Sacred Tao Song mantras carry Tao love, which melts all blockages and transforms all life.

Sacred Tao Song mantras carry Tao forgiveness, which brings inner joy and inner peace.

Sacred Tao Song mantras carry Tao compassion, which boosts energy, stamina, vitality, and immunity.

Sacred Tao Song mantras carry Tao light, which heals, prevents sickness, rejuvenates, and transforms every aspect of life, including relationships and finances.

At 11:00 p.m. Eastern Daylight Time on May 27, 2011, as I was meditating, The Tao Committee told me:

"Zhi Gang, we are giving you sacred mantras from the Source that you can share with humanity."

I replied, "I am extremely honored to receive the sacred mantras and teaching."

The Tao Committee told me, "These sacred Tao mantras carry the power to remove all types of blockages. Humanity can use them to self-clear bad karma in order to transform health, relationships, and finances."

I immediately bowed to The Tao Committee 108 times to show my deepest gratitude.

Then The Tao Committee started to give me the sacred Tao mantras. They gave them to me line by line. As soon as I received them, I chanted them. My whole body shone with incredible rainbow light and crystal light. The Tao Committee also told me there was invisible light within. The frequency and vibration were incredible. My heart and soul were deeply moved. I bowed my head one thousand times to the floor to show my honor and gratitude to The Tao Committee.

I am extremely happy and excited, as well as most humbled, to bring these sacred Tao Song mantras from the Source to humanity and Mother Earth. I will share these sacred Tao Song mantras in chapter 3, "Sacred Tao Song Mantras for Removing Soul Mind Body Blockages to Transform All Life."

These sacred Tao Song mantras are extremely powerful. I started to teach them in a workshop the very next day, May 28, 2011. I taught the participants one of the sacred Tao Song mantras for the first Soul House:[2]

> *Hei Ya You Tao* (pronounced *hay yah yoe dow*)
> *Hei Ya You Tao*
> *Hei Ya You Tao*
> *Hei Ya You Tao*
> *Hei Ya You Tao . . .*

Here are a few comments from those who were present at the workshop.

> *The Tao light and Tao love of the Tao mantra are still radiating into every cell and space of my body, cleansing, washing, and healing all. Thank you, Master Sha.*
> *G. R.*

---

2. The first Soul House is a space at the bottom of the torso. I will explain this in detail in chapter 2.

Since I was a child, I have always dreamed of uplifting my consciousness, purifying fully, and becoming as full of the highest love and forgiveness as our beloved spiritual fathers and mothers. I feel in this process that great openings are occurring for me in all aspects of my life. My emotions are balanced, my mind is much quieter and clearer, my energy is balanced, and I am so much more connected to my soul. There are no words for the gratitude I feel to you, Tao, and the Divine for these priceless treasures.

Thank you. Thank you. Thank you. Love you. Love you. Love you.

With endless gratitude and love,
M. M.

Tao, which is the Source of countless planets, stars, galaxies, and universes, had never before released these sacred Tao Song mantras.

The power of these sacred Tao Song mantras cannot be explained in words or comprehended by thoughts.

They are some of the highest sacred treasures for humanity to self-heal all sickness in the spiritual, mental, emotional, and physical bodies, as well as to increase immunity for preventing sickness.

They are sacred gifts to rejuvenate the soul, heart, mind, and body of humanity.

They are sacred tools to transform relationships and finances.

They are sacred pearls to prolong life.

They are essential sacred keys for immortality.

Learn them.

Chant them.

Sing them.
Benefit from them.
Transform all life with them.

I love my heart and soul
I love all humanity
Join hearts and souls together
Love, peace and harmony
Love, peace and harmony

TAO SONG
AND
TAO DANCE

Foundation of Tao Song

SOUL LANGUAGE AND Soul Song are the foundation of Tao Song. I offered comprehensive teaching about Soul Language and Soul Song in the first book of the Soul Power Series, *Soul Wisdom: Practical Soul Treasures to Transform Your Life.* In this book, I will give you the essence that you need for study and understanding of Tao Song.

Soul Language

In October 1994 I traveled from Canada back to China to study with Dr. and Master Zhi Chen Guo, my most beloved spiritual father and master. Nearly twenty thousand people gathered in his healing center. They spoke Soul Language together. The vibration was beyond comprehension. I could feel heat penetrating my body. This was extremely fascinating to me. Never before had I experienced such a huge number of people speaking Soul Language together.

I really wanted to bring out my own Soul Language. I followed the teaching. I chanted the divine code San San Jiu Liu Ba Yao Wu (3396815 in Chinese, pronounced *sahn sahn jeo leo bah yow woo*). To bring out your Soul Language, the technique is to chant San San Jiu Liu Ba Yao Wu as fast as you can.[1] I chanted so fast, yet after ten days my Soul Language still could not flow out.

Back in Canada in 1996, I really wanted to teach Soul Language. I asked Heaven to bless me to bring out my Soul Language and my Soul Language translation abilities. Heaven saw my sincere heart's desire to spread this powerful teaching. This time, when I chanted San San Jiu Liu Ba Yao Wu continuously and chanted faster and faster, my Soul Language quickly flowed out. A strange voice came out of my mouth. It sounded like "bababababababababa. . . ." It was so fast that it shocked me. I was extremely excited. My body was shaking and I felt a lot of heat. I was so happy and grateful that my Soul Language had come out.

I then asked Heaven to open my Soul Language Channel further so I could translate my Soul Language. In 1994 at Master Guo's healing center, I had learned the basic principles for translating Soul Language. But because I could not flow out my Soul Language at that time, even after practicing diligently for ten days, of course I could not translate my Soul Language either when I was at Master Guo's center.

After I finally flowed out my Soul Language in 1996, I applied the basic teaching for translating Soul Language. I asked Heaven to bless me. I started to speak my Soul Language. As I continued to flow my Soul Language, I suddenly heard a few simple sentences in my mind: "I am very happy to speak my Soul

---

1. See pp. 26–27 of *Soul Communication: Opening Your Spiritual Channels for Success and Fulfillment* (Toronto/New York: Heaven's Library/Atria Books, 2008).

Language. I am honored to teach Soul Language. I will apply Soul Language for healing and rejuvenation." I was so excited to hear these few sentences in my head as my Soul Language flowed out. This was the beginning of my Soul Language translation.

I share my personal experience of bringing out my Soul Language and beginning to translate my Soul Language because Soul Language is the foundation of Tao Song.

WHAT IS SOUL LANGUAGE?

There are thousands of languages on Mother Earth. There is only one Soul Language.

Soul Language is the voice and language of the soul. Although everyone's Soul Language sounds different, Soul Language is the universal language. All souls understand Soul Language. All souls communicate through Soul Language.

A human being consists of soul, mind, and body. Soul is spirit. Mind is consciousness. Body includes all of the systems, organs, tissues, and cells.

Everyone speaks his or her native language. We learn and speak our native language through our minds, which is our consciousness. As we grow up and go to school, many of us start to study a second language. To learn and speak any language is to use the mind.

A physical human being does not usually speak Soul Language. A newborn baby, however, definitely speaks Soul Language, which is the baby's soul voice. Before a baby can speak a human language, the baby makes all kinds of sounds—*baba, woo, yaya, da ha hu*. We call this "baby talk," but these sounds are actually the baby's soul voice and Soul Language. They carry meaning. They can be translated to human language and understood. When an infant starts to speak a human language, the baby's Soul Language usually stops.

SIGNIFICANCE, BENEFITS, AND POWER OF SOUL LANGUAGE

Soul Language carries soul frequency and vibration, which can transform the frequency and vibration of your systems, organs, tissues, and cells. Soul Language carries your soul's love, forgiveness, compassion, and light. Soul Language has great significance and power, including the following points:

- The Soul Language Channel is a major spiritual channel that allows one to communicate with the Soul World.
- Soul Language carries soul love, which melts all blockages and transforms all life.
- Soul Language carries soul forgiveness, which brings inner joy and inner peace.
- Soul Language carries soul compassion, which boosts energy, stamina, vitality, and immunity.
- Soul Language carries soul light, which heals, prevents sickness, rejuvenates, and transforms all life, including relationships and finances.
- Soul Language is a soul treasure for self-healing your spiritual, mental, emotional, and physical bodies.
- Soul Language is a soul treasure for boosting your energy, stamina, vitality, and immunity.
- Soul Language is a soul treasure for rejuvenating your soul, heart, mind, and body.

- Soul Language is a soul treasure for advancing your Tao journey, whose final destiny is to reach immortality.

BRING OUT YOUR SOUL LANGUAGE

Now I will share with you and humanity how to speak Soul Language.

Anyone can bring out his or her Soul Language by applying the teaching here. As you follow the teaching and bring out your Soul Language, you will understand Soul Language much better.

Apply the Four Power Techniques I have shared in all of my books:

Body Power. Sit up straight. Put the tip of your tongue as close as you can to the roof of your mouth without touching. Contract your anus for a few seconds and then release. Put your hands in the Soul Light Era Prayer Position by gently covering your Message Center[2] with your left palm. Put your right hand in the traditional prayer position with fingers pointing up in front of the left hand. See figure 1.

Soul Power. Say *hello:*

> *Dear Divine,*
> *Dear Tao,*

---

2. The Message Center, also known as the heart chakra, is a fist-sized energy center located in the center of your chest, behind the sternum. The Message Center is very important for developing soul communication abilities and for healing. It is also the love center, forgiveness center, karma center, emotional center, life transformation center, soul enlightenment center, and more. Clearing blockages from your Message Center and opening and developing your Message Center are key to your ability to communicate with your own soul and other souls.

Figure 1. Soul Light Era Prayer Position

*Dear soul mind body of all spiritual fathers and moth-
     ers in all layers of Heaven and on Mother Earth,*
Dear Heaven,
Dear Mother Earth,
Dear countless planets, stars, galaxies, and universes,
I love you, honor you, and appreciate you.
Please bring my Soul Language out.
I am extremely grateful.
Thank you. Thank you. Thank you.

Mind Power. Concentrate and focus on your Message Center.
Visualize bright golden light or bright rainbow light radiating in
your Message Center.

Sound Power. As Dr. and Master Zhi Chen Guo was meditating early one morning in 1974, he received the divine code San San Jiu Liu Ba Yao Wu (3396815 in Chinese, pronounced *sahn sahn jeo leo bah yow woo*) from the Divine. This divine code is the sacred key to bring out your Soul Language and to offer divine healing, blessing, and life transformation. This sacred code has power beyond comprehension. San San Jiu Liu Ba Yao Wu (3396815) is powerful because:

- It was created by the Divine. When you chant this sacred code, the Divine comes to help you.
- It has divine calling power. When you chant this sacred code, countless saints, buddhas, healing angels, archangels, ascended masters, lamas, gurus, kahunas, and all other types of spiritual fathers and mothers will respond.
- It carries a special vibration to stimulate the body in a sacred pattern. The sound of each number vibrates and stimulates the cells in a particular area of the body:

    San (3) stimulates the chest.

    Jiu (9) stimulates the lower abdomen.

    Liu (6) stimulates the ribs.

    Ba (8) stimulates the navel.

    Yao (1) stimulates the head.

    Wu (5) stimulates the stomach.

When you chant *San San Jiu Liu Ba Yao Wu* (3396815), energy flows in the body as shown in figure 2.

Energy starts to vibrate in the chest, and then flows to the lower abdomen. From there it moves to the ribs and then goes

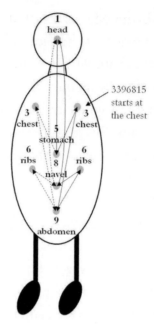

Figure 2. 3396815 promotes energy flow in the body

to the navel. Next it radiates to the head. Finally it moves down to the stomach. This movement of energy in the body is a sacred healthy pattern. Moving energy in this pattern just by chanting San San Jiu Liu Ba Yao Wu is sacred divine healing and rejuvenation.

I have shared the sacred divine code 3396815 in almost all of my books, including *Power Healing*,[3] published in 2002. In the years since, thousands of people all over the world have applied this divine mantra to develop their Soul Language.

Chant *San San Jiu Liu Ba Yao Wu* (3396815), pronounced *sahn sahn jeo leo bah yow woo*, as quickly as possible. Suddenly a special sound that you have never heard before could flow out.

---

3. *Power Healing: The Four Keys to Energizing Your Body, Mind, and Spirit* (San Francisco: HarperSanFrancisco, 2002).

It could sound like "ba ba ba ba ba" or "la la la la la la la la" or "ei ya ya ya ya you," or "he he he he he he he." It could sound more complicated than these examples. It could sound like humming or singing. Everyone's Soul Language has its own sound.

Generally speaking, Soul Language has a repetitive quality in the beginning. As you continue to speak Soul Language, it can change from day to day. Soul Language does not follow any formula. It expresses the nature of soul very well. The soul has freedom and flexibility. Therefore, Soul Language is expressed in a variety of tones and sounds.

Practice to bring out your Soul Language now.

Chant aloud:

> 3396815—*sahn sahn jeo leo bah yow woo*
> 3396815—*sahn sahn jeo leo bah yow woo*
> 3396815—*sahn sahn jeo leo bah yow woo*
> 3396815—*sahn sahn jeo leo bah yow woo*
> 3396815—*sahn sahn jeo leo bah yow woo*
> 3396815—*sahn sahn jeo leo bah yow woo*
> 3396815—*sahn sahn jeo leo bah yow woo* . . .

Chant faster! Chant even faster!! Chant as fast as you can!!! Let go of the desire to pronounce the words correctly. Your special sound could flow out.

In order to confirm that you are really speaking Soul Language, stop the special sound. Then start chanting 3396815 (*sahn sahn jeo leo bah yow woo*) again. Chant as fast as you can. In a short time your special sound could flow out again. Then stop the special voice again, and go back to chanting 3396815 (*sahn sahn jeo leo bah yow woo*). Chant as fast as you can. The special voice could flow out again quickly.

Repeat this process a few times. Then you can be sure that your Soul Language has flowed out.

A young woman in Georgia studied the Soul Language teaching in my book *Soul Wisdom*.[4] She did the practice. Her Soul Language could not come out. She did the practice again. Her Soul Language still could not come out. She practiced a third time. Still her Soul Language could not come out. Then she said, "I will do it one more time. If my Soul Language does not come out this time, I may never flow out my Soul Language." She chanted 3396815 for the fourth time. In a few minutes, her Soul Language suddenly flowed out. Her body was shaking.

This can happen for many people when their Soul Language flows out. Their bodies could really shake. Their hearts could beat very fast. They could feel very hot. In 2002 I taught a workshop in Fairfield, Iowa, as part of a tour for my book *Power Healing*. A chiropractor in the workshop chanted 3396815 and his Soul Language flowed out. He was so excited that he started running and literally jumping around the room.

Your Soul Language has been hidden within you for decades or even many lifetimes. When your Soul Language comes out, it could be a dramatic explosion for your body. Do not be nervous. If you have an extremely strong response to your Soul Language, you can send a Soul Order[5] aloud or silently to tell your body, "Stop. Stop. Stop." Your Soul Language and your bodily reactions could stop instantly.

---

4. *Soul Wisdom: Practical Soul Treasures to Transform Your Life* (Toronto/New York: Heaven's Library/Atria Books, 2008).

5. For more on Soul Orders, see chapter 4 of *The Power of Soul: The Way to Heal, Rejuvenate, Transform, and Enlighten All Life* (Toronto/New York: Heaven's Library/Atria Books, 2009).

Soul Language carries soul frequency and vibration with soul love, forgiveness, compassion, and light.

Soul frequency and vibration can transform the frequency and vibration of your mind, body, systems, organs, and cells.

Soul love melts all blockages and transforms all life.

Soul forgiveness brings inner joy and inner peace.

Soul compassion boosts energy, stamina, vitality, and immunity.

Soul light heals, prevents sickness, rejuvenates soul, heart, mind, and body, and transforms relationships, finances, and every aspect of life.

The power of Soul Language is beyond words, comprehension, and imagination.

Some people flow out their Soul Language the first time they practice chanting *San San Jiu Liu Ba Yao Wu* as fast as possible. Some people flow out their Soul Language after practicing a few times. Remember to chant *San San Jiu Liu Ba Yao Wu* at least three to five minutes per time. Some people may need to chant for ten to twenty minutes to bring out their Soul Language. Some people may need to practice more than ten times to flow out their Soul Language. Have no attachment. Just by chanting *San San Jiu Liu Ba Yao Wu,* you could receive remarkable healing and rejuvenation.

There are thousands of heart-touching and moving healing stories from chanting *San San Jiu Liu Ba Yao Wu* (3396815). I will share one story with you. An acupuncturist in a workshop I taught at the Omega Institute in New York shared that she had learned San San Jiu Liu Ba Yao Wu from my book *Power Healing*. She was overweight. She grabbed the teaching from *Power Healing* and said, "Let me chant *San San Jiu Liu Ba Yao Wu* to lose weight." Applying the teaching from *Power Healing*, she said *hello* (Soul Power):

> *Dear soul mind body of San San Jiu Liu Ba Yao Wu,*
> *I love you.*
> *You have the power to help me lose weight.*
> *Please help me lose weight.*
> *I am very grateful.*
> *Thank you.*

Then she chanted *San San Jiu Liu Ba Yao Wu* many times a day for a few minutes each time. After five days she lost five pounds. She was excited and shared her results with her husband. Her husband also started to chant *San San Jiu Liu Ba Yao Wu* to lose weight. After five days he achieved a similar result. The two of them shared their experience and this simple soul healing practice with their friends. A few of their friends also received great results by chanting *San San Jiu Liu Ba Yao Wu* to lose weight.

How does San San Jiu Liu Ba Yao Wu work for losing weight? San San Jiu Liu Ba Yao Wu (3396815) is a sacred divine code and mantra that can remove soul mind body blockages underlying weight challenges. It promotes energy flow throughout the whole body. This increases metabolism to assist in losing weight.

San San Jiu Liu Ba Yao Wu can remove soul mind body blockages for any health condition. What you need to do is apply it. Ancient wisdom says:

Zhou bu li kou

"Zhou" means *mantra*. "Bu" means *not*. "Li" means *leave*. "Kou" means *mouth*.

"Zhou bu li kou" (pronounced *joe boo lee koe*) means *chant a mantra nonstop*. You can chant a mantra out loud or silently. Chanting out loud is yang chanting. It vibrates the bigger cells and spaces in the body. Chanting silently is yin chanting. It vibrates the smaller cells and spaces. Both ways work, but during the day it is better to chant silently. When you practice silent chanting, it can become a habit. When chanting a mantra nonstop becomes a habit, the benefits are enormous. Words are not enough to express the benefits of chanting a mantra nonstop.

Chant *San San Jiu Liu Ba Yao Wu* again and again. Your Soul Language will flow out. Be patient and confident. Do not give up. Keep chanting *San San Jiu Liu Ba Yao Wu* as much as possible. Every moment you are chanting, you are receiving benefits for healing, rejuvenation, longevity, and transformation of relationships, finances, and every aspect of life, because this sacred divine code and mantra brings divine frequency and vibration with divine love, forgiveness, compassion, and light to humanity, Mother Earth, and countless planets, stars, galaxies, and universes.

This is your service. It is Service Xiu Lian. "Xiu Lian" (pronounced *sheo lyen*) means *the totality of one's spiritual journey*. Service Xiu Lian simply means you just serve, and then Heaven blesses you and transforms your life. When you chant *San San Jiu Liu Ba Yao Wu,* when you chant any Divine Soul Song or Tao Song, you are serving. Therefore, Heaven is blessing you every time you chant. Every moment you are chanting, you are receiving:

- healing
- rejuvenation
- transformation of your body's frequency and vibration from head to toe, skin to bone

- prolongation of life
- transformation of your relationships
- transformation of your finances

In addition, your chanting benefits humanity, Mother Earth, and all universes.

In one sentence: You are transforming every aspect of your life.

APPLY SOUL LANGUAGE TO TRANSFORM YOUR HEALTH, RELATIONSHIPS, AND FINANCES

Let me lead you in some practices to apply Soul Language to transform every aspect of your life.

Transform Health

Apply Soul Language to transform your health. Use the Four Power Techniques.

Body Power. Sit up straight. Put the tip of your tongue as close as you can to the roof of your mouth without touching. Contract your anus slightly for a few seconds. Put your hands on your lower abdomen below your navel in the Yin Yang Palm Hand Position.[6] (See figure 3.)

Soul Power. Say *hello:*

---

6. Grip your left thumb with the fingers of your right hand and make a fist. Wrap all four fingers of the left hand over the right hand. Grip your left thumb with about 75–80 percent of your maximum strength. This is the Yin Yang Palm Hand Position.

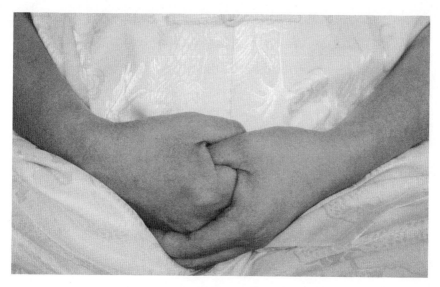

Figure 3. Yin Yang Palm Hand Position

Dear Divine,
Dear Tao,
Dear soul mind body of all spiritual fathers and moth-
ers in all layers of Heaven and on Mother Earth,
Dear Heaven,
Dear Mother Earth,
Dear countless planets, stars, galaxies, and universes,
Dear San San Jiu Liu Ba Yao Wu,
Dear my Soul Language,
Dear Sha's Golden Healing Ball,[7]
Dear Divine Love Peace Harmony Rainbow Light
Ball,[8]

---

7. A spiritual gift and mantra received directly from the Divine by Master Sha on December 7, 1995. See *Sha's Golden Healing Ball: The Perfect Gift*, revised edition (Heaven's Library, 2010).
8. Another divine spiritual gift to humanity, Master Sha received the Divine Love Peace Harmony Rainbow Light Ball on December 7, 2010. See *Divine Love Peace Harmony Rainbow Light Ball: Transform You, Humanity, Mother Earth, and All Universes* (Heaven's Library, 2010).

I love you, honor you, and appreciate you.
Please heal my _____ (make a request for healing
    of your spiritual body, mental body, emotional
    body, or physical body).
I am extremely grateful.
Thank you. Thank you. Thank you.

Mind Power. Concentrate or focus your mind on the area or on the health condition for which you are requesting healing. Visualize bright golden light or bright rainbow light radiating in the area of your request.

Sound Power. Chant:

> *San San Jiu Liu Ba Yao Wu*
> *San San Jiu Liu Ba Yao Wu*
> *San San Jiu Liu Ba Yao Wu*
> *San San Jiu Liu Ba Yao Wu*
> *San San Jiu Liu Ba Yao Wu*
> *San San Jiu Liu Ba Yao Wu*
> *San San Jiu Liu Ba Yao Wu . . .*

If your Soul Language has flowed out, chant your Soul Language continuously. If your Soul Language has not flowed out, continue to chant 3396815 (pronounced *sahn sahn jeo leo bah yow woo*). You can chant silently or aloud.

Chant for three to five minutes per time, three to five times per day. There is no time limit. The more you chant and the longer you chant, the better the results you could receive. For chronic and life-threatening conditions, always remember to chant a minimum of two hours per day. The more you chant, the better.

Transform Relationships

Apply Soul Language to transform your relationships. Use the Four Power Techniques.

Body Power. Sit up straight. Put the tip of your tongue as close as you can to the roof of your mouth without touching. Contract your anus slightly for a few seconds. Put your hands on your lower abdomen, below your navel, in the Jin Dan Da Tao Xiu Lian Hand Position. (See figure 4.)

Soul Power. Say *hello:*

> *Dear Divine,*
> *Dear Tao,*
> *Dear soul mind body of all spiritual fathers and mothers in all layers of Heaven and on Mother Earth,*

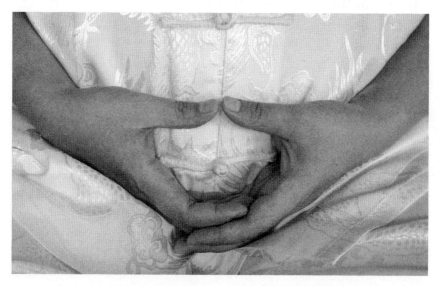

Figure 4. Jin Dan Da Tao Xiu Lian Hand Position

Dear Heaven,
Dear Mother Earth,
Dear countless planets, stars, galaxies, and universes,
Dear San San Jiu Liu Ba Yao Wu,
Dear my Soul Language,
Dear Sha's Golden Healing Ball,
Dear Divine Love Peace Harmony Rainbow Light Ball,
I love you, honor you, and appreciate you.
Please bless the relationships between _____ and me
    (name relationships for which you are requesting
    a blessing).
I am extremely grateful.
Thank you. Thank you. Thank you.

Mind Power. Concentrate or focus your mind on the people, pets, organizations, or more for whom you are requesting a blessing. Visualize bright golden light or bright rainbow light radiating among the relationships.

Sound Power. Chant aloud:

San San Jiu Liu Ba Yao Wu
San San Jiu Liu Ba Yao Wu
San San Jiu Liu Ba Yao Wu
San San Jiu Liu Ba Yao Wu
San San Jiu Liu Ba Yao Wu
San San Jiu Liu Ba Yao Wu
San San Jiu Liu Ba Yao Wu . . .

Chant *San San Jiu Liu Ba Yao Wu* as fast as you can to bring out your Soul Language and continue to chant your Soul Language. You may then chant your Soul Language silently (if you can) or aloud.

Chant for three to five minutes per time, three to five times per day. There is no time limit. The more you chant and the longer you chant, the better the results you could receive. For very challenging relationships, always remember to chant a minimum of two hours per day. The more you chant, the better.

Transform Finances

Apply Soul Language to transform your finances. Use the Four Power Techniques.

Body Power. Sit up straight. Put the tip of your tongue as close as you can to the roof of your mouth without touching. Contract your anus slightly for a few seconds. Put your hands in the Soul Light Era Prayer Position. (See figure 1 on page 6.)

Soul Power. Say *hello:*

> *Dear Divine,*
> *Dear Tao,*
> *Dear soul mind body of all spiritual fathers and mothers*
>   *in all layers of Heaven and on Mother Earth,*
> *Dear Heaven,*
> *Dear Mother Earth,*
> *Dear countless planets, stars, galaxies, and universes,*
> *Dear San San Jiu Liu Ba Yao Wu,*
> *Dear my Soul Language,*
> *Dear Sha's Golden Healing Ball,*
> *Dear Divine Love Peace Harmony Rainbow Light Ball,*

I love you, honor you, and appreciate you.
Please bless my finances and/or my business.
I am extremely grateful.
Thank you. Thank you. Thank you.

Mind Power. Concentrate or focus your mind on your finances and/or your business. Visualize bright golden light or bright rainbow light radiating in your finances and/or your business.

Sound Power. Chant aloud:

> *San San Jiu Liu Ba Yao Wu* (pronounced *sahn sahn*
>   *jeo leo bah yow woo*)
> *San San Jiu Liu Ba Yao Wu*
> *San San Jiu Liu Ba Yao Wu*
> *San San Jiu Liu Ba Yao Wu*
> *San San Jiu Liu Ba Yao Wu*
> *San San Jiu Liu Ba Yao Wu*
> *San San Jiu Liu Ba Yao Wu . . .*

Chant *San San Jiu Liu Ba Yao Wu* as fast as you can to bring out your Soul Language and continue to chant your Soul Language. You may then chant your Soul Language silently or aloud.

Chant for three to five minutes per time, three to five times per day. There is no time limit. The more you chant and the longer you chant, the better the results you could receive. For significant financial and/or business challenges, always remember to chant a minimum of two hours per day. The more you chant, the better.

I cannot emphasize the following sentences enough. I write these sentences in many of my books. I speak these sentences in many of my workshops and teleconferences. They are an essential part of my teaching. Please chant them as mantras. They are extremely powerful mantras. I cannot express the importance of these sentences enough.

Soul Language carries soul frequency and vibration, which can transform the frequency and vibration of your health, relationships, and finances.

Soul Language carries soul love, which melts all blockages.

Soul Language carries soul forgiveness, which brings inner joy and inner peace.

Soul Language carries soul compassion, which boosts energy, stamina, vitality, and immunity.

Soul Language carries soul light, which heals, prevents sickness, purifies and rejuvenates the soul, heart, mind, and body, and transforms relationships, finances, and every aspect of life.

Soul Language is the foundation of Soul Song, Divine Soul Song, and Tao Song. Soul Song is the song of Soul Language. First speak Soul Language. Then transform your Soul Language to Soul Song.

Soul Song

After bringing out your Soul Language, the next step is to sing Soul Song.

WHAT IS SOUL SONG?

Soul Song is the song of your soul. In fact, Soul Song is the song of your Soul Language. To sing a Soul Song you must bring out your Soul Language first. Then transform your Soul Language to Soul Song.

SIGNIFICANCE, BENEFITS, AND POWER OF SOUL SONG

Soul Song has a higher frequency and vibration than Soul Language. This is important wisdom. Many of you will be able to feel and experience more power for healing, rejuvenation, and transformation of relationships and finances when you sing a Soul Song as compared to speaking your Soul Language.

What Soul Language can do, Soul Song can do better.

BRING OUT YOUR SOUL SONG

To bring out your Soul Song is very simple. This is the way to do it.

Apply the Four Power Techniques:

Body Power. Sit up straight. Put the tip of your tongue as close as you can to the roof of your mouth without touching. Contract your anus slightly for a few seconds. Put your hands in the Soul Light Era Prayer Position (figure 1, page 6).

Soul Power. Say *hello:*

> *Dear Divine,*
> *Dear Tao,*

Dear soul mind body of all spiritual fathers and mothers
in all layers of Heaven and on Mother Earth,
Dear Heaven,
Dear Mother Earth,
Dear countless planets, stars, galaxies, and universes,
Dear San San Jiu Liu Ba Yao Wu,
Dear my Soul Language,
Dear Sha's Golden Healing Ball,
Dear Divine Love Peace Harmony Rainbow Light Ball,
I love you, honor you, and appreciate you.
Please transform my Soul Language to Soul Song.
I am extremely grateful.
Thank you. Thank you. Thank you.

Mind Power. Concentrate or focus your mind on your Message Center (heart chakra). Visualize bright golden light or bright rainbow light radiating in your Message Center.

Sound Power. Chant aloud:

San San Jiu Liu Ba Yao Wu (pronounced sahn sahn
jeo leo bah yow woo)
San San Jiu Liu Ba Yao Wu
San San Jiu Liu Ba Yao Wu
San San Jiu Liu Ba Yao Wu
San San Jiu Liu Ba Yao Wu
San San Jiu Liu Ba Yao Wu
San San Jiu Liu Ba Yao Wu . . .

As you chant *San San Jiu Liu Ba Yao Wu* (3396815), let your Soul Language come out first. Then slow down your chanting of Soul Language and transform the chanting to singing. Your Soul Song will come out naturally.

Continue to sing your Soul Song for three to five minutes per time, three to five times per day. There is no time limit. The more you sing and the longer you sing, the better the results you could receive for transformation of every aspect of life, including relationships and finances.

APPLY SOUL SONG TO TRANSFORM YOUR HEALTH, RELATIONSHIPS, AND FINANCES

I am honored to lead you to apply the Four Power Techniques in one practice to transform your health, relationships, and finances together.

Body Power. Sit up straight. Put the tip of your tongue as close as you can to the roof of your mouth without touching. Contract your anus slightly for a few seconds. Put both hands on your lower abdomen, below your navel, in the Jin Dan Da Tao Xiu Lian Hand Position (see figure 4 on page 17).

Soul Power. Say *hello:*

> *Dear Divine,*
> *Dear Tao,*
> *Dear soul mind body of all spiritual fathers and mothers*
>   *in all layers of Heaven and on Mother Earth,*
> *Dear Heaven,*
> *Dear Mother Earth,*
> *Dear countless planets, stars, galaxies, and universes,*
> *Dear San San Jiu Liu Ba Yao Wu,*

Dear Sha's Golden Healing Ball,
Dear Divine Love Peace Harmony Rainbow Light Ball,
Dear my Soul Song,
I love you, honor you, and appreciate you.
Please transform my health, relationships, and finances
(request a specific healing blessing, a relationship
blessing, and a financial blessing).
I am extremely grateful.
Thank you. Thank you. Thank you.

Mind Power. Concentrate or focus your mind on your requests for your health, healing, relationships, finances, and business. Visualize bright golden light or bright rainbow light radiating on these requests.

Sound Power. Chant aloud:

San San Jiu Liu Ba Yao Wu (pronounced *sahn sahn*
jeo leo bah yow woo)
San San Jiu Liu Ba Yao Wu
San San Jiu Liu Ba Yao Wu
San San Jiu Liu Ba Yao Wu
San San Jiu Liu Ba Yao Wu
San San Jiu Liu Ba Yao Wu
San San Jiu Liu Ba Yao Wu . . .

First bring out your Soul Language, then turn it to Soul Song. Continue to sing your Soul Song for three to five minutes per time, three to five times per day. There is no time limit. The more you sing and the longer you sing, the better the results you could receive for transformation of every aspect of life, including health, healing, relationships, and finances.

Soul Song is extremely powerful. Soul Song carries soul love, which melts all blockages. Soul Song carries soul forgiveness, which brings inner joy and inner peace. Soul Song carries soul compassion, which boosts energy, stamina, vitality, and immunity. Soul Song carries soul light, which heals, prevents sickness, rejuvenates, and transforms all life, including relationships and finances.

Sing your Soul Song anytime and anywhere. You can sing your Soul Song silently or aloud to transform all life. Develop a habit of singing your Soul Song nonstop. The benefits for transformation of health, relationships, and finances are beyond comprehension.

Tao Song

Tao is the Source. Tao is the creator of countless planets, stars, galaxies, and universes. Tao is the creator of Heaven and Mother Earth. Tao is The Way of all life. Tao is the universal principles and laws.

To sing a Tao Song is to bring Source power to you, your loved ones, humanity, and wan ling (all souls, pronounced *wahn ling*) in countless planets, stars, galaxies, and universes.

WHAT IS TAO SONG?

Tao Song is song from the Source. Source power cannot be explained in words or comprehended by thoughts. Tao Song has already created many miracles. It will create millions and billions of miracles for humanity and for wan ling in countless planets, stars, galaxies, and universes.

Tao Song carries Tao frequency and vibration with Tao love, forgiveness, compassion, and light that can transform the frequency and vibration of all life.

SIGNIFICANCE, BENEFITS, AND POWER OF TAO SONG

Tao Song has the power and abilities to:

- heal your spiritual, mental, emotional, and physical bodies
- heal the spiritual, mental, emotional, and physical bodies of others
- boost energy, stamina, vitality, and immunity
- rejuvenate soul, heart, mind, and body
- achieve *fan lao huan tong* (pronounced *fahn lao* [rhymes with *now*] *hwahn tawng*), which means *transform old age to the health and purity of the baby state*
- prolong life
- increase intelligence
- transform relationships
- transform finances
- transform humanity, Mother Earth, and countless planets, stars, galaxies, and universes

I will offer sacred Tao Song mantras for you to chant and sing in chapter 3. You will learn and experience a lot of practice for healing, rejuvenation, prolonging life, and transforming relationships and finances.

In this chapter, I have explained what Soul Language is; the significance, benefits, and power of Soul Language; and how to apply Soul Language for healing and for transforming relationships and finances. In one sentence:

Soul Language is the foundation for Soul Song, Divine Soul Song, and Tao Song.

I have also explained what Soul Song is; the significance, benefits, and power of Soul Song; and how to apply Soul Song for healing and for transforming relationships and finances. In one sentence:

Soul Song carries a higher frequency and vibration than Soul Language for healing, rejuvenation, and transformation of relationships and finances.

I have also explained what Tao Song is and its significance, benefits, and power. I will lead you to practice Tao Song in chapter 3. In one sentence:

Tao Song is song from the Source that carries the highest frequency and vibration for healing, rejuvenation, longevity, immortality, and transformation of all life.

The Sacred and Most Important Areas for Healing the Spiritual, Mental, Emotional, and Physical Bodies

A HUMAN BEING HAS a soul, mind, and body. A human being has different systems, organs, cells, cell units, DNA and RNA, and tiny matter inside the cells. A human being also has spaces. There are spaces between the organs and spaces between the cells. Spaces are the key for health.

Message Energy Matter Theory

I have shared the Message Energy Matter Theory in my earlier books. This is a very important theory for healing and more. I need to share it with you again. Here is the essence of Message Energy Matter Theory:

- A cell is the smallest functioning unit of the body.
- A cell constantly vibrates by contracting and expanding.
- When cells contract, matter inside the cells transforms to energy outside of the cells.
- When cells expand, energy outside of the cells transforms to matter inside the cells.
- The transformation between matter inside the cells and energy outside of the cells should be in relative balance. If this balance is broken, sickness occurs.
- Soul is message. In scientific study, soul is information.
- Matter and energy are both carriers of message. Message is soul. Soul is the boss. Soul can direct and balance the transformation between matter inside the cells and energy outside of the cells.
- Love, forgiveness, compassion, light, grace, peace, and harmony are messages. To give these messages to the body is to offer soul healing. These messages can balance the transformation between matter inside the cells and energy outside of the cells. This is the secret of how soul healing works.

Message Energy Matter Theory explains very well how to balance the transformation between matter inside the cells and energy outside of the cells. Message Energy Matter Theory explains very well how spiritual healing or soul healing works. It also explains how prayer works. There are countless heart-touching and moving stories in history that demonstrate the power of spiritual healing, soul healing, and prayer.

The most important wisdom for healing is to remove soul blockages. Soul blockages are blockages due to bad karma.

Karma is the record of one's services in all lifetimes, past and present. Karma is divided into good karma and bad karma. Good karma includes love, care, compassion, sincerity, honesty, generosity, kindness, and much more. Bad karma includes killing, harming, taking advantage of others, stealing, cheating, and more.

Karma is cause and effect. Good karma brings blessings to one's life, including good health, harmonious relationships, and comfortable finances. Bad karma brings lessons to one's life. These lessons may include challenges in health, relationships, finances, and any aspect of life. In one sentence:

Karma is the root cause of success and failure in every aspect of life.

The best way to self-clear bad karma is to offer service unconditionally to others. To offer service is to make others happier and healthier. To offer service is to bring love, peace, and harmony to you, your family, your loved ones, humanity, Mother Earth, and countless planets, stars, galaxies, and universes.

The fastest way to clear bad karma is to receive Divine Karma Cleansing from chosen divine servants who have been given the divine authority and honor to offer this special divine service. As I explained in the first section of this book ("Soul Power Series"), the Divine chose me as a servant of humanity and the Divine in July 2003. To this day, August 23, 2011, I have created twenty-three divine servants for the Divine. These divine servants can offer Divine Karma Cleansing for humanity, pets, and more.

Later in this book, I will explain Divine Karma Cleansing and lead you in many practices to self-clear bad karma.

Seven Soul Houses

A human being lives in a house. Your beloved soul lives in your body. Your body is the house for your soul. The Divine taught me that there are seven Soul Houses within the body. See figure 5.

WHAT ARE THE SEVEN SOUL HOUSES?

Your beloved soul can move within your body. Some souls can even travel outside the body. However, your soul generally re-

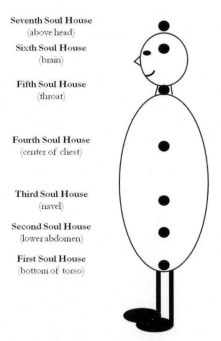

Figure 5. Seven Soul Houses in the human body

sides in one of the seven Soul Houses in your body. All seven Soul Houses are located along the central channel of the body. The central channel starts at the Hui Yin (pronounced *hway yeen*) acupuncture point, a tiny but very important acupuncture point located in the perineum, between the genitals and the anus. From the Hui Yin acupuncture point, go straight upward through the body to the top of the head, where the central channel will end at the Bai Hui (pronounced *bye hway*) acupuncture point. To locate the Bai Hui acupuncture point, imagine a line from the top of one ear going over the head to the top of the other ear. Imagine another line from the tip of the nose going up and over the top of the head to the nape of the neck. The Bai Hui acupuncture point is located where these two lines intersect.

First Soul House

The first Soul House is located at the center of the bottom of your torso and is fist-sized.

Second Soul House

The second Soul House is located at the center of the body in the lower abdomen, between the bottom of the lower abdomen and the level of the navel. It is also fist-sized.

Third Soul House

The third Soul House is located at the center of the body at the level of the navel and is fist-sized.

Fourth Soul House

The fourth Soul House is located at the center of the body in the middle of the chest behind the sternum and is fist-sized.

Fifth Soul House

The fifth Soul House is located at the center of the body in the middle of the throat and is fist-sized.

Sixth Soul House

The sixth Soul House is located at the center of the body in the middle of the brain and is fist-sized.

Seventh Soul House

The seventh Soul House is located just above the Bai Hui acupuncture point at the top of the head and is fist-sized. The seventh Soul House is the only Soul House that lies outside the physical body.

SIGNIFICANCE, BENEFITS, AND POWER
OF THE SEVEN SOUL HOUSES

Each Soul House has its own significance. Each Soul House carries its own benefits. Each Soul House brings its own power.

First Soul House

The first Soul House includes the Hui Yin acupuncture point. "Hui" means *accumulation*. "Yin" means *message energy matter of yin.* In traditional Tao teachings and in traditional Chinese medicine, the most important healing principle is to balance yin and yang.

Yin yang is an ancient philosophy that summarizes everything in the universe. Yang represents the nature of fire, including heat, upward movement, excitement, and more. Yin represents the nature of water, including cold, downward movement, calmness, and more.

It is important to develop and strengthen the Hui Yin area because it is the energy pump that will provide all of the energy necessary for the remaining Soul Houses.

Every system, every organ, every cell, and every DNA and RNA has yin yang nature. The Hui Yin acupuncture point accumulates the soul, mind, and body of the whole body's yin. Soul mind body is message energy matter. The Hui Yin point is one of the most important acupuncture points for balancing yin and yang in the whole body. It is a sacred spot. Because the first Soul House includes the Hui Yin acupuncture point, the significance, benefits, and power of the first Soul House can be summarized as follows:

- The first Soul House gathers the message energy matter of the yin of the entire body.
- It is the key Soul House for healing the whole body, because it includes the Hui Yin acupuncture point, which is the vital acupuncture point for healing all kinds of sickness. Every organ, every cell, and every DNA and RNA needs yin yang balance. The Hui Yin point can serve to balance yin and yang in every part of the body. Therefore, to do practices for the Hui Yin acupuncture point is to heal all kinds of sickness.

- It is the foundation energy center for the other six Soul Houses.
- It and the Hui Yin point are key for gaining Tao abilities.
- It is the key Soul House for healing and rejuvenation of the reproductive system and immune system; for healing the anus, rectum, and sexual organs; and for increasing sexual power.
- The soul mind body of relationship blockages is expressed in the first Soul House. Soul blockages are bad karma. Mind blockages include negative mindsets, negative beliefs, negative attitudes, ego, and attachments. Body blockages include blockages in energy and matter.
- The first Soul House is the sacred power house for developing confidence and stability.
- It is the sacred power house for longevity.
- It is the sacred power house for singing Tao Song, Divine Soul Song, and Soul Song. It is the sacred power house for all singing and chanting.
- It is the sacred power house for connecting to Mother Earth.
- The Hui Yin communicates with Mother Earth. Mother Earth represents yin. Heaven represents yang.

In ancient Tao teaching, the Hui Yin area is named Hai Di Lun. "Hai" means *sea*. "Di" means *bottom*. "Lun" means *gear*. "Hai Di Lun" (pronounced *hye dee lwun*) means *the gear at the bottom of the sea*. It is the source of foundation energy for the whole body, just like the engine of a car. Without an engine, a car cannot move. Without a powerful Hui Yin or Hai Di Lun, a human being cannot have strong energy, stamina, vitality, or immunity.

The Hui Yin area, Hai Di Lun, or first Soul House is the key for rejuvenation and longevity. I began to teach immortality in the eighth book of the Soul Power Series, *Tao II*,[1] and will teach you more in this book. I cannot emphasize enough that the first Soul House is the number one place that you must highly develop for your Tao journey, which is the immortal journey.

How can you know that you have a highly developed first Soul House? I will release the secret now. When you chant the sacred Tao Song mantra for the first Soul House (I will teach you this in chapter 3), you may feel a warm, tingling sensation. You could feel a pulse beating in the Hui Yin area. If these feelings stop after you stop the practice, you have not highly developed your first Soul House. When you have a highly developed first Soul House, which is the Hui Yin area, you will have a warm feeling there all of the time, day and night. Remember this signal. If you have not reached this level, you need to do more practice. In one sentence:

It is vital to highly develop the first Soul House, which is the Hui Yin area, for healing, rejuvenation, longevity, and immortality.

Second Soul House

The significance, benefits, and power of the second Soul House can be summarized as follows:

---

1. *Tao II: The Way of Healing, Rejuvenation, Longevity, and Immortality* (Toronto/New York: Heaven's Library/Atria Books, 2010).

- The second Soul House is the key for empowering the Lower Dan Tian, a fist-sized foundational energy center that is centered 1.5 cun^2 below the navel and 2.5 cun inside the front of the body.
- It is also the key Soul House for healing the large intestine.
- It is the sacred power house for developing energy, stamina, and vitality.
- It is the sacred power house for rejuvenation.
- It is the sacred power house for losing weight.

Third Soul House

The significance, benefits, and power of the third Soul House can be summarized as follows:

- The third Soul House is the key for empowering, healing, and rejuvenating the Water element, which includes the kidneys, urinary bladder, ears, and bones in the physical body, as well as for healing fear in the emotional body.
- It is the key for empowering, healing, and rejuvenating the Wood element, which includes the liver, gallbladder, eyes, and tendons in the physical body, as well as for healing anger in the emotional body.
- It is also the key for healing the stomach and small intestine.

---

2. Cun (pronounced *tsoon*) is a Chinese unit of measurement. This "personal inch" measure is equivalent to the width of one's top thumb joint. Hence, it varies from person to person.

- It is the key Soul House for healing and rejuvenating the urinary system and musculoskeletal system.
- It is key for empowering the Snow Mountain Area and Ming Men acupuncture point, which is located on the back directly behind the navel. The Snow Mountain Area is a foundational energy center at the base of the spine and in front of the tailbone. It is known to yogis as the kundalini, to Taoists as the Golden Urn, and to traditional Chinese medicine practitioners as the Ming Men area, which means Gate of Life. The Snow Mountain Area or Ming Men area is divided into Ming Men fire and Ming Men water. Ming Men fire is the most important yang in the body. Ming Men water is the most important yin in the body.

  Let me give you an example. Millions of people suffer from hypertension, diabetes, or menopause. From the standpoint of energy, matter, and traditional Chinese medicine, all three of these unhealthy conditions are due to an insufficiency of Ming Men water. Sacred Tao Song mantra practice to develop the third Soul House is sacred healing for hypertension, diabetes, and menopause.
- The third Soul House supplies energy food for the brain and Third Eye.
- It is the sacred power house for developing courage, strength, fortitude, and persistence to overcome challenges.
- It is the sacred power house for developing jing (matter).

Fourth Soul House

The significance, benefits, and power of the fourth Soul House can be summarized as follows:

- The fourth Soul House is the key for empowering, healing, and rejuvenating the Fire element, which includes the heart, small intestine, tongue, and all blood vessels in the physical body, as well as for healing depression and anxiety in the emotional body.
- It is the key for empowering, healing, and rejuvenating the Metal element, which includes the lungs, large intestine, skin, and nose in the physical body, as well as for healing sadness and grief in the emotional body.
- It is the key for empowering, healing, and rejuvenating the Earth element, which includes the spleen, stomach, mouth, lips, gums, teeth, and muscles in the physical body, as well as for healing worry in the emotional body.
- It is also the key Soul House for healing and rejuvenating the circulatory system, respiratory system, lymphatic system, and digestive system.
- It is the karma house.
- The soul mind body of financial blockages is expressed in the fourth Soul House.
- The fourth Soul House is the key Soul House for empowering the Message Center. Also known as the heart chakra, the Message Center is a fist-sized energy center located in the center of your chest, behind the sternum. The Message Center is very important

for developing soul communication abilities and for healing. It is also the love center, forgiveness center, karma center, emotional center, life transformation center, soul enlightenment center, and more.

- It is the sacred power house for soul communication with the Divine, Tao, and all kinds of spiritual fathers and mothers, as well as with the soul mind body of Heaven, Mother Earth, and countless planets, stars, galaxies, and universes.
- It is the sacred power house for the Soul Language Channel.
- It is the sacred power house for the Direct Soul Communication Channel.
- It is the sacred power house for the Direct Knowing Channel.
- It is the sacred power house for love, forgiveness, compassion, light, peace, harmony, purity, gratitude, obedience, loyalty, devotion, generosity, kindness, sincerity, and honesty.
- It is the sacred power house for expression and speaking truth.
- It is the sacred power house for developing Tao Song power of Tao presence.
- It is the sacred power house for developing Tao Song power of breath.
- It is the sacred power house to connect with humanity.
- It is the sacred power house for developing qi (vital energy or life force).

Fifth Soul House

The significance, benefits, and power of the fifth Soul House can be summarized as follows:

- The fifth Soul House is the key for healing and rejuvenating the thyroid, vocal cords, and throat.
- It is the sacred power house for developing willpower.

Sixth Soul House

The significance, benefits, and power of the sixth Soul House can be summarized as follows:

- The sixth Soul House is the key for empowering, healing, and rejuvenating the central nervous system, peripheral nervous system, and endocrine system.
- It is the key for developing the Third Eye.
- It is the key for developing intelligence and wisdom.
- It is the key for developing all brain functions.
- It is the sacred power house for developing concentration and memory.
- It is the sacred power house for developing intuitive abilities.
- It is the sacred power house for developing shen (soul or message or information).
- It is the sacred power house for developing Tao Song power of Tao hearing.

Seventh Soul House

The significance, benefits, and power of the seventh Soul House can be summarized as follows:

- The seventh Soul House includes the Bai Hui acupuncture point and sits directly above it.
- It is the sacred power house to connect with Heaven, the Divine, and Tao.
- It is the sacred power house of consciousness.
- It is the sacred power house for the highest soul standing.

The seven Soul Houses are the seven sacred spaces of the body. They connect with the Five Elements, which are Wood, Fire, Earth, Metal, and Water. They also connect with the various systems, organs, and tissues. In addition, they connect with the emotions. It is very important to understand the significance, benefits, and power of each Soul House. When you do practice for a particular Soul House, you receive the benefits for that Soul House and everything that is associated with that Soul House. To heal the seven Soul Houses is to heal the soul mind body of the entire body, from head to toe, skin to bone.

Developing the seven Soul Houses is vital not only for healing, but also for rejuvenation, longevity, and immortality. In my Tao teaching, to rejuvenate is to reach *fan lao huan tong* (pronounced *fahn lao* [rhymes with *now*] *hwahn tawng*), which means to transform old age to the health and purity of the baby state. Fan lao huan tong is an ancient traditional Tao term. Fan lao huan tong is a dream for most. Some Tao saints have reached fan lao huan tong, but they are very rare. In the present historic period, we have a great opportunity to create more saints to reach fan lao huan tong in order to become better servants.

The sixth and eighth books of the Soul Power Series, *Tao I: The Way of All Life* and *Tao II: The Way of Healing, Rejuvenation, Longevity, and Immortality*, plus this book and my future books on Tao reveal the essence of ancient secrets from traditional Tao teaching. Even more, they reveal new secrets, wisdom, knowledge, and practical treasures and techniques given to me directly by the Divine and The Tao Committee. I am extremely honored to be a servant of traditional Tao lineages and to be the servant of the Divine and Tao to share Tao secrets, wisdom, knowledge, and practical treasures and techniques with humanity. These new sacred Tao teachings and practices could lead many people to reach fan lao huan tong and to live a long, long life. Finally, some top saints will reach immortality. This Tao journey cannot be explained in words or comprehended by thoughts.

SOUL MIND BODY BLOCKAGES IN THE SEVEN SOUL HOUSES AND THEIR IMPACT ON HEALTH, RELATIONSHIPS, AND FINANCES

I have just explained the significance, benefits, and power of the seven Soul Houses. Each Soul House connects with different systems and organs. Each Soul House carries different powers and abilities. If you have a blockage in any Soul House, the systems, organs, powers, and abilities related with that specific Soul House will be affected. I cannot stress enough the importance of studying and understanding the significance and benefits of the seven Soul Houses, as well as their power and abilities. You will understand that if you have soul mind body blockages in a specific Soul House, challenges in health for related systems and organs, challenges in relationships, challenges in finances, and challenges in the power and abilities related to that Soul House could occur.

Wai Jiao

My spiritual father and mentor, Dr. and Master Zhi Chen Guo, discovered the Wai Jiao (pronounced *wye jee-yow*) after fifty years of clinical research and practice with thousands of patients.

WHAT IS THE WAI JIAO?

The Wai Jiao is the biggest space in the body. It is located in front of the spinal column and back ribs. It also extends up into the head. In fact, the Wai Jiao includes the backsides of the skull cavity, chest cavity, and abdominal cavity.

SIGNIFICANCE, BENEFITS, AND POWER OF THE WAI JIAO

The Wai Jiao is the sea of energy inside of the body. In order to understand the Wai Jiao better, you need to understand San Jiao first. San Jiao (pronounced *sahn jee-yow*) is a major teaching of traditional Chinese medicine that has been recorded for about five thousand years. Sometimes called the Triple Burner or Triple Warmer, "San Jiao" means *three areas*. The three areas are the Upper Jiao, Middle Jiao, and Lower Jiao.

The Upper Jiao is the body's space above the diaphragm. It includes the heart, lungs, and brain.

The Middle Jiao is the body's space between the diaphragm and the level of the navel. It includes the liver, gallbladder, pancreas, stomach, and spleen.

The Lower Jiao is the body's space from the level of the navel down to the bottom of the abdomen. It includes the small and large intestines, urinary bladder, kidneys, reproductive organs, and sexual organs.

San Jiao is the pathway of qi and body fluid. If San Jiao flows, one is healthy. If San Jiao is blocked, one is sick.

My most beloved spiritual father, Dr. and Master Zhi Chen Guo, discovered the Wai Jiao. It is absolutely sacred wisdom that humanity had not known before.

Energy blockages within San Jiao flow horizontally to the Wai Jiao.

For example, if one has heart or lung issues, the related energy blockages will move from the Upper Jiao to the upper part of the Wai Jiao.

If one has liver, gallbladder, pancreas, stomach, or spleen issues, the related energy blockages will move from the Middle Jiao to the middle part of the Wai Jiao.

If one has small intestine, large intestine, urinary bladder, kidney, reproductive organ, or sexual organ issues, the related energy blockages will move from the Lower Jiao to the lower part of the Wai Jiao.

Therefore, clearing the Wai Jiao is the key to clearing energy blockages. *The Yellow Emperor's Internal Classic*, the authority book of traditional Chinese medicine, states: "If qi flows, one is healthy. If qi is blocked, one is sick. If qi flows, blood follows. If qi is blocked, blood is stagnant." To promote free flow of energy in the Wai Jiao is to remove all energy blockages in the body.

To clear energy blockages in the Wai Jiao is vital. To clear soul blockages in the Wai Jiao is even more important. Soul blockages in the Wai Jiao are bad karma in the Wai Jiao. Why is it so important to clear these blockages? Soul is the boss. *Heal the soul first; then healing of the mind and body will follow.*

Since the Divine chose me as a servant of humanity and the Divine in July 2003, I have had the authority and honor to offer Divine Karma Cleansing and Divine Soul Mind Body Transplants. The fifth book of my Soul Power Series, *Divine Soul Mind Body Healing and Transmission System,*[3] explains this divine healing system.

This divine healing system has created thousands of soul healing miracles on Mother Earth. I have offered Divine Karma Cleansing to more than one hundred thousand people all over the world.

Karma is divided into good karma and bad karma. Good karma is created when a person and his or her ancestors offer love, forgiveness, compassion, light, generosity, care, kindness, integrity, and more to others. This good service in one's previous lifetimes and in this lifetime blesses the person and his or her descendants in this lifetime and in future lifetimes with good health, good relationships, and good finances.

Bad karma is created when a person and his or her ancestors offer unpleasant actions, behaviors, speech, and thoughts, such as killing, harming, taking advantage, cheating, stealing, and more to others. This unpleasant service in one's previous lifetimes and in this lifetime brings lessons to the person and his or her descendants in this lifetime and in future lifetimes. These

---

3. *Divine Soul Mind Body Healing and Transmission System: The Divine Way to Heal You, Humanity, Mother Earth, and All Universes* (Toronto/New York: Heaven's Library/Atria Books, 2009).

lessons include sickness, broken relationships, and financial challenges.

There is a place in Heaven named the Akashic Records. All of one's actions, behaviors, and thoughts, good and bad, from all lifetimes are recorded there. Every soul has his or her own book in the Akashic Records. All of one's lifetimes and also all of one's ancestors' lifetimes are recorded.

All of one's actions, behaviors, and thoughts from all lifetimes can offer good service or bad service, which creates good karma or bad karma. Therefore, the Akashic Records are the record of all karma.

In addition to clearing soul blockages in the Wai Jiao, it is also vital to clear soul blockages in the seven Soul Houses and Tao Song Channel (see page 49). I emphasize that one of the most important issues for healing and for transformation of relationships, finances, and every aspect of life is to clear soul blockages in the Wai Jiao, seven Soul Houses, and Tao Song Channel. Soul is the boss. Clear bad karma, which is soul blockages. Next, clear mind blockages, which include negative mind-sets, negative attitudes, negative beliefs, ego, and attachments. Also clear body blockages, which include energy and matter blockages.

Clear the soul blockages first; then clearing of the mind and body blockages will follow.

Clear soul blockages in the seven Soul Houses.

Clear soul blockages in the Wai Jiao.

Clear soul blockages in the Tao Song Channel.

Then, clearing of the mind blockages and body blockages in the seven Soul Houses, Wai Jiao, and Tao Song Channel will follow.

SOUL MIND BODY BLOCKAGES IN THE WAI JIAO AND THEIR
IMPACT ON HEALTH, RELATIONSHIPS, AND FINANCES

If the Wai Jiao is blocked, any kind of sickness in any system,
organ, cells, DNA, and RNA could occur. Chanting and singing
sacred Tao Song mantras to clear soul mind body blockages in
the seven Soul Houses, Wai Jiao, and Tao Song Channel is the
way to heal all sickness. The power of the Tao Song mantras for
the seven Soul Houses, Wai Jiao, and Tao Song Channel that I
will introduce in the next chapter cannot be expressed by words
or comprehended by thoughts.

The Wai Jiao is not only the key for healing sickness in your
spiritual, mental, emotional, and physical bodies, it is also the
key for healing relationships and finances. If you have relationship and financial challenges, you also have soul mind body
blockages in the Wai Jiao. To clear the Wai Jiao is also to transform relationships and finances.

Tao Song Channel

The Tao Song Channel starts at the Hui Yin acupuncture point,
flows up through the seven Soul Houses to the Bai Hui acupuncture point at the top of the head, and then flows down in front
of the spinal column through the Wai Jiao, returning to the Hui
Yin acupuncture point.

WHAT IS THE TAO SONG CHANNEL?

The Tao Song Channel is the internal channel of a human being.
It connects with Tao. Generally speaking, a person has many soul
mind body blockages in the Tao Song Channel due to mistakes

one has made in one's present lifetime and all past lifetimes. To clear the Tao Song Channel is to remove soul mind body blockages in the Tao Song Channel in order to align with Tao.

If your Tao Song Channel is completely pure and open, Tao frequency and vibration, with Tao love, forgiveness, compassion, and light, will radiate from your body to humanity, Mother Earth, and countless planets, stars, galaxies, and universes.

SIGNIFICANCE, BENEFITS, AND POWER
OF THE TAO SONG CHANNEL

The Tao Song Channel has unlimited significance, benefits, and power. Let me share some major ones. The Tao Song Channel:

- connects with Tao
- gathers Tao frequency and vibration, with Tao love, forgiveness, compassion, and light
- gathers the jing qi shen (matter energy soul) of Tao to transform your jing qi shen to Tao jing qi shen
- is the sacred path to heal the spiritual, mental, emotional, and physical bodies
- is the Tao power house to transform your relationships and finances
- is the sacred Tao temple for purifying your soul, heart, mind, and body
- is the Tao power house to increase your power for healing, rejuvenation, longevity, and immortality
- is the sacred Tao instrument to develop Tao abilities
- is an unconditional universal servant to serve humanity, Mother Earth, and all universes
- is the key for your Tao journey

SOUL MIND BODY BLOCKAGES IN THE TAO SONG
CHANNEL AND THEIR IMPACT ON HEALTH,
RELATIONSHIPS, AND FINANCES

If one's Tao Song Channel is blocked, one could:

- lack energy, stamina, vitality, and immunity
- have one's soul get lost
- be mentally confused
- suffer emotional imbalances, including anger, depression, anxiety, worry, sadness, fear, guilt, and more
- suffer sickness in the physical body, including pain, inflammation, tumors, cancer, and more
- have relationship blockages
- have financial blockages

In one sentence:

**The Tao Song Channel is key for health,
relationships, and finances.**

Five Elements

Five Elements is one of the most important theories and practices in traditional Chinese medicine. It uses the five elements of nature—wood, fire, earth, metal, and water—to summarize and categorize the internal organs, sensory organs, bodily tissues, emotional body, and more.

Five Elements theory has guided millions of people in history to heal sickness and to rejuvenate soul, heart, mind, and body.

Systems, organs, and cells can all be categorized into the Five

Elements. Balancing the Five Elements is one of the key healings in traditional Chinese medicine.

Expanding the wisdom, there are countless planets in the universe. They can be categorized into Wood planets, Fire planets, Earth planets, Metal planets, and Water planets.

Countless stars, galaxies, and universes can also be categorized into the Five Elements. Balancing the Five Elements is one of the key healings for countless planets, stars, galaxies, and universes.

WHAT ARE THE FIVE ELEMENTS?

The Five Elements are Wood, Fire, Earth, Metal, and Water.

Wood Element

The Wood element includes the liver, gallbladder, eyes, and tendons in the physical body, anger in the emotional body, and more.

Fire Element

The Fire element includes the heart, small intestine, tongue, and blood vessels—including all arteries, veins, and capillaries—in the physical body, anxiety and depression in the emotional body, and more.

Earth Element

The Earth element includes the spleen, stomach, mouth, lips, gums, teeth, and muscles in the physical body, worry in the emotional body, and more.

Metal Element

The Metal element includes the lungs, large intestine, nose, and skin in the physical body, sadness and grief in the emotional body, and more.

Water Element

The Water element includes the kidneys, urinary bladder, ears, and bones in the physical body, fear in the emotional body, and more.

See figure 6 on pages 54–55 for more on the Five Elements in the body and beyond.

The Five Elements have the following relationships:

- generating
- controlling
- overcontrolling
- reverse controlling

The *generating* relationship can be understood as the mother-son relationship. The mother gives birth to the son and feeds the son. The mother generates and nourishes the son. There are five mother-son pairs within the Five Elements:

Element	Yin Organ	Yang Organ	Body Tissue	Body Fluid	Sense	Unbalanced Emotion	Balanced Emotion
Wood	Liver	Gall-bladder	Tendons Nails	Tears	Eyes Sight	Anger	Patience
Fire	Heart	Small Intestine	Blood Vessels	Sweat	Tongue Taste	Depression Anxiety Excitability	Joy
Earth	Spleen	Stomach	Muscles	Saliva	Mouth Lips Speech	Worry	Love Compassion
Metal	Lung	Large Intestine	Skin	Mucus	Nose Smell	Grief Sadness	Courage
Water	Kidney	Urinary Bladder	Bones Joints	Urine	Ears Hearing	Fear	Calmness

Figure 6. Five Elements

- Wood generates (is the mother of) Fire.
- Fire generates Earth.
- Earth generates Metal.
- Metal generates Water.
- Water generates Wood.

See figure 7. These relationships can be seen in the natural world, where wood ignites to start a fire, a fire produces ash, earth can be mined for metal, metal carries water (as in a bucket or a pipe), and plants grow from spring rain.

Applying this to the organs of the body, a healthy mother organ nourishes the son organ. Therefore, a liver (Wood element) with balanced soul, energy, and matter (shen qi jing) and without blockages will fully nourish the soul, energy, and matter of the heart (Fire element). In the same way, a healthy heart will nourish the spleen (Earth element), a healthy spleen will nourish the lungs (Metal element), healthy lungs will nourish the kid-

Finger	Taste	Color	Weather	Season	Direction	Phase	Energy
Index	Sour	Green	Windy	Spring	East	New Yang	Generative
Middle	Bitter	Red	Hot	Summer	South	Full Yang	Expansive
Thumb	Sweet	Yellow	Damp	Change of seasons	Central	Yin/Yang Balance	Stabilizing
Ring	Hot	White	Dry	Autumn	West	New Yin	Contracting
Little	Salty	Blue	Cold	Winter	North	Full Yin	Conserving

neys (Water element), and healthy kidneys will nourish the liver (Wood element).

The generating or mother-son relationships among the Five Elements are extremely important. In chapter 3 I will teach you

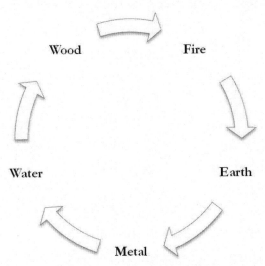

Figure 7. Generating relationship

Tao Song mantras to heal and rejuvenate each element and to empower the elements to nourish and balance each other.

The *controlling* relationship shows the order of dominance or control among the Five Elements:

- Wood controls Earth.
- Earth controls Water.
- Water controls Fire.
- Fire controls Metal.
- Metal controls Wood.

See figure 8.

In the natural world, wood draws nutrients from earth, earth dams water, water puts out fire, fire melts metal, and metal chops wood.

The *overcontrolling* and *reverse controlling* relationships are unbalanced relationships that can be used to describe and explain pathological conditions in the organs of the body. These

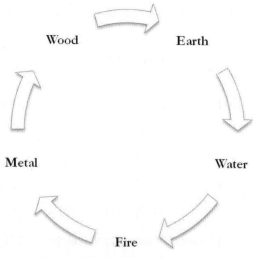

Figure 8. Controlling relationship

relationships and conditions are caused by soul mind body or message energy matter blockages.

Five Elements theory can be used to guide us on how to balance the physical body, emotional body, mental body, and spiritual body. It can be applied to balance nature. It can be used to balance planets, stars, galaxies, and universes.

SIGNIFICANCE, BENEFITS, AND POWER
OF THE FIVE ELEMENTS

Five Elements is one of the major universal laws. Its significance and power cannot be emphasized enough. Everyone and everything on Mother Earth and in countless planets, stars, galaxies, and universes can be categorized by the Five Elements. To balance the Five Elements is to balance humanity, Mother Earth, and countless planets, stars, galaxies, and universes.

In one sentence:

The Five Elements are a key for health, relationships, finances, and every aspect of life.

Five Elements is ancient teaching of traditional Tao and traditional Chinese medicine. It is a universal law. Study, understand, and apply the Five Elements to balance humanity, Mother Earth, and countless planets, stars, galaxies, and universes.

SOUL MIND BODY BLOCKAGES IN THE FIVE ELEMENTS AND
THEIR IMPACT ON HEALTH, RELATIONSHIPS, AND FINANCES

The Five Elements theory can go much deeper. The Five Elements can be subdivided. For example, the heart belongs to the

Fire element. But the heart itself carries the natures of Wood, Fire, Earth, Metal, and Water. The kidney belongs to the Water element. The kidney itself carries the natures of all five elements. In fact, every organ carries all five elements. Every cell has the five-element nature. Every tiny matter in the universe has the five-element nature.

If a person is sick, you can find out which elements are not balanced if you have open spiritual channels. Major healing will result from balancing those elements.

For challenges and imbalances in relationships, finances, and any aspect of your life, you can apply Five Elements theory to balance your relationships, finances, and any aspect of your life. In chapter 3, I will teach you how to balance your health, relationships, and finances through the Five Elements.

Sacred Tao Song Mantras for Removing Soul Mind Body Blockages to Transform All Life

*I*N MY BOOK *Soul Mind Body Medicine*[1] and in the Soul Power Series, I have shared with humanity that the root cause of all sickness is bad karma. Sickness is caused by blockages in soul, mind, and body. The soul blockages are the root blockage. This root blockage is bad karma.

You have had hundreds of lifetimes as a human being. Some of you have had more than one thousand lifetimes as a human being. Some ancient, high-level saints may have had thousands of lifetimes as a human being and continue to reincarnate on Mother Earth. They are chosen servants. They return to Mother

---

1. *Soul Mind Body Medicine: A Complete Soul Healing System for Optimum Health and Vitality* (Novato, California: New World Library, 2006).

Earth to accomplish their divine tasks to serve humanity and to be unconditional, Total GOLD[2] servants.

In all of your lifetimes, you have developed soul mind body blockages in health, emotions, the mind, relationships, finances, and more. To heal your health, unbalanced emotions, mind, and more, and to transform your relationships, finances, and every aspect of your life, you must remove soul mind body blockages.

Remove Soul Mind Body Blockages

You have learned earlier in this book about soul mind body blockages in health, relationships, and finances. Soul blockages are bad karma. Mind blockages include negative mind-sets, negative beliefs, negative attitudes, ego, attachment, and more. Body blockages include energy blockages and matter blockages. According to my teachings in *Soul Mind Body Medicine* and the Soul Power Series, in order to heal your health, relationships, and finances, you must remove soul mind body blockages in health, relationships, and finances.

There are two ways to clear your soul mind body blockages. The first way is to self-clear them. I encourage everyone to use this way. I emphasize it in my workshops and in my books. I teach and lead you in many practices to self-clear your soul mind body blockages. The second way to clear your soul mind body blockages is the divine way. Only a very limited number of people can offer this second way to humanity. Those who can are special servants, vehicles, and channels of the Divine. They are

---

2. Total GOLD means total gratitude, total obedience, total loyalty, and total devotion to the Divine and Tao.

given divine authority and ability to offer divine removal of soul mind body blockages.

In July 2003 I was chosen as a divine servant, vehicle, and channel. I was honored to be given the divine authority and ability to offer Divine Karma Cleansing and removal of soul mind body blockages as well as to offer Divine Soul Mind Body Transplants. I was also given the honor to create a system of Divine Soul Healers, which has four levels. The highest level is a divine servant, vehicle, and channel.

At this time (September 2011), more than twenty divine servants, vehicles, and channels can offer the divine way to remove soul mind body blockages in health, relationships, and finances, and also offer Divine Soul Mind Body Transplants for health, relationships, and finances. They can also offer divine blessings for an organization, for a city, for a country, for Mother Earth, and for all universes. These divine servants are traveling all over the world to offer Divine Karma Cleansing and Divine Soul Mind Body Transplants to serve individuals, families, humanity, organizations, cities, countries, and Mother Earth.

It is important to know how to self-clear soul mind body blockages to transform your health, relationships, and finances. The seventh book of my Soul Power Series, *Divine Transformation: The Divine Way to Self-clear Karma to Transform Your Health, Relationships, Finances, and More,*[3] is a special book that focuses on the vital wisdom and practices of self-clearing bad karma (soul blockages), as well as mind blockages and body blockages. Pay attention to this book. Learn and apply the secrets, wisdom,

---

3. *Divine Transformation: The Divine Way to Self-clear Karma to Transform Your Health, Relationships, Finances, and More* (Toronto/New York: Heaven's Library/Atria Books, 2010).

knowledge, and practical techniques—and especially the Divine Downloads—in this book to transform every aspect of your life, including health, relationships, and finances.

Now in this book, I am delighted to reveal Tao treasures to empower you further to self-clear soul mind body blockages in your health, relationships, and finances. I was honored to receive these sacred Tao Song mantras on May 27, 2011. These are priceless Tao treasures that every human being can apply to self-clear soul mind body blockages in every aspect of life. These sacred Tao Song mantras are extremely powerful because they carry Tao frequency and vibration with Tao love, forgiveness, compassion, and light.

Tao is the Source. Tao is the creator. Tao is The Way. Tao is the universal principles and laws. Tao creates Heaven, Mother Earth, and countless planets, stars, galaxies, and universes. Tao creates Tao Song. Tao Song is sacred Tao mantras that can transform all life. Tao gave these sacred Tao Songs and Tao mantras to me to pass to humanity. I am extremely honored, blessed, and humbled.

Sacred Tao Song Mantras for Healing the Spiritual, Mental, Emotional, and Physical Bodies

A human being has spiritual, mental, emotional, and physical bodies. Soul is the boss of a human being. Therefore to heal, one must be sure to remove soul blockages. This healing secret can be summarized in one sentence:

Heal the soul first; then healing of the mind, body, and every aspect of life will follow.

Tao Song is secret and sacred Tao mantras that carry Tao frequency and vibration. Tao frequency and vibration can transform the frequency and vibration of one's body, including one's systems, organs, cells, DNA, and RNA, as well as transform relationships, finances, and all blockages in one's life.

Tao Song also carries Tao love, forgiveness, compassion, and light. I repeat these sentences many times. In my workshops worldwide, in my regular weekly blessings for humanity—almost every day and at every opportunity, I share this teaching.

These sentences are themselves a Tao mantra. When you read these sentences, when you hear me speak them, you are receiving blessings from Tao. Read them again and again. Repeat them again and again. Each time you are receiving blessings from Tao.

Tao Song carries Tao frequency and vibration with Tao love, forgiveness, compassion, and light, which can transform the frequency and vibration of all life.

Tao love melts all blockages and transforms all life.

Tao forgiveness brings inner joy and inner peace.

Tao compassion boosts energy, stamina, vitality, and immunity.

Tao light heals, prevents sickness, purifies and rejuvenates soul, heart, mind, and body, and transforms relationships, finances, and every aspect of life.

Every time you see these sentences, do not think you know this wisdom and quickly skip through them. Go into the condition and read them slowly. Remember the secret of Sound Power, one of the Four Power Techniques that I have shared with humanity. Sound Power can be summarized in one sentence:

What you chant is what you are.

Now I share with you a secret of reading:

What you read is what you are.

When you read these five sentences, you are invoking Tao frequency and vibration with Tao love, forgiveness, compassion, and light. You are becoming Tao frequency, Tao vibration, Tao love, Tao forgiveness, Tao compassion, and Tao light. Be aware of this one of the most important wisdoms and practices. In fact, stop reading now and repeat these five sacred sentences for three to five minutes. If you can do it longer, even better. Go into the condition. Become Tao frequency and vibration with Tao love, forgiveness, compassion, and light.

DO NOT CREATE NEW BAD KARMA

Why should a person not read negative books or see negative images in magazines or movies? Because the negativity pollutes the soul, heart, mind, and body. As with the land, water, and air, once the soul, heart, mind, and body are polluted, it takes time to remove the pollution. For example, a pregnant woman should not watch negative, dark, or sexual movies, because that negativity and unpleasantness will pollute the unborn child, who is constantly receiving messages and learning in the womb. This pollution could affect the child for years, decades, even lifetimes.

In the spiritual journey, everybody understands the old saying "See no evil. Hear no evil. Speak no evil." I add, "Think no evil." To advance on your spiritual journey, you have to pay attention to these four "no evils." This is the key to purifying your soul, heart, mind, and body. You must not allow negativity and impurity to affect your soul, heart, mind, and body.

If you are a true spiritual being, you will understand the teaching more deeply. There is an ancient statement:

Zhong sheng wei guo, pu sa wei yin.

"Zhong sheng" (pronounced *jawng shung*) means *normal human being*. "Wei" (pronounced *way*) means *afraid*. "Guo" (pronounced *gwaw*) means *result*. A normal human being is afraid of the result. For example, when someone has a medical checkup, such as a CT scan, an MRI, or a biopsy, and the result is a diagnosis of cancer, the person could become very afraid. When someone is fired from his or her job, or his or her business fails, the person could become afraid, upset, and worried. When someone loses a beloved spouse or partner, that one could become very sad, angry, or afraid. Generally speaking, when people experience any unpleasant results in life, they could become afraid, worried, concerned, or upset.

Life-threatening sicknesses, financial challenges, relationship losses, and more are *results* in one's life. "Zhong sheng wei guo" means *when normal human beings have an unpleasant result, they are afraid, worried, and concerned.*

"Pu sa" (pronounced *poo sah*) means *bodhisattva*. "Wei" (pronounced *way*) means *afraid*. "Yin" (pronounced *yeen*) means *cause*. Bodhisattvas are enlightened masters. They understand karma. They pay great attention to "see no evil, hear no evil, speak no evil, think no evil," because they understand that when they create bad karma, unpleasant results will follow.

Zhong sheng wei guo, pu sa wei yin teaches that if you are not a highly enlightened spiritual being, you do not understand the power of bad karma. When you have disasters in life, you become afraid. A highly enlightened spiritual master is more afraid of the cause than of the result. A highly developed spiritual being does not want to create bad karma (the cause), because the bad karma will bring bad results (lessons, even disasters). Karma is cause and effect.

I have taught my students worldwide that it is easy to create new bad karma. What you say could hurt others. You could behave badly toward others. You could have an angry, critical, or complaining attitude toward others. You may think about taking advantage of others. You could have worse thoughts about really harming others. In daily life, it is very difficult to avoid creating some negative, improper, hurtful, or harmful actions, behavior, speech, and thoughts and to avoid seeing and hearing polluted things.

To minimize the new bad karma that you create, the important wisdom is:

**When you do, say, hear, or think something
improper, apologize instantly as follows:**

Dear Divine,
Dear Tao,
Dear Heaven and Mother Earth,
Dear all of my spiritual fathers and mothers,
I am sorry to have said this.
I am sorry to have behaved like this.
I am sorry to have thought this.
I am sorry that I have forgotten love, peace, and
*   harmony.*
Please forgive me.

Then chant:

Divine forgiveness
Divine forgiveness
Divine forgiveness
Divine forgiveness
Divine forgiveness
Divine forgiveness
Divine forgiveness . . .

If you transform your improper speech, behavior, and thoughts instantly in this way, you will not create new bad karma. *Zhong sheng wei guo, pu sa wei yin* is to teach us to be highly disciplined in our daily life, especially in actions, behaviors, speech, thoughts, hearing, and more.

If you create bad karma but do not apologize instantly, Heaven and the Akashic Records will record this bad karma. All of your bad karma accumulates. When your bad karma becomes heavy, you will start to learn karmic lessons. These lessons could include sickness, broken relationships, financial challenges, all kinds of emotional imbalances such as anger, fear, worry, depression, anxiety, and more.

Let me share a top secret for preventing new bad karma: **chant silently nonstop**. Tao Song is sacred Tao mantras that you can chant in your soul, heart, mind, and body nonstop. It is not necessary to chant out loud. You can chant silently. I have shared these two ways to chant in my earlier books.

To chant out loud is to vibrate the bigger cells and spaces in the body.

To chant silently is to vibrate the smaller cells and spaces.

To chant is to purify your soul, heart, mind, and body.

To chant is to serve.

To chant is to heal.

To chant is to rejuvenate.

To chant is to transform relationships, finances, and every aspect of life.

To chant is to enlighten your soul, heart, mind, and body.

If you can make it a habit to chant all of the time, you will avoid creating new bad karma. At the same time, you will self-clear the bad karma you have accumulated through all of your lifetimes, little by little. After many years of chanting, service, and purification, you could clear all of your bad karma from all of your lifetimes completely. If you have very heavy bad karma, it could be very difficult to completely self-clear all of it in this way, but it could be possible. It also depends on how committed you are to serving unconditionally and selflessly. In addition, it depends on how well you discipline your actions, behaviors, speech, and thoughts.

The Buddha, Shi Jia Mo Ni Fo or Siddhartha Gautama, the founder of Buddhism, created eighty-four thousand spiritual methods in his forty-nine years of spiritual teaching. One of his most powerful teachings is jing tu zong. "Jing" means *pure.* "Tu" means *land.* "Zong" means *special style.* "Jing tu zong" (pronounced *jing too dzong*) means *Pure Land style.* The teaching of jing tu zong emphasizes chanting one mantra, Na Mo A Mi Tuo Fo (pronounced *nah maw ah mee twaw faw*).

"Na mo" are words of honor to a special esteemed being. It means *I honor and appreciate you.* A Mi Tuo Fo (Amitabha in Sanskrit) is a great ancient buddha. Shi Jia Mo Ni Fo introduced A Mi Tuo Fo to his students.

A Mi Tuo Fo was an emperor in ancient times, before this "turn" or incarnation of Mother Earth. Mother Earth has been destroyed and reborn many times. A Mi Tuo Fo's time on Mother Earth was billions of years ago. While he was an emperor, he found his spiritual father. He gave up his emperor's position and went on his spiritual journey. He made forty-eight vows and created a realm in Heaven where there is no fighting, no ego, and no attachment. This place is named the Pure Land. A Mi Tuo Fo has gathered millions and millions of buddhas and bodhisattvas in the Pure Land. Millions of Buddhist practitioners and students in history have chanted *Na Mo A Mi Tuo Fo.* Na Mo A Mi Tuo Fo is the most popular Buddhist mantra. Go to any Buddhist temple in any part of the world and you will hear this chant.

Why do I mention this Buddhist teaching? I am not teaching Buddhism. I am sharing this powerful teaching to help you and humanity understand the true power of chanting.

In Buddhist teaching, when you are angry, you chant *Na Mo A Mi Tuo Fo.* Chant and your anger will disappear. When you have pain, chant *Na Mo A Mi Tuo Fo* and your pain could disappear. When you have relationship challenges, chant *Na Mo A Mi Tuo Fo* and you could receive huge blessings.

Many serious Buddhist practitioners in history have suffered from life-threatening conditions such as cancer. These serious Buddhist practitioners understand karma very well because Buddhist teaching emphasizes karma, which is cause and effect.

A major Buddhist teaching is that karma from past lives affects this life. Karma from this life will affect future lives. Karma cannot be separated from past, present, and future lives. When many Buddhist practitioners learn they have a "hopeless" life-threatening condition, they know that they are dying and they realize that the root cause is bad karma. What do they do? They start to chant *Na Mo A Mi Tuo Fo* seriously, day and night. I have read a Chinese book of sacred teachings that records many cases of people who chanted *Na Mo A Mi Tuo Fo* day and night for two or three months. Then suddenly one night they see A Mi Tuo Fo and other buddhas come to them in a dream to remove all of their blockages. The next day they experience a miraculous healing. There are thousands of stories in history from all over the world about the miraculous healings and blessings from chanting *Na Mo A Mi Tuo Fo.*

How does this chant work? A Mi Tuo Fo is a top buddha. He is a servant of humanity. He is a divine servant, vehicle, and channel. The Divine gave him the honor to offer miracle healing. When a person chants *Na Mo A Mi Tuo Fo*, A Mi Tuo Fo will come to help. People with difficult cases chant day and night for months. Every moment one is chanting, A Mi Tuo Fo is helping. In a few months, a miracle could happen. For some people, a miracle happens quickly.

Why do some people take months to heal chronic and life-threatening conditions by chanting *Na Mo A Mi Tuo Fo* while others can receive miracle healings instantly? It depends on one's karmic condition. The heavier one's bad karma, the longer it takes to clear it. A person who has lighter karma could recover much faster.

I am sharing the mantra Na Mo A Mi Tuo Fo to tell you and humanity that chanting is one of the most powerful ways to receive healing blessings. People have not paid enough attention to chanting.

I came to Canada in 1990. I have been in the west for twenty-one years. I started to offer spiritual teaching in 1992. In the west meditation is much more popular than chanting. But in the last few years more and more people in the west have started to chant. I share the history of the mantra Na Mo A Mi Tuo Fo to emphasize the power of chanting special mantras.

Tao Song is sacred Tao mantras. A mantra is a calling and a spiritual gathering tool. When you chant a Tao mantra, you could be very surprised by what you can see if your Third Eye is open. You could see A Mi Tuo Fo, Mother Mary, Guan Yin, Jesus, the Medicine Buddha, Saint Germain, and many more holy beings. You may not have called them. Why did they come? The answer is simple.

Tao Song is sacred Tao mantras. Tao is the Source. When you chant Source mantras, buddhas, holy saints, healing angels, lamas, gurus, and all kinds of spiritual fathers and mothers will be there to offer you healing and blessing. This is the sacred power of chanting and singing Tao Song.

SEVEN SOUL HOUSES

A human being lives in a house. A soul is a golden light being. A soul also needs to live in a house. A human being has seven Soul Houses. See figure 5 on page 32.

Many people understand the seven energy chakras. People may not understand the wisdom that the seven energy chakras are the seven Soul Houses. A human being's main soul (the "body soul") resides in one of these seven Soul Houses.

Modern medical science has mapped and charted the circulatory system, the nervous system, and more. Anatomy can describe the structure and location of the major arteries, veins, and nerves in the body. Traditional Chinese medicine has mapped and charted the meridians, which are the pathways of qi (vital energy or life force) in the body. For example, there are fourteen regular meridians. Every major organ has an associated meridian. More than three hundred sixty acupuncture points lie along the meridians. Unlike the blood vessels and the nerves, the physical eye cannot see the meridians. Only advanced spiritual beings with a highly developed Third Eye may be able to see the meridians.

In *Soul Mind Body Medicine* and the books of the Soul Power Series, I have shared with humanity that the body has a soul system, which means that in addition to a blood vessel chart, a nerve chart, a meridian chart, and more, there is a soul chart inside the body. However, it is impossible to create a physical picture of this soul chart. Remember my teaching in the Soul Power Series: Every system has a soul. Every organ has a soul. Every cell has a soul. Every DNA and RNA has a soul. The brain has billions of cells. Every cell has a soul, which is a golden light being. How can we show these billions of souls in a chart?

Every organ has a soul. Every meridian has a soul. Every acupuncture point has a soul. Now I want to share with you and humanity that every space has many, many souls. The abdominal cavity, the chest cavity, and the skull cavity each has millions and billions of souls. Therefore, when you highly develop your Third

Eye, you could be very surprised. When you scan a human being from head to toe, skin to bone, you will see countless souls moving inside the body.

In ancient Tao teaching, a human being has three internal treasures that I explained in detail in my book *Tao II: The Way of Healing, Rejuvenation, Longevity, and Immortality*.[4] These three internal treasures are jing, qi, and shen.

Jing is matter. Qi is energy. Shen is soul. In scientific study, shen is information or message. Conventional modern medicine pays attention to jing, which is matter. Your physician may order blood tests to measure biochemical changes within the cells. You may have an ultrasound, CT scan, or MRI to discover cysts, tumors, or other structural imbalances, which are all matter issues. When you have surgery, matter is removed. When you take medication, it is to adjust the function and balance of the cells, which are matter. Conventional modern medicine pays great attention to matter. However, modern medicine pays little or no attention to soul. Generally speaking, modern medicine separates body and soul.

Traditional Chinese medicine and many other healing modalities focus on qi, which is energy. *The Yellow Emperor's Internal Classic*, the authority book of traditional Chinese medicine, states, "When qi flows, one is healthy. When qi is blocked, one is sick." In traditional Chinese medicine, any sickness can be explained as a blockage in qi. Healing in traditional Chinese medicine is offered in three major ways: Chinese herbs, acupuncture, and Tui Na, which is Chinese massage. They all aim to promote the flow of qi. The basic theory and wisdom is that qi belongs to

---

4. *Tao II: The Way of Healing, Rejuvenation, Longevity, and Immortality* (Toronto/New York: Heaven's Library/Atria Books, 2010).

yang, while blood belongs to yin. If qi flows, blood follows. If qi is blocked, blood is stagnant. The healing theories and methods of traditional Chinese medicine can be summarized in one sentence:

To heal is to promote the flow of qi.

I am extremely honored that the Divine and Tao guided me to create Soul Mind Body Medicine and the Soul Power Series. My teaching and healing emphasize shen, which is soul. A human being has a soul. Every system has a soul. Every organ has a soul. Every cell has a soul. Every tissue has a soul. Soul blockages, which are bad karma, are the root blockages for health challenges, as well as for challenges in relationships, finances, and every aspect of life.

When a person has killed others, abused others, taken advantage of others, cheated, stolen, and done all kinds of harmful and hurtful unpleasant things to others in this lifetime and in all past lifetimes, the soul carries the bad karma that was created. The body soul carries karma. The souls of systems, organs, and cells also carry karma. The souls of spaces also carry karma.

Many people have received an organ transplant, such as a heart, kidney, or liver transplant. There are many stories of a recipient's personality changing after the transplant. This is often because the donor's heart, kidney, or liver carries bad karma. Once this bad karma of the organ is in and with the recipient, it will affect him or her. Some people who receive an organ transplant could be very lucky if they receive a karma-free organ.

Do not worry about your bad karma. You have no control over your previous actions, behaviors, speech, and thoughts. Be sincerely sorry for your mistakes, but do not feel guilty. The key is to learn how to self-clear bad karma. The other key is to stop creating new bad karma. In this book, I give you the highest treasures: sacred Source mantras to empower you to self-clear your bad karma and transform your health, relationships, and finances.

As I explained earlier, the seven Soul Houses are the major spaces inside the body. Spaces carry countless souls. A person with heavy bad karma could have thousands of dark souls sitting in a single Soul House. These dark souls come to us to teach us our karmic lessons.

On Mother Earth and in countless planets, stars, galaxies, and universes, there are two kinds of souls. There are two sides, which are yin and yang. There are Light Side souls. There are Dark Side souls. Both sides exist together.

Light Side souls include healing angels, archangels, ascended masters, lamas, gurus, kahunas, buddhas, bodhisattvas, Tao saints, holy saints, all other kinds of saints, all kinds of spiritual fathers and mothers, the leaders and workers of the Akashic Records, Heaven's generals and soldiers, the Divine, and Tao. The task of the Light Side souls is to offer love, forgiveness, compassion, light, peace, healing, harmony, grace, sincerity, honesty, generosity, kindness, purity, integrity, and more.

Dark Side souls include demons, monsters, ghosts, and more. The task of the Dark Side souls is to give karmic lessons and to damage. If a person has heavy bad karma due to killing, harming, taking advantage of others, cheating, stealing, and more in all lifetimes, then according to the law of karma, the person must learn lessons. The lessons could include sickness, challenging or broken relationships, financial challenges, business failures, and more. Dark Side souls are on duty to block your health, relationships, and finances. This is the duty of the Dark Side souls.

Many people have not opened their spiritual channels. They cannot see Dark Side souls. Some people who have opened their spiritual channels *can* see Dark Side souls. Karma cleansing is to clear dark souls.

There are two ways to clear your bad karma. One way is to self-clear your bad karma. The other way is the divine way.

You self-clear bad karma by offering unconditional or selfless service to others. To serve is to make others happier and healthier. Unconditional and selfless service includes doing volunteer work for spiritual groups, for charitable organizations, and for all types of good services; donating to support those who are homeless, hungry, or sick; supporting animals; protecting the environment; educating; healing; and much, much more.

When a person offers this good service, Heaven records the service and offers Heaven's virtue, which is expressed in Heaven's flowers. These flowers are red, golden, rainbow, purple, and crystal. These Heaven's flowers are spiritual currency. If a person receives enough spiritual currency by offering unconditional, selfless service, the Divine and Tao will forgive the person's spiritual debt, and then dark souls inside the person's body will leave. This is the process of self-clearing karma.

The other way to clear bad karma is Divine Karma Cleansing. Divine Karma Cleansing can only be offered by a special servant chosen by the Divine. When this chosen servant offers Divine Karma Cleansing, Heaven's generals and soldiers appear to remove dark souls inside the person. In history, the servants who have been given this kind of honor and authority are rare.

REMOVE SOUL MIND BODY BLOCKAGES
IN THE SEVEN SOUL HOUSES

A human being consists of soul, mind, and body. I have written *Soul Mind Body Medicine* and eight books in the Soul Power Series. I have explained in all of my books that sickness is due to soul mind body blockages. Now I will explain in detail what soul mind body blockages are.

Soul Blockages

Soul blockages are bad karma. There are many kinds of bad karma. Let me summarize the major types of soul blockages:

- **Personal Karma**—Personal bad karma is created by the mistakes one has made in all of one's lifetimes. Mistakes are harmful and hurtful actions, behaviors, speech, and thoughts, including killing, harming, taking advantage of others, stealing, cheating, and more. Your personal bad karma is carried by your soul. It is also recorded in the Akashic Records.
- **Ancestral Karma**—Everyone has an ancestral tree—parents, grandparents, great-grandparents, and so on. This is the ancestral tree from one's present lifetime. A person could have had, for example, eight hundred lifetimes. The person has an ancestral tree from each lifetime. In seven hundred of those lifetimes, for example, one could have had completely different fathers and mothers. In other lifetimes, the person could have had the same father or the same mother. The total ancestral tree of a person is the

combination of the ancestral trees from all of one's lifetimes.

There is a famous statement from ancient times:

Qian ren zai shu, hou ren cheng liang
前人栽树, 后人乘凉

"Qian ren" (pronounced *chyen wren*) means *ancestors*. "Zai shu" (pronounced *dzye shoo*) means *plant tree*. "Hou ren" (pronounced *hoe wren*) means *descendants*. "Cheng liang" (pronounced *chung lyahng*) means *enjoy shade*. "Qian ren zai shu, hou ren cheng liang" means *ancestors plant the tree, descendants enjoy the shade.* This expresses that when your ancestors create good karma with love, care, compassion, sincerity, honesty, generosity, kindness, purity, integrity, and more, they are planting a tree. Their descendants, including you and your descendants, enjoy the shade of the tree. This shade is the blessings one receives from one's ancestors' good karma. The blessings include good health, good relationships, good finances, good children, great intelligence, and success in every aspect of life.

Qian ren zao nie, hou ren zao yang
前人造孽, 后人遭殃

"Qian ren" (pronounced *chyen wren*) means *ancestors*. "Zao nie" (pronounced *dzow nyeh*) means *do bad things, including killing, harming, taking advantage of others, and much more.* "Hou ren" (pronounced *hoe wren*) means *descendants.* "Zao yang" (pronounced *dzow yahng*) means *receive disasters.*

"Qian ren zao nie, hou ren zao yang" means *ancestors create bad karma, descendants receive disasters.* These disasters include sickness, broken relationships, financial challenges, difficult children, and more.

- o **Ancestral karma on fathers' side**—All ancestral trees on the fathers' side from all of your lifetimes have created bad karma as explained earlier. The law of karma says that this bad karma will affect you and your descendants in this lifetime and in future lifetimes.

- o **Ancestral karma on mothers' side**—All ancestral trees on the mothers' side from all of your lifetimes have created bad karma. This bad karma will affect you and your descendants in this lifetime and in future lifetimes.

- **Relationship Karma**—A human being has many types of relationships. Your parents brought you into the world. Your grandparents brought your parents into the world. You may have a spouse, partner, boyfriend, or girlfriend. You may have colleagues, business associates, a boss, or employees. There are all kinds of relationships. Generally speaking, a person has had hundreds of lifetimes. One could accumulate bad karma in any relationship in all lifetimes. This bad relationship karma is also carried by your soul and recorded in the Akashic Records.

Some people cannot find a true love. They may get married two or three times. They may have many

boyfriends or girlfriends. Yet, they never feel they
have found a true love. Some people always find it
difficult to have good relationships in the workplace.
Some people have difficulties in their family relationships.

The root cause of relationship difficulties is bad
karma. If some people treat you very badly, it is very
likely that you treated them badly in past lifetimes or
in this lifetime.

I would like to share a story. An author came to
tell me, "I have a contract with a world-renowned
author who has made millions and millions of dollars. We coauthored one of this writer's most success-
ful books. This person totally forgot me and enjoyed
all of the benefits. My lawyer told me that he could
easily get one million dollars for me without even
going to court. I have the written contract as evi-
dence. This writer is very famous. My lawyer guar-
antees that he can do this for me." She asked for my
opinion.

I connected with the Akashic Records. I spoke
with the leaders of Akashic Records and asked them
to open this lady's book in the Akashic Records.
After I did a short reading, I gave her my suggestion
that she should *not* sue the other author. She asked
me why. I told her, "According to the Akashic Records, you cheated this man in past lifetimes. Your
lawyer is correct. If you sue this author, you will get
at least one million dollars from him. But the karma
between the two of you will continue."

She was sad to hear this but she respected my soul

reading. A little later she went to India, where she met Sathya Sai Baba and another world-renowned guru. Both of these gurus also told her that she cheated this other author in past lifetimes. Therefore, she should not initiate a lawsuit. With the additional spiritual guidance from these two gurus, she felt better. She did not sue the other author. Her life has been peaceful ever since.

- **Mental Body Karma**—If a person has hurt or damaged others in this lifetime or in past lifetimes in ways that caused mental issues such as mental confusion and mental disorders in others, this hurt or harm creates bad mental body karma.

- **Emotional Body Karma**—If a person has hurt or damaged others in this lifetime or in past lifetimes in ways that caused others to suffer emotional imbalances, this hurt or harm creates bad emotional body karma. Emotional imbalances include anger, depression, anxiety, worry, grief, sadness, fear, guilt, and more.

- **Organ and System Karma**—A human being has a soul. A bodily system has a soul. An organ has a soul. If a person has heavy bad karma, some of this bad karma could go to the soul of a system or the soul of an organ. A person could also have directly hurt the systems or organs of others in past lifetimes or in this lifetime. The bad karma carried by the souls of the systems and the souls of the organs could severely damage the systems or organs.

- **Cell Karma**—Each system and each organ consists of millions and billions of cells. If a person directly hurt the cells of others in past lifetimes, this creates bad cell karma. A person could also have such heavy bad personal karma (karma carried by the body soul) that some of it goes to the cellular level. Bad cell karma can be a root cause of all kinds of physical pain and sickness.

- **Curses**—Light Side souls bless people with love, forgiveness, compassion, and light that can bring healing, rejuvenation, longevity, and transformation of relationships and finances. Millions of people pray to Light Side souls to bless their lives. Dark Side souls can curse people. On Mother Earth, some people pray to Dark Side souls to curse others. Generally speaking, curses can manifest in two ways: (1) Dark souls such as demons, monsters, and ghosts directly come to you to bother you, block you, and cause pain and suffering. (2) The Dark Side creates and sends dark spiritual instruments such as knives and swords to stay with you and hurt you.

- **Negative Memories**—Souls have memory. Souls have great memory. Souls carry many memories. For example, someone could have leg pain and yet no one can find any reason for the pain. There is no growth, no damage, no infection. What is the explanation? This pain could come from soul memories. The person's leg could have been cut off in past lifetimes. The negative memories of these traumas are carried by the person's soul. The memory is so strong that the person actually experiences physical pain in the leg with no physical reason.

  Negative memories can be created by pain, physical sickness, trauma, accidents, emotional imbalances, mental confusion, relationship blockages, financial suffering, and more. Removing these negative memories is vital for transforming health, emotions, mindsets, attitudes, relationships, finances, and more.

- **Vows**—In the spiritual journey, many saints and buddhas have made serious vows to the Divine and Tao. When they accomplish their good vows, their souls are uplifted to higher realms of Heaven. Some have been uplifted to the divine realm.

  When a soul is uplifted to the divine realm, this soul stops reincarnation. In the human realm, there are all types of workshops, seminars, and retreats offered by all kinds of speakers and trainers. In the divine realm, the Divine offers the teaching. In the divine realm, a soul can receive divine teaching regularly. The honor for this soul is beyond imagination.

  The universe can be divided into yin and yang. As there are good vows, understand that there are also unpleasant vows. Here are some major kinds of unpleasant vows:

  + **Vow against the divine mission**—In past lifetimes and in this lifetime, some people directly fight with the divine mission. For whatever reasons, these people do not like the Divine. They go against the Divine. They could do all kinds of things, say all kinds of words, and have all kinds of behaviors to fight with the Divine. This creates huge bad karma.

  + **Vow to follow a wrong spiritual teacher**— Many people in the spiritual journey follow a wrong spiritual teacher in their lifetimes. They may not be aware that they are following a wrong spiritual teacher. They may have made a sincere vow to serve the mission of a wrong spiritual teacher. Unfortunately, this creates bad karma.

How do you know whether you are following a right or a wrong spiritual teacher? The standard is simple and straightforward. Is the spiritual teacher serving humanity unconditionally or is the teacher serving himself? This is the important principle to distinguish between a right spiritual teacher and a wrong spiritual teacher.

✦ **Vow of poverty**—Some people make a vow of poverty. If you carry this kind of vow, it is very hard to achieve financial abundance.

✦ **Relationship vow**—Some people make a vow to their wife or husband, girlfriend or boyfriend, or partner that they will love them forever for all future lifetimes. They may marry or live together for a few years and then separate. This kind of vow creates bad karma.

✦ **Vow to the Dark Side**—Some people make a vow to the Dark Side to harm people in all kinds of ways. This creates very serious bad karma.

• **Voodoo Sources**—A voodoo source is a group of dark souls who harm people through curses and other Dark Side methods. Voodoo sources can cause huge disasters for one's health, relationships, and finances.

• **Space Karma**—A human being has two kinds of spaces: bigger spaces and smaller spaces. Bigger spaces are the spaces between organs. Smaller spaces are the spaces between cells. Space karma is karma carried by the bigger spaces. Karma carried by the smaller spaces is considered to be part of the cell karma described above.

- **Karma in the Seven Soul Houses, Wai Jiao, and Tao Song Channel**—In chapter 2 I explained the significance, benefits, and power of the seven Soul Houses, the Wai Jiao, and the Tao Song Channel. Bad karma in these nine spaces will adversely affect their benefits and power. The blockages and imbalances in these nine spaces can affect health, relationships, finances, intelligence, and more.

Mind Blockages

Mind is consciousness. A human being has a consciousness. Every system, organ, cell, cell unit, DNA, RNA, space between the organs, space between the cells, and tiny matter inside the cells has a consciousness. Mind blockages include negative mind-sets, negative beliefs, negative attitudes, ego, and attachments.

Body Blockages

Body blockages include energy blockages and matter blockages. Energy blockages occur in the spaces between the organs and the cells. Matter blockages occur inside the cells.

SACRED TAO SONG MANTRAS TO SELF-CLEAR SOUL MIND
BODY BLOCKAGES IN THE SEVEN SOUL HOUSES

The Source gave me sacred Tao mantras on May 27, 2011. Now
I will share these sacred Tao Song mantras to empower you and
humanity to remove soul mind body blockages from every Soul
House and to develop the power of every Soul House. See the "A
Special Gift" section on pages 311–313 for instructions on how to
access video recordings of me singing the sacred Tao Song mantras
that I share in this book. You can learn the proper melodies and
practice with me just as though you were in a workshop with me.

First Soul House

Let me lead you to apply the sacred Tao Song mantras to remove
soul mind body blockages from the first Soul House and to develop the power of the first Soul House. First I want to review
the essential wisdom and knowledge about the first Soul House,
including its location, significance, benefits, and power.

The first Soul House is a fist-sized space located at the center
of the bottom of your lower abdomen. The first Soul House is
the foundation energy center for all seven Soul Houses, the Wai
Jiao, and the Tao Song Channel. It is also the key energy center
for healing the whole body, especially the reproductive system
and immune system, as well as for the anus, rectum, and sexual
organs. It is key for increasing sexual power. It is the key Soul
House for enhancing relationships. It is the key Soul House for
developing the power of your own Tao Song. It is the key power
house for developing your confidence and stability. The first Soul
House connects with Mother Earth and gathers the soul, mind,
and body of yin from the whole body.

Apply the Four Power Techniques to self-clear soul mind body blockages from the first Soul House and develop the power of the first Soul House.

Body Power. Sit up straight. Put the tip of your tongue as close as you can to the roof of your mouth without touching. Males, sit on your left palm facing the Hui Yin area. Females, sit on your right palm facing the Hui Yin area. Place the other palm over the bottom of your lower abdomen and pubic area. Alternatively, you can put both palms on your lower abdomen below your navel or one palm over the other below your navel.

Soul Power. Say *hello*:

> *Dear Divine,*
> *Dear Tao,*
> *Dear Heaven, Mother Earth, and countless planets,*
>   *stars, galaxies, and universes,*
> *Dear all saints, including Tao saints, holy saints, and*
>   *all other saints, buddhas, bodhisattvas, healing*
>   *angels, archangels, ascended masters, lamas, gurus,*
>   *kahunas, and all spiritual fathers and mothers on*
>   *Mother Earth and in all layers of Heaven,*
> *Dear my ancestors,*
> *Dear Tao Song,*
> *I love you, honor you, and appreciate you.*
> *When I sing the Tao Song mantras for the first Soul*
>   *House, please clear soul mind body blockages in my*
>   *first Soul House and develop my first Soul House.*
> *I am very grateful.*
> *Thank you. Thank you. Thank you.*

Mind Power. Focus on your first Soul House, which is the fist-sized space located at the bottom of your lower abdomen in the central channel of your torso. It includes the Hui Yin acupuncture point and the space directly above. Visualize a golden light ball or a rainbow light ball rotating counterclockwise in this area. If your Third Eye is open, observe whatever images you receive.

Sound Power. Chant or sing silently or aloud:

> *Hei Ya You Tao* (pronounced *hay yah yoe dow*)
> *Hei Ya You Tao*
> *Hei Ya You Tao*
> *Hei Ya You Tao*
> *Hei Ya You Tao*
>
> *Hei Ya You Tao*
> *Hei Ya You Tao*
> *Hei Ya You Tao*
> *Hei Ya You Tao*
> *Hei Ya You Tao*
>
> *Hei Ya You Tao*
> *Hei Ya You Tao*
> *Hei Ya You Tao*
> *Hei Ya You Tao*
> *Hei Ya You Tao*
>
> *Hei Ya You Tao*
> *Hei Ya You Tao*
> *Hei Ya You Tao*
> *Hei Ya You Tao*
> *Hei Ya You Tao . . .*

Chant or sing for three to five minutes now. There is no time limit for this. The longer you chant and the more you chant, the better.

If your Third Eye is open, as you practice more and more, you will see dark beings and dark shadows leave from your first Soul House. You may also see a golden light ball or a rainbow light ball rotating counterclockwise in this area. This golden light ball or rainbow light ball is the Jin Dan[5] of your first Soul House. It takes time to form this Jin Dan. The initial size of this Jin Dan could be about 10 percent of the size of a small grain of rice.

To remove soul mind body blockages from your first Soul House and to highly develop its power, one must practice at least two hours a day. If you create a warm feeling in the Hui Yin area and can keep the warmth all the time, congratulations! That is your ultimate goal and achievement in developing the first Soul House.

How fast can you develop the first Soul House and Hui Yin area? Everybody is different. If your soul has been seriously on the spiritual journey for hundreds of lifetimes, you could develop much faster. If your soul has not practiced in past lifetimes, you could take much longer. But Tao Song is a Source mantra and Source treasure. It will speed the removal of soul mind body blockages from the first Soul House and speed the development

---

5. "Jin Dan" means *golden light ball*. This special golden light ball is a oneness ball that gathers the shen qi jing (soul energy matter) of Heaven, Mother Earth, humanity, and countless universes. The body can have a Jin Dan. Every system, every organ, every cell, every DNA, and every RNA can have a Jin Dan. Energy centers, Soul Houses, and more can have a Jin Dan. No one is born with a Jin Dan. It takes special practice to build any Jin Dan. Sacred Tao Song mantras are one of the most powerful practices to build a Jin Dan. For more on the significance, benefits, and power of the Jin Dan, see *Tao I: The Way of All Life*.

of the First Soul House for everyone. The power of this Tao Song is beyond your comprehension. Practice more and more.

Here are some comments from some of my students after doing this practice:

> *Thank you, Master Sha, for the beautiful Hui Yin practice. I saw a beautiful golden light spinning in that area. Much darkness left my body. I seemed then to be floating in an empty space, free of this dimension. It seemed as though I was born into a divine space. What a profound experience. I am very happy and grateful to you, the Divine, and Tao forever. Thank you. Thank you. Thank you.*
> *K.M.*

> *Dear Master Sha, thank you for the great blessing for the first Soul House. When the blessing came, the high frequency light filled my first Soul House light ball. It began to rotate counterclockwise. Instantly, this very fine frequency light shot up my central channel and out through the top of my head. I suddenly went into a stillness. Then my entire body became saturated with this very special light. I knew that my body was transforming to a light body! Thank you!*
> *M.S.*

There is an ancient statement:

Zhi guan geng yun, bu guan shou huo
只管耕耘, 不管收获

"Zhi guan" (pronounced *jr gwahn*) means *just do it*. "Geng yun" (pronounced *gung ywun*) means *farming, including sowing the seeds, fertilizing, watering, tilling the soil.* This tells us to be a farmer, just do the right job for planting. "Bu guan" (pronounced *boo gwahn*) means *do not think*. "Shou huo" (pronounced *sho hwaw*) means *harvest.* "Zhi guan geng yun, bu guan shou huo" means *do the proper planting, including fertilizing, watering, and tilling the soil, but do not think about the harvest and a good harvest will come.*

This teaches us that when you do spiritual practice, for example, to remove soul mind body blockages and develop the first Soul House, you need to apply the Four Power Techniques, including singing or chanting *Hei Ya You Tao.* Put your mind on the first Soul House. Say *hello* for a blessing and use the proper hand and body positions. This is *Zhi guan geng yun.* Do not expect results. The results will come by themselves. The warm feeling in the Hui Yin area will come and remain longer and longer. I emphasize again that this is how you will know that you have highly developed your Hui Yin area: you will feel warmth in the Hui Yin area all the time. This is *bu guan shou huo.*

Some people do not follow this important spiritual principle. They expect too much. They keep thinking, "I want heat in my Hui Yin area. I want heat in my Hui Yin area all the time." If you expect too much, you could produce an uncomfortable, dry, burning feeling. This happens because when you use your mind too much, internal fire is produced.

Let me explain further with another example.

When you boil water in a pot, eventually the water will boil away. Then you cannot continue to fire the pot because it will burn the pot. In spiritual practice, this is called *burning the dry pot.*

I share this to help you avoid any side effects of meditation. Millions of people in the world meditate seriously, but they may not achieve good results if they do not know this sacred principle. I am releasing these sacred principles and techniques of meditation. They can be summarized in one sentence:

Shi xiang fei xiang
似想非想

"Xiang" (pronounced *shyahng*) means *thinking* or *visualizing*. When one meditates, what is one doing? To meditate is to use the mind. To meditate is to think, to visualize, and to concentrate. "Shi" (pronounced *shr*) means *seems*. "Shi xiang" means *you seem to think*. "Fei" (pronounced *fay*) means *no*. "Fei xiang" means *not think*. "Shi xiang fei xiang" means that when you meditate you seem to think of an area of the body for a moment, then you stop thinking of that area for a moment. You alternate thinking and not thinking. Think, visualize, or concentrate on an area for a short time, and then forget about it for a short time. Repeat this process over and over. This is the top secret for meditation.

In summary, when you meditate, do not focus on one area too much. Focus for a while and then leave the area for a while. Repeat this process. Follow nature's way. Relax. *Zhi guan geng yun, bu guan shou huo.* Just practice. If you feel no response in the area, it simply means you need to practice more. Do not be upset or irritated. The more irritated or upset you are, the more you will not develop. For example, millions of people want to open their Third Eye. They put too much intention on the Third Eye, which could cause side effects such as the "burning the dry pot" syndrome, which is a very uncomfortable feeling of dry heat. This could result in serious headaches, anxiety, and more.

Another major secret that I share with you and humanity is that when you meditate or practice, you may develop heat, tingling, and comfort in the Hui Yin area and the first Soul House. You will feel it more and more. Then suddenly this feeling disappears. You may think, "My goodness, what is happening now? My heat has disappeared. Why am I going downhill? I want to develop this heat. The heat came, but now it has disappeared." You could be frustrated.

Let me share with you another top secret. This is the process for everyone's spiritual journey. This is the spiritual law that the Divine and Tao apply to every spiritual being. Are you persistent? If you give up, you could lose your spiritual journey. You may think, "Oh, it does not work!" If you give up, do you know what could happen? You could come back in your next life to do the same thing. If you give up again in your next lifetime, you will need to learn the same lessons in another future lifetime. These lessons could be repeated for many lifetimes. Do not give up. Persist. Trust. Practice. *Zhi guan geng yun, bu guan shou huo.* One day, you will feel the heat, vibration, and comfort again. The heat from your Hui Yin will radiate down your legs to the tips of your toes. The heat will radiate up through your whole body to the top of your head. This is the first step of your advanced development.

Let me share with you another story. My second spiritual sister, the second daughter of Dr. and Master Zhi Chen Guo, developed advanced Third Eye abilities. One day her Third Eye suddenly closed. She asked her father, "Can my Third Eye open again?" Master Guo answered, "Your Third Eye will never open again." She said in her heart, "I *will* open my Third Eye again. I have to do hard practice." She did practice very hard, from 10:00 p.m. to 5:00 a.m. every night. About one and a half years later, her Third Eye reopened. Her Third Eye abilities were much more advanced than before.

Master Guo gave the message "Your Third Eye will never open again" to his second daughter in order to remove expectation and attachment from her. Because she had unshakable confidence and great persistence, she received great results. *Zhi guan geng yun, bu guan shou huo.* Never expect. Just do your practice. This is the important principle and teaching.

DUN WU AND LING GAN

When you read my books, read them more than once because there are secrets hidden within. When you read them a second or third time, you will suddenly have "aha!" moments. In spiritual study, there are two kinds of important "aha!" moments: Dun Wu and Ling Gan.

"Dun Wu" (顿悟, pronounced *dwun woo*) means *sudden realization.* When you read the book, when you practice, suddenly you realize the secret hidden within the book. You have received the secret of the secret by yourself. That is Dun Wu. No Dun Wu, no development. Without Dun Wu, you cannot be considered a wise person. Dun Wu is an "aha!" moment of sudden realization of the truth when you focus on a specific topic. For example, you could receive an "aha!" moment of spiritual wisdom and secrets while you are doing spiritual practice. When you realize the truth, your mind is on that topic.

The next "aha!" moment for a wise person is Ling Gan. "Ling Gan" (灵感, pronounced *ling gahn*) means *in some special condition you suddenly understand the truth of nature, or you suddenly discover scientific findings.* For example, when Newton saw an apple fall from a tree, he suddenly discovered gravity.

More recently, Professor Ruijuan Xiu was at the beach. She saw the waves lapping at the shore again and again. Suddenly she realized that the flow of the capillary system in the body was just like the waves on the shore. This realization was a great scientific insight and finding on how the capillary system works. This is Ling Gan.

Ling Gan means a scientist wants to know the truth or a spiritual seeker wants to have spiritual discoveries. They have tried so hard yet could not get an answer. When they suddenly receive the answer, their mind is not on the topic; something suddenly stimulates their mind, and they receive the answer and find the truth. This is Ling Gan.

Dun Wu and Ling Gan can be developed by everyone. Spiritual practice will help you to develop Dun Wu and Ling Gan. Blessings from Heaven, Mother Earth, the Divine, and Tao will help one develop Dun Wu and Ling Gan. Scientists have Dun Wu and Ling Gan because they have thought about the subject of their research for a long time. They put their heart and soul into it. In fact, they are doing deep meditation all of the time. Suddenly, Heaven, Mother Earth, the Divine, and Tao give them a big blessing. Suddenly they realize the truth and have a scientific finding through Dun Wu or Ling Gan. Therefore, Dun Wu and Ling Gan are the secrets of the "aha!" moment for the wise person, intelligent person, and highly developed spiritual being. You will understand that when you study Tao you will develop your own Dun Wu and Ling Gan. I wish you to have Dun Wu and Ling Gan as soon and as often as possible.

Let us continue to self-clear soul mind body blockages from the first Soul House and develop the first Soul House. We will apply the second sacred Tao Song mantra for the first Soul House.

Body Power. Sit up straight. Put the tip of your tongue as close as you can to the roof of your mouth without touching. Males, sit on your left palm facing the Hui Yin area. Females, sit on your right palm facing the Hui Yin area. Place the other palm over the bottom of your lower abdomen and pubic area. Alternatively, you can put both palms on your lower abdomen below your navel or one palm over the other below your navel.

Soul Power. As in the previous practice (see page 87), say *hello* to connect with the Divine, Tao, and all kinds of spiritual fathers and mothers, as well as with Heaven, Mother Earth, and countless planets, stars, galaxies, and universes.

Mind Power. Focus on your *first* Soul House. Visualize a golden light ball or a rainbow light ball rotating counterclockwise in that area. If your Third Eye is open, observe whatever images you receive.

Sound Power. Chant or sing silently or aloud:

> *Hei Ya You Zhong* (pronounced *hay yah yoe jawng*)
> *Hei Ya You Zhong*
> *Hei Ya You Zhong*
> *Hei Ya You Zhong*
> *Hei Ya You Zhong*
>
> *Hei Ya You Zhong*
> *Hei Ya You Zhong*
> *Hei Ya You Zhong*
> *Hei Ya You Zhong*
> *Hei Ya You Zhong*
>
> *Hei Ya You Zhong*
> *Hei Ya You Zhong*

Hei Ya You Zhong
Hei Ya You Zhong
Hei Ya You Zhong

Hei Ya You Zhong
Hei Ya You Zhong
Hei Ya You Zhong
Hei Ya You Zhong
Hei Ya You Zhong . . .

Chant or sing for three to five minutes now. There is no time limit. The more you chant, the better.

At this moment I am flowing this book in the Toronto Love Peace Harmony Centre. I am leading about thirty students to practice chanting this Tao Song for twenty to thirty minutes. I asked for feedback from the participants.

Linda Dupuis, a Divine Healing Hands Practitioner, shared, "When I first started to chant, my body felt extreme heat moving straight up through my central channel. It took me a few minutes to cool down. When I first started the practice I was tired, and now I feel more energy."

Lily Jain, doctoral candidate of Naturopathic Medicine, shared, "When I was chanting the Tao Song, I felt a lot of heat from the Hui Yin area to the Message Center and then to the top of my head. I felt a lot of vibration and a tremendous amount of heat. I felt like I was transported to a heavenly place, surrounded by golden light and with tremendous peace. I did not want to stop chanting."

Marsha Green, Doctor of Psychology, shared, "I felt a great deal of heat and vibration. I still feel a pulsing in the center of my body that is rotating counterclockwise. The focus is in the bottom of my torso. I feel extremely grateful to be here. I feel like I'm in a heavenly place."

Linda Brown, Doctor of Naturopathic Medicine, said, "When we were chanting, I was feeling a great deal of vibration in the Hui Yin area and it extended throughout my body. Now, several minutes after completing the chanting, I am still feeling a strong buzzing in the Hui Yin area, as well as in my hands. In fact, all of my cells are buzzing."

Tracy Drynan, Doctor of Chiropractic, acupuncturist, and martial artist, said, "The feeling of warmth and expansion of flow through my legs and through my back area was equal to what an hour or two of qi gong or tai chi practice would generate. This is amazing. This is a wonderful way to rebuild the body and feel vital. The warmth, tingling, and aliveness I feel within myself make me very happy."

Lydia Maes, Divine Healing Hands Practitioner, shared, "I felt a lot of vibration and heat in the Hui Yin area. I am very excited because I usually do not feel in that area. Then the heat went away. I could also see and feel the golden ball rotating in that area, which was a first for me."

Lynne Nusyna, Psychotherapist and one of my Worldwide Representatives, said, "I was very touched by the teachings that Master Sha presented as they were simple yet profound truth. The practices that were shared by Master Sha this evening provide the foundation for these very special teachings that are now being introduced to all on Mother Earth. I am so very grateful to be present as this new wisdom is being shared and to learn directly from the Master how to build a strong foundation for my Tao body and to be able to demonstrate Tao abilities."

Melalilia Uriarte said, "With the practice we just did, I was perspiring so much. I am a dancer and I usually do not perspire."

Venier Wing Sang Wong said, "Thank you, Master Sha. You have blessed me tremendously. I have breast cancer. You had cleared the bad karma of my seven Soul Houses, Wai Jiao, and Tao Song Channel. Shortly afterward, my abdomen expanded. I looked like I was five or six months pregnant. I saw with my Third Eye that cells were expanded. Blockages were removed in the first Soul House. Today when you led us in this practice, it happened again. My abdomen expanded and the energy moved up through my body. The degree of energy that was moving and moving was so powerful. Tao Song is incredibly powerful. I remember you led us in a Hui Yin practice a few years ago. I used to do that practice for one half hour and I remember such intense heat. I remember seeing Mother Earth shoot out of my body. I am so grateful to you for saving my life and taking us through this rebirth. We absolutely can self-clear karma with this. I am so grateful to you, Master Sha."

Jessica shares, "Thank you so much, Master Sha. When we were chanting today, my energy and matter circles were flowing. I have a lot of gas in my stomach now. I do not feel a lot of heat, but feel very cold. I feel a tingling sensation in my Hui Yin area. I am trying not to fight the feelings that I get. It is okay to feel this. *Follow nature's way.*"

I thank all who have shared their experiences. You can see that the power of Tao Song blessed everyone instantly. Chant Tao Songs more and more to receive more and more healing, blessing, and life transformation.

Now I am releasing the third sacred Tao Song mantra to self-clear soul mind body blockages from the first Soul House and to develop the first Soul House.

Apply the same Body Power, Soul Power, and Mind Power. For Sound Power, chant or sing silently or aloud:

Hei Ya You Ling (pronounced *hay yah yoe ling*)
Hei Ya You Ling
Hei Ya You Ling
Hei Ya You Ling
Hei Ya You Ling

Hei Ya You Ling
Hei Ya You Ling
Hei Ya You Ling
Hei Ya You Ling
Hei Ya You Ling

Hei Ya You Ling
Hei Ya You Ling
Hei Ya You Ling
Hei Ya You Ling
Hei Ya You Ling

Hei Ya You Ling
Hei Ya You Ling
Hei Ya You Ling
Hei Ya You Ling
Hei Ya You Ling . . .

Chant or sing for three to five minutes now. There is no time limit. The more you chant, the better.

Now I am releasing the fourth sacred Tao Song mantra to remove soul mind body blockages from the first Soul House and to develop the first Soul House.

Apply the Four Power Techniques.

Body Power. Sit up straight. Put the tip of your tongue as close as you can to the roof of your mouth without touching. Males, sit on your left palm facing the Hui Yin area. Females, sit on your right palm facing the Hui Yin area. Place the other palm over the bottom of your lower abdomen and pubic area. Alternatively, you can put both palms on your lower abdomen below your navel or one palm over the other below your navel.

Soul Power. Say *hello:*

> *Dear Divine,*
> *Dear Tao,*
> *Dear Heaven, Mother Earth, and countless planets,*
> *stars, galaxies, and universes,*
> *Dear all saints, including Tao saints, holy saints and*
> *all other saints, buddhas, bodhisattvas, healing*
> *angels, archangels, ascended masters, lamas, gurus,*
> *kahunas, and all spiritual fathers and mothers in*
> *Mother Earth and in all layers of Heaven,*
> *Dear my ancestors,*
> *Dear Tao Song,*
> *I love you, honor you, and appreciate you.*
> *When I sing the Tao Song mantras for the first Soul*
> *House, please clear the soul mind body blockages in*
> *my first Soul House and develop my first Soul*
> *House.*
> *I am very grateful.*
> *Thank you. Thank you. Thank you.*

Mind Power. Focus on your first Soul House, which is the fist-sized space located at the bottom of your lower abdomen in the central channel of your torso. It includes the Hui Yin area and the space directly above. Visualize a golden light ball or a rainbow light ball rotating counterclockwise in this area. If your Third Eye is open, observe whatever images you receive.

Sound Power. Chant or sing silently or aloud:

Hei Ya You Xu (pronounced *hay yah yoe shü*)
Hei Ya You Xu
Hei Ya You Xu
Hei Ya You Xu
Hei Ya You Xu

Hei Ya You Xu
Hei Ya You Xu
Hei Ya You Xu
Hei Ya You Xu
Hei Ya You Xu

Hei Ya You Xu
Hei Ya You Xu
Hei Ya You Xu
Hei Ya You Xu
Hei Ya You Xu

Hei Ya You Xu
Hei Ya You Xu
Hei Ya You Xu
Hei Ya You Xu
Hei Ya You Xu . . .

Chant or sing for three to five minutes now. There is no time limit. The more you chant, the better.

Now I am releasing the fifth sacred Tao Song mantra to remove soul mind body blockages from the first Soul House and to develop the first Soul House.

Apply the Four Power Techniques as above and chant or sing silently or aloud:

Hei Ya You Kong (pronounced *hay yah yoe kawng*)
Hei Ya You Kong
Hei Ya You Kong
Hei Ya You Kong
Hei Ya You Kong

Hei Ya You Kong
Hei Ya You Kong
Hei Ya You Kong
Hei Ya You Kong
Hei Ya You Kong

Hei Ya You Kong
Hei Ya You Kong
Hei Ya You Kong
Hei Ya You Kong
Hei Ya You Kong

Hei Ya You Kong
Hei Ya You Kong
Hei Ya You Kong
Hei Ya You Kong
Hei Ya You Kong . . .

Chant or sing for three to five minutes now. There is no time limit. The more you chant, the better.

You have learned the five sacred Tao Song mantras to remove soul mind body blockages in the first Soul House and to develop the first Soul House. Now we will put the five sacred Tao Song mantras together.

Apply the same Four Power Techniques as stated earlier.

Chant or sing silently or aloud:

> *Hei Ya You Tao*
> *Hei Ya You Tao*
> *Hei Ya You Tao*
> *Hei Ya You Tao*
> *Hei Ya You Tao*
>
> *Hei Ya You Zhong*
> *Hei Ya You Zhong*
> *Hei Ya You Zhong*
> *Hei Ya You Zhong*
> *Hei Ya You Zhong*
>
> *Hei Ya You Ling*
> *Hei Ya You Ling*
> *Hei Ya You Ling*
> *Hei Ya You Ling*
> *Hei Ya You Ling*
>
> *Hei Ya You Xu*
> *Hei Ya You Xu*
> *Hei Ya You Xu*
> *Hei Ya You Xu*
> *Hei Ya You Xu*

Hei Ya You Kong
Hei Ya You Kong
Hei Ya You Kong
Hei Ya You Kong
Hei Ya You Kong . . .

Chant or sing for three to five minutes now. There is no time limit. The more times you chant and the longer you chant per time, the better.

These sacred Tao Songs are sounds from the Source. As I mentioned previously in this chapter, the Source gave me these sacred Tao Song mantras on May 27, 2011. I am extremely grateful. There are no words that can express enough my greatest gratitude for receiving this priceless, extraordinary power. Humanity, Mother Earth, and countless planets, stars, galaxies, and universes can receive benefits from these sacred Tao Song mantras that are beyond any imagination and comprehension.

Second Soul House

Now let me lead you to apply the sacred Tao Song mantras to remove soul mind body blockages from the second Soul House and to develop the power of the second Soul House. First I will review the essential wisdom and knowledge about the second Soul House, including its location, significance, benefits, and power.

The second Soul House is a fist-sized space located at the center of the body between the first Soul House and the level of the navel. It is the key area for empowering the Lower Dan Tian, one of your foundation energy centers. It is also the key for healing the large intestine. It is the sacred power house for developing energy, stamina, and vitality, for rejuvenation, and for losing weight.

Apply the Four Power Techniques to self-clear soul mind body blockages from the second Soul House and develop the second Soul House.

Body Power. Sit up straight. Put the tip of your tongue as close as you can to the roof of your mouth without touching. Males, sit on your left palm facing the Hui Yin area. Females, sit on your right palm facing the Hui Yin area. Place the other palm over the bottom of your lower abdomen and pubic area. Alternatively, you can put both palms on your lower abdomen below your navel or one palm over the other below your navel.

Soul Power. Say *hello:*

> *Dear Divine,*
> *Dear Tao,*
> *Dear Heaven, Mother Earth, and countless planets,*
>   *stars, galaxies, and universes,*
> *Dear all saints, including Tao saints, holy saints, and*
>   *all other saints, buddhas, bodhisattvas, healing*
>   *angels, archangels, ascended masters, lamas, gurus,*
>   *kahunas, and all spiritual fathers and mothers on*
>   *Mother Earth and in all layers of Heaven,*
> *Dear my ancestors,*
> *Dear Tao Song,*
> *I love you, honor you, and appreciate you.*
> *When I sing the Tao Song mantras for the second Soul*
>   *House, please clear soul mind body blockages in my*

> *second Soul House and develop my second Soul*
> *House.*
> *I am very grateful.*
> *Thank you. Thank you. Thank you.*

Mind Power. Focus your mind on your first Soul House. This is the most important principle for singing a Tao Song. It does not matter where you offer healing and rejuvenation in your body; always put your mind on the *first* Soul House.

I am going to release the most important secret for singing Tao Song. It can be summarized in one sentence. Remember this wisdom:

> **When you sing Tao Song or any song, put**
> **your mind on the first Soul House.**

I have not received any physical teaching or training for singing. The Divine and Tao have trained me to put my mind on the first Soul House to sing Soul Songs, Divine Soul Songs, and Tao Songs. The Divine and Tao have trained me to *always* put my mind on the first Soul House: when I speak, sing, or teach. All the time, I keep my mind on the first Soul House. The first Soul House is the most important Soul House for healing, rejuvenation, longevity, and immortality. To keep your mind on your first Soul House is to develop its power. This is the most important secret that I release for singing Tao Song. When you sing a Tao Song, visualize a golden light ball or a rainbow light ball rotating counterclockwise in the first Soul House.

Sound Power. Chant or sing silently or aloud:

Heng Ya You Tao (pronounced *hung yah yoe dow*)
Heng Ya You Tao
Heng Ya You Tao
Heng Ya You Tao
Heng Ya You Tao

Heng Ya You Tao
Heng Ya You Tao
Heng Ya You Tao
Heng Ya You Tao
Heng Ya You Tao

Heng Ya You Tao
Heng Ya You Tao
Heng Ya You Tao
Heng Ya You Tao
Heng Ya You Tao

Heng Ya You Tao
Heng Ya You Tao
Heng Ya You Tao
Heng Ya You Tao
Heng Ya You Tao . . .

Let us next chant the second sacred Tao Song mantra for the second Soul House.

Chant or sing silently or aloud:

Heng Ya You Zhong (pronounced *hung yah yoe jawng*)
Heng Ya You Zhong

Heng Ya You Zhong
Heng Ya You Zhong
Heng Ya You Zhong

Heng Ya You Zhong
Heng Ya You Zhong
Heng Ya You Zhong
Heng Ya You Zhong
Heng Ya You Zhong

Heng Ya You Zhong
Heng Ya You Zhong
Heng Ya You Zhong
Heng Ya You Zhong
Heng Ya You Zhong

Heng Ya You Zhong
Heng Ya You Zhong
Heng Ya You Zhong
Heng Ya You Zhong
Heng Ya You Zhong . . .

Continue to self-clear soul mind body blockages from the second Soul House and develop the second Soul House with the third, fourth, and fifth sacred Tao Song mantras:

Heng Ya You Ling (pronounced *hung yah yoe ling*)
Heng Ya You Ling
Heng Ya You Ling
Heng Ya You Ling
Heng Ya You Ling

Heng Ya You Ling
Heng Ya You Ling
Heng Ya You Ling
Heng Ya You Ling
Heng Ya You Ling

Heng Ya You Ling
Heng Ya You Ling
Heng Ya You Ling
Heng Ya You Ling
Heng Ya You Ling

Heng Ya You Ling
Heng Ya You Ling
Heng Ya You Ling
Heng Ya You Ling
Heng Ya You Ling . . .

Heng Ya You Xu (pronounced *hung yah yoe shü*)
Heng Ya You Xu
Heng Ya You Xu
Heng Ya You Xu
Heng Ya You Xu

Heng Ya You Xu
Heng Ya You Xu
Heng Ya You Xu
Heng Ya You Xu
Heng Ya You Xu

Heng Ya You Xu
Heng Ya You Xu
Heng Ya You Xu
Heng Ya You Xu
Heng Ya You Xu

Heng Ya You Xu
Heng Ya You Xu
Heng Ya You Xu
Heng Ya You Xu
Heng Ya You Xu . . .

Heng Ya You Kong (pronounced *hung ya yoe kawng*)
Heng Ya You Kong
Heng Ya You Kong
Heng Ya You Kong
Heng Ya You Kong

Heng Ya You Kong
Heng Ya You Kong
Heng Ya You Kong
Heng Ya You Kong
Heng Ya You Kong

Heng Ya You Kong
Heng Ya You Kong
Heng Ya You Kong
Heng Ya You Kong
Heng Ya You Kong

Heng Ya You Kong
Heng Ya You Kong
Heng Ya You Kong
Heng Ya You Kong
Heng Ya You Kong . . .

Chant or sing for three to five minutes now. There is no time limit. The more you chant and the longer you chant per time, the better.

If you have health issues related to the second Soul House, you absolutely need to chant more. There is no time limit. For rejuvenation and longevity, you need to chant much more. Tao Song carries the power, frequency, and vibration of the Source. This power cannot be expressed in any words or comprehended by any thoughts. My teaching for many years has emphasized: *If you want to know if a pear is sweet, taste it.* If you want to know if Tao Song is powerful, experience it.

My students shared their experience of this practice and blessing:

> *Thank you, dear Master Sha and dear Divine and Tao, for the extraordinary blessing for the second Soul House. Everything feels very clear and full of beautiful light. My heart is content. All my gratitude.*
> *K.M.*

> *I am totally blissed and in stillness and oneness within myself. It is a wonderful feeling. I am very grateful.*
> *C.L.*

Chant or sing Tao Song mantras more and more. They can transform your health, relationships, and finances beyond comprehension.

Third Soul House

Now let me lead you to apply the sacred Tao Song mantras to remove soul mind body blockages from the third Soul House and develop the power of the third Soul House. I will explain the essence of the location of the third Soul House, as well as the significance, benefits, and power of this Soul House. The third Soul House is a fist-sized space located at the center of the body at the level of the navel.

The third Soul House has great significance, benefits, and power. It is the key Soul House for empowering, healing, and rejuvenating the Water element and the Wood element. The Water element includes the kidneys, urinary bladder, ears, and bones in the physical body and fear in the emotional body. The Wood element includes the liver, gallbladder, eyes, and tendons in the physical body and anger in the emotional body. The third Soul House is also key for healing the stomach, small intestine, urinary system, and musculoskeletal system. It also empowers the Snow Mountain Area and Ming Men acupuncture point. It is the sacred power house for developing courage, strength, and fortitude to overcome challenges and for developing jing, which is matter.

Apply the Four Power Techniques to self-clear soul mind body blockages from the third Soul House and develop the third Soul House.

Body Power. Sit up straight. Put the tip of your tongue as close as you can to the roof of your mouth without touching. Males, sit on your left palm facing the Hui Yin area. Females, sit on your right palm facing the Hui Yin area. Place the other palm over the bottom of your lower abdomen and pubic area. Alternatively, you can put both palms on your lower abdomen below your navel or one palm over the other below your navel.

Soul Power. Say *hello:*

> *Dear Divine,*
> *Dear Tao,*
> *Dear Heaven, Mother Earth, and countless planets,*
>   *stars, galaxies, and universes,*
> *Dear all saints, including Tao saints, holy saints, and*
>   *all other saints, buddhas, bodhisattvas, healing*
>   *angels, archangels, ascended masters, lamas, gurus,*
>   *kahunas, and all spiritual fathers and mothers on*
>   *Mother Earth and in all layers of Heaven,*
> *Dear my ancestors,*
> *Dear Tao Song,*
> *I love you, honor you, and appreciate you.*
> *When I sing the Tao Song mantras for the third Soul*
>   *House, please clear soul mind body blockages in my*
>   *third Soul House and develop my third Soul House.*
> *I am very grateful.*
> *Thank you. Thank you. Thank you.*

Mind Power. Again, focus your mind on your *first* Soul House. I have explained the importance of this in my discussion above about the second Soul House. Visualize a golden light ball or a rainbow light ball rotating counterclockwise in the area of your first Soul House. If your Third Eye is open, observe whatever images you receive.

Sound Power. Chant or sing silently or aloud:

Hong Ya You Tao (pronounced *hawng yah yoe dow*)
Hong Ya You Tao
Hong Ya You Tao
Hong Ya You Tao
Hong Ya You Tao

Hong Ya You Tao
Hong Ya You Tao
Hong Ya You Tao
Hong Ya You Tao
Hong Ya You Tao

Hong Ya You Tao
Hong Ya You Tao
Hong Ya You Tao
Hong Ya You Tao
Hong Ya You Tao

Hong Ya You Tao
Hong Ya You Tao
Hong Ya You Tao
Hong Ya You Tao
Hong Ya You Tao . . .

Let us continue by chanting the second sacred Tao Song mantra for the third Soul House.

Chant or sing silently or aloud:

Hong Ya You Zhong (pronounced *hawng yah yoe jawng*)
Hong Ya You Zhong

Hong Ya You Zhong
Hong Ya You Zhong
Hong Ya You Zhong

Hong Ya You Zhong
Hong Ya You Zhong
Hong Ya You Zhong
Hong Ya You Zhong
Hong Ya You Zhong

Hong Ya You Zhong
Hong Ya You Zhong
Hong Ya You Zhong
Hong Ya You Zhong
Hong Ya You Zhong

Hong Ya You Zhong
Hong Ya You Zhong
Hong Ya You Zhong
Hong Ya You Zhong
Hong Ya You Zhong . . .

Continue to self-clear soul mind body blockages from the third Soul House and develop the third Soul House with the third, fourth, and fifth sacred Tao Song mantras:

Hong Ya You Ling (pronounced *hawng ya yoe ling*)
Hong Ya You Ling
Hong Ya You Ling
Hong Ya You Ling
Hong Ya You Ling

Hong Ya You Ling
Hong Ya You Ling
Hong Ya You Ling
Hong Ya You Ling
Hong Ya You Ling

Hong Ya You Ling
Hong Ya You Ling
Hong Ya You Ling
Hong Ya You Ling
Hong Ya You Ling

Hong Ya You Ling
Hong Ya You Ling
Hong Ya You Ling
Hong Ya You Ling
Hong Ya You Ling . . .

Hong Ya You Xu (pronounced *hawng ya yoe shü*)
Hong Ya You Xu
Hong Ya You Xu
Hong Ya You Xu
Hong Ya You Xu

Hong Ya You Xu
Hong Ya You Xu
Hong Ya You Xu
Hong Ya You Xu
Hong Ya You Xu

Hong Ya You Xu
Hong Ya You Xu

Hong Ya You Xu
Hong Ya You Xu
Hong Ya You Xu

Hong Ya You Xu
Hong Ya You Xu
Hong Ya You Xu
Hong Ya You Xu
Hong Ya You Xu . . .

Hong Ya You Kong (pronounced *hawng ya yoe kawng*)
Hong Ya You Kong
Hong Ya You Kong
Hong Ya You Kong
Hong Ya You Kong

Hong Ya You Kong
Hong Ya You Kong
Hong Ya You Kong
Hong Ya You Kong
Hong Ya You Kong

Hong Ya You Kong
Hong Ya You Kong
Hong Ya You Kong
Hong Ya You Kong
Hong Ya You Kong

Hong Ya You Kong
Hong Ya You Kong
Hong Ya You Kong

Hong Ya You Kong
Hong Ya You Kong . . .

Chant or sing for three to five minutes now. There is no time limit for this. The longer you chant and the more you chant, the better.

Every Soul House has its own power and significance. Therefore, the practice with each Soul House is unique. If you have health challenges related to a specific Soul House, make sure you practice more with that Soul House. To chant is to transform your frequency to Tao frequency. To chant is to heal. To chant is to rejuvenate. To chant is to reach *fan lao huan tong*, which is to transform old age to the health and purity of the baby state. To chant is to prolong life. To chant is to move in the direction of immortality.

I asked my Tao Song workshop participants to share their experience of this practice for the third Soul House.

> *The blessing for our third Soul House gives me a feeling of sweating and heat that was marvelous for my kidneys. Thank you, Master Sha. Thank you, Tao.*
> *T.S.*

> *Dear Master Sha, the second Soul House and the third Soul House are gleefully singing and dancing. Thank you.*
> *D.T.*

Now let us move on to the fourth Soul House.

Fourth Soul House

The fourth Soul House is a fist-sized space located at the center of the body in the chest behind the sternum.

The fourth Soul House is very significant. This Soul House is the key for empowering, healing, and rejuvenating the Fire element, Metal element, and Earth element. The Fire element includes the heart, small intestine, tongue, and blood vessels, including large and small arteries, capillary system, and small and large veins. The Fire element also connects with depression and anxiety in the emotional body. The Metal element includes the lungs, large intestine, skin, and nose in the physical body and connects with sadness and grief in the emotional body. The Earth element includes the spleen, stomach, mouth, lips, gums, teeth, and muscles in the physical body and connects with worry in the emotional body. The fourth Soul House is also the key Soul House for healing and rejuvenation of the circulatory system, respiratory system, lymphatic system, and digestive system.

The fourth Soul House is also the key Soul House for empowering the Message Center, which is the Soul Language center, soul communication center, direct knowing center, karma center, healing center, love, forgiveness, compassion, and light center, life transformation center, and soul enlightenment center.

This Soul House is the sacred power house for expression and speaking truth. It is also the power house for developing Tao Song power of Tao presence and for developing Tao Song power of breath. The fourth Soul House is the power house to develop qi, which is vital energy or life force.

Apply the Four Power Techniques to self-clear soul mind body blockages from the fourth Soul House and develop the fourth Soul House.

Body Power. Sit up straight. Put the tip of your tongue as close as you can to the roof of your mouth without touching. Males, sit on your left palm facing the Hui Yin area. Females, sit on your right palm facing the Hui Yin area. Place the other palm over the bottom of your lower abdomen and pubic area. Alternatively, you can put both palms on your lower abdomen below your navel or one palm over the other below your navel.

Soul Power. Say *hello:*

> *Dear Divine,*
> *Dear Tao,*
> *Dear Heaven, Mother Earth, and countless planets,*
>   *stars, galaxies, and universes,*
> *Dear all saints, including Tao saints, holy saints, and*
>   *all other saints, buddhas, bodhisattvas, healing*
>   *angels, archangels, ascended masters, lamas, gurus,*
>   *kahunas, and all spiritual fathers and mothers on*
>   *Mother Earth and in all layers of Heaven,*
> *Dear my ancestors,*
> *Dear Tao Song,*
> *I love you, honor you, and appreciate you.*
> *When I sing the Tao Song mantras for the fourth Soul*
>   *House, please clear soul mind body blockages in my*
>   *fourth Soul House and develop my fourth Soul*
>   *House.*
> *I am very grateful.*
> *Thank you. Thank you. Thank you.*

Mind Power. Focus your mind on your *first* Soul House. Visualize a golden light ball or a rainbow light ball rotating counterclockwise in that area. If your Third Eye is open, observe whatever images you receive.

Sound Power. Chant or sing silently or aloud:

> *Ah Ya You Tao* (pronounced *ah yah yoe dow*)
> *Ah Ya You Tao*
> *Ah Ya You Tao*
> *Ah Ya You Tao*
> *Ah Ya You Tao*
>
> *Ah Ya You Tao*
> *Ah Ya You Tao*
> *Ah Ya You Tao*
> *Ah Ya You Tao*
> *Ah Ya You Tao*
>
> *Ah Ya You Tao*
> *Ah Ya You Tao*
> *Ah Ya You Tao*
> *Ah Ya You Tao*
> *Ah Ya You Tao*
>
> *Ah Ya You Tao*
> *Ah Ya You Tao*
> *Ah Ya You Tao*
> *Ah Ya You Tao*
> *Ah Ya You Tao . . .*

Let us continue by chanting the second sacred Tao Song mantra for the fourth Soul House.

Chant or sing silently or aloud:

Ah Ya You Zhong (pronounced *ah yah yoe jawng*)
Ah Ya You Zhong
Ah Ya You Zhong
Ah Ya You Zhong
Ah Ya You Zhong

Ah Ya You Zhong
Ah Ya You Zhong
Ah Ya You Zhong
Ah Ya You Zhong
Ah Ya You Zhong

Ah Ya You Zhong
Ah Ya You Zhong
Ah Ya You Zhong
Ah Ya You Zhong
Ah Ya You Zhong

Ah Ya You Zhong
Ah Ya You Zhong
Ah Ya You Zhong
Ah Ya You Zhong
Ah Ya You Zhong . . .

Continue to self-clear soul mind body blockages from the fourth Soul House and develop the fourth Soul House with the third, fourth, and fifth sacred Tao Song mantras:

Ah Ya You Ling (pronounced *ah yah yoe ling*)
Ah Ya You Ling
Ah Ya You Ling

Ah Ya You Ling
Ah Ya You Ling

Ah Ya You Ling
Ah Ya You Ling
Ah Ya You Ling
Ah Ya You Ling
Ah Ya You Ling

Ah Ya You Ling
Ah Ya You Ling
Ah Ya You Ling
Ah Ya You Ling
Ah Ya You Ling

Ah Ya You Ling
Ah Ya You Ling
Ah Ya You Ling
Ah Ya You Ling
Ah Ya You Ling . . .

Ah Ya You Xu (pronounced *ah yah yoe shü*)
Ah Ya You Xu
Ah Ya You Xu
Ah Ya You Xu
Ah Ya You Xu

Ah Ya You Xu
Ah Ya You Xu
Ah Ya You Xu
Ah Ya You Xu
Ah Ya You Xu

Ah Ya You Xu
Ah Ya You Xu
Ah Ya You Xu
Ah Ya You Xu
Ah Ya You Xu

Ah Ya You Xu
Ah Ya You Xu
Ah Ya You Xu
Ah Ya You Xu
Ah Ya You Xu . . .

Ah Ya You Kong (pronounced *ah yah yoe kawng*)
Ah Ya You Kong
Ah Ya You Kong
Ah Ya You Kong
Ah Ya You Kong

Ah Ya You Kong
Ah Ya You Kong
Ah Ya You Kong
Ah Ya You Kong
Ah Ya You Kong

Ah Ya You Kong
Ah Ya You Kong
Ah Ya You Kong
Ah Ya You Kong
Ah Ya You Kong

Ah Ya You Kong
Ah Ya You Kong

Ah Ya You Kong
Ah Ya You Kong
Ah Ya You Kong . . .

Chant or sing for three to five minutes now. There is no time limit for this. The longer you chant and the more you chant, the better.

The Tao Song mantras for the fourth Soul House are extremely important. These Tao Song mantras are key to opening the spiritual channels (Soul Language Channel, Direct Soul Communication Channel, Third Eye Channel, Direct Knowing Channel) and to heal the Fire, Earth, and Metal elements. These Tao Song mantras also bring Tao love, forgiveness, compassion, and light to your fourth Soul House. This Tao Song is vital to self-clear all types of karma, including financial karma.

Practice more and more. The benefits are unlimited.

Next is the fifth Soul House.

Fifth Soul House

The fifth Soul House is a fist-sized space located at the center of the body in the center of the throat.

The fifth Soul House is the key for healing and rejuvenation of the thyroid, vocal cords, and throat. It is also the sacred power house for developing willpower and for developing Tao Song power of overtones, resonance, and voice range from lowest to highest.

Apply the Four Power Techniques to self-clear soul mind body blockages from the fifth Soul House and develop the fifth Soul House.

Body Power. Sit up straight. Put the tip of your tongue as close as you can to the roof of your mouth without touching. Males, sit on your left palm facing the Hui Yin area. Females, sit on your right palm facing the Hui Yin area. Place the other palm over the bottom of your lower abdomen and pubic area. Alternatively, you can put both palms on your lower abdomen below your navel or one palm over the other below your navel.

Soul Power. Say *hello:*

> *Dear Divine,*
> *Dear Tao,*
> *Dear Heaven, Mother Earth, and countless planets,*
>   *stars, galaxies, and universes,*
> *Dear all saints, including Tao saints, holy saints, and*
>   *all other saints, buddhas, bodhisattvas, healing*
>   *angels, archangels, ascended masters, lamas, gurus,*
>   *kahunas, and all spiritual fathers and mothers on*
>   *Mother Earth and in all layers of Heaven,*
> *Dear my ancestors,*
> *Dear Tao Song,*
> *I love you, honor you, and appreciate you.*
> *When I sing the Tao Song mantras for the fifth Soul*
>   *House, please clear soul mind body blockages in my*
>   *fifth Soul House and develop my fifth Soul House.*
> *I am very grateful.*
> *Thank you. Thank you. Thank you.*

Mind Power. Focus your mind on your *first* Soul House. Visualize a golden light ball or a rainbow light ball rotating counterclockwise in that area. If your Third Eye is open, observe whatever images you receive.

Sound Power. Chant or sing silently or aloud:

Xi Ya You Tao (pronounced *shee yah yoe dow*)
Xi Ya You Tao
Xi Ya You Tao
Xi Ya You Tao
Xi Ya You Tao

Xi Ya You Tao
Xi Ya You Tao
Xi Ya You Tao
Xi Ya You Tao
Xi Ya You Tao

Xi Ya You Tao
Xi Ya You Tao
Xi Ya You Tao
Xi Ya You Tao
Xi Ya You Tao

Xi Ya You Tao
Xi Ya You Tao
Xi Ya You Tao
Xi Ya You Tao
Xi Ya You Tao . . .

Let us continue by chanting the second sacred Tao Song mantra for the fifth Soul House.

Chant or sing silently or aloud:

Xi Ya You Zhong (pronounced *shee yah yoe jawng*)
Xi Ya You Zhong
Xi Ya You Zhong
Xi Ya You Zhong
Xi Ya You Zhong

Xi Ya You Zhong
Xi Ya You Zhong
Xi Ya You Zhong
Xi Ya You Zhong
Xi Ya You Zhong

Xi Ya You Zhong
Xi Ya You Zhong
Xi Ya You Zhong
Xi Ya You Zhong
Xi Ya You Zhong

Xi Ya You Zhong
Xi Ya You Zhong
Xi Ya You Zhong
Xi Ya You Zhong
Xi Ya You Zhong . . .

Continue to self-clear soul mind body blockages from the fifth Soul House and develop the fifth Soul House with the third, fourth, and fifth sacred Tao Song mantras:

Xi Ya You Ling (pronounced *shee yah yoe ling*)
Xi Ya You Ling
Xi Ya You Ling

Xi Ya You Ling
Xi Ya You Ling

Xi Ya You Ling
Xi Ya You Ling
Xi Ya You Ling
Xi Ya You Ling
Xi Ya You Ling

Xi Ya You Ling
Xi Ya You Ling
Xi Ya You Ling
Xi Ya You Ling
Xi Ya You Ling

Xi Ya You Ling
Xi Ya You Ling
Xi Ya You Ling
Xi Ya You Ling
Xi Ya You Ling . . .

Xi Ya You Xu (pronounced *shee yah yoe shü*)
Xi Ya You Xu
Xi Ya You Xu
Xi Ya You Xu
Xi Ya You Xu

Xi Ya You Xu
Xi Ya You Xu
Xi Ya You Xu
Xi Ya You Xu
Xi Ya You Xu

Xi Ya You Xu
Xi Ya You Xu
Xi Ya You Xu
Xi Ya You Xu
Xi Ya You Xu

Xi Ya You Xu
Xi Ya You Xu
Xi Ya You Xu
Xi Ya You Xu
Xi Ya You Xu . . .

Xi Ya You Kong (pronounced *shee yah yoe kawng*)
Xi Ya You Kong
Xi Ya You Kong
Xi Ya You Kong
Xi Ya You Kong

Xi Ya You Kong
Xi Ya You Kong
Xi Ya You Kong
Xi Ya You Kong
Xi Ya You Kong

Xi Ya You Kong
Xi Ya You Kong
Xi Ya You Kong
Xi Ya You Kong
Xi Ya You Kong

Xi Ya You Kong
Xi Ya You Kong

Xi Ya You Kong
Xi Ya You Kong
Xi Ya You Kong . . .

Chant or sing for three to five minutes now. There is no time limit for this. The longer you chant and the more you chant, the better.

To develop a powerful Tao Song with the qualities of overtones, resonance, and voice range from lowest to highest, you need to practice the Tao Song mantras for the fifth Soul House a lot. Remember the most important principle: **when you sing a Tao Song, *always* put your mind on the first Soul House**. I emphasize this because your vocal cords are in the throat, but your mind must be on the first Soul House. This is the most important secret I shared when I offered the teaching on the second Soul House a little earlier. If you put your mind on the first Soul House, you will continue to increase your singing power beyond words. If you instead put your mind on your throat and vocal cords, you could easily damage them.

Now let me lead you to practice the sacred Tao Song mantras for the sixth Soul House.

Sixth Soul House

The sixth Soul House is a fist-sized space located in the center of the body in the center of the brain.

This Soul House is the power house for empowering, healing, and rejuvenating the central nervous system, peripheral nervous system, endocrine system, and all brain functions, including concentration, memory, intuitive abilities, intelligence, wisdom, and more. The sixth Soul House is also the power house for developing the Third Eye. It is the power house for developing shen, which is soul, information, or message.

Apply the Four Power Techniques to self-clear soul mind body blockages from the sixth Soul House and develop the sixth Soul House.

Body Power. Sit up straight. Put the tip of your tongue as close as you can to the roof of your mouth without touching. Males, sit on your left palm facing the Hui Yin area. Females, sit on your right palm facing the Hui Yin area. Place the other palm over the bottom of your lower abdomen and pubic area. Alternatively, you can put both palms on your lower abdomen below your navel or one palm over the other below your navel.

Soul Power. Say *hello:*

> *Dear Divine,*
> *Dear Tao,*
> *Dear Heaven, Mother Earth, and countless planets,*
>   *stars, galaxies, and universes,*
> *Dear all saints, including Tao saints, holy saints, and*
>   *all other saints, buddhas, bodhisattvas, healing*
>   *angels, archangels, ascended masters, lamas, gurus,*
>   *kahunas, and all spiritual fathers and mothers on*
>   *Mother Earth and in all layers of Heaven,*
> *Dear my ancestors,*
> *Dear Tao Song,*
> *I love you, honor you, and appreciate you.*
> *When I sing the Tao Song mantras for the sixth Soul*
>   *House, please clear soul mind body blockages in my*
>   *sixth Soul House and develop my sixth Soul House.*

I am very grateful.
Thank you. Thank you. Thank you.

Mind Power. Focus your mind on your *first* Soul House. Visualize a golden light ball or a rainbow light ball rotating counterclockwise in that area. If your Third Eye is open, observe whatever images you receive.

Sound Power. Chant or sing silently or aloud:

Yi Ya You Tao (pronounced *yee yah yoe dow*)
Yi Ya You Tao
Yi Ya You Tao
Yi Ya You Tao
Yi Ya You Tao

Yi Ya You Tao
Yi Ya You Tao
Yi Ya You Tao
Yi Ya You Tao
Yi Ya You Tao

Yi Ya You Tao
Yi Ya You Tao
Yi Ya You Tao
Yi Ya You Tao
Yi Ya You Tao

Yi Ya You Tao
Yi Ya You Tao
Yi Ya You Tao

Yi Ya You Tao
Yi Ya You Tao . . .

Let us continue by chanting the second sacred Tao Song mantra for the sixth Soul House.
Chant or sing silently or aloud:

Yi Ya You Zhong (pronounced *yee yah yoe jawng*)
Yi Ya You Zhong
Yi Ya You Zhong
Yi Ya You Zhong
Yi Ya You Zhong

Yi Ya You Zhong
Yi Ya You Zhong
Yi Ya You Zhong
Yi Ya You Zhong
Yi Ya You Zhong

Yi Ya You Zhong
Yi Ya You Zhong
Yi Ya You Zhong
Yi Ya You Zhong
Yi Ya You Zhong

Yi Ya You Zhong
Yi Ya You Zhong
Yi Ya You Zhong
Yi Ya You Zhong
Yi Ya You Zhong . . .

Continue to self-clear soul mind body blockages from the sixth Soul House and develop the sixth Soul House with the third, fourth, and fifth sacred Tao Song mantras:

Yi Ya You Ling (pronounced *yee yah yoe ling*)
Yi Ya You Ling
Yi Ya You Ling
Yi Ya You Ling
Yi Ya You Ling

Yi Ya You Ling
Yi Ya You Ling
Yi Ya You Ling
Yi Ya You Ling
Yi Ya You Ling

Yi Ya You Ling
Yi Ya You Ling
Yi Ya You Ling
Yi Ya You Ling
Yi Ya You Ling

Yi Ya You Ling
Yi Ya You Ling
Yi Ya You Ling
Yi Ya You Ling
Yi Ya You Ling . . .

Yi Ya You Xu (pronounced *yee yah yoe shü*)
Yi Ya You Xu
Yi Ya You Xu

Yi Ya You Xu
Yi Ya You Xu

Yi Ya You Xu
Yi Ya You Xu
Yi Ya You Xu
Yi Ya You Xu
Yi Ya You Xu

Yi Ya You Xu
Yi Ya You Xu
Yi Ya You Xu
Yi Ya You Xu
Yi Ya You Xu

Yi Ya You Xu
Yi Ya You Xu
Yi Ya You Xu
Yi Ya You Xu
Yi Ya You Xu . . .

Yi Ya You Kong (pronounced *yee yah yoe kawng*)
Yi Ya You Kong
Yi Ya You Kong
Yi Ya You Kong
Yi Ya You Kong

Yi Ya You Kong
Yi Ya You Kong
Yi Ya You Kong
Yi Ya You Kong
Yi Ya You Kong

Yi Ya You Kong
Yi Ya You Kong
Yi Ya You Kong
Yi Ya You Kong
Yi Ya You Kong

Yi Ya You Kong
Yi Ya You Kong
Yi Ya You Kong
Yi Ya You Kong
Yi Ya You Kong . . .

Chant or sing for three to five minutes now. There is no time limit for this. The longer you chant and the more you chant, the better.

The sixth Soul House is very important for developing mind intelligence. In fact, it is vital for developing all brain functions and abilities. This Soul House is also vital for developing Third Eye spiritual abilities. It is the key for soul development. When your soul sits in the sixth Soul House, your soul is preparing to reach the seventh Soul House. From the sixth Soul House to the seventh Soul House is a major step for soul development. When your soul is uplifted from the sixth Soul House to the seventh Soul House, your soul will be free to do soul travel. Why does a soul need to soul travel? The soul will go to Heaven, Mother Earth, and countless planets, stars, galaxies, and universes, as well as to the Source to gather nutrients. Then your soul will bring these nutrients back from Heaven, Mother Earth, countless planets, stars, galaxies, and universes, and the Source to nourish your physical body. This is a vital step for longevity and immortality.

My ten-year Tao training includes a sequence of annual Tao

retreats. I will start to teach and train my Tao students to do soul travel in the third year of the ten-year program.

The last Soul House is the seventh Soul House.

Seventh Soul House

The seventh Soul House is a fist-sized space located just above the center of the top of the head.

The seventh Soul House includes the Bai Hui (pronounced *bye hway*) acupuncture point (located at the center of the top of the head), which gathers the yang of the whole body. This is the sacred power house to connect with Heaven, the Divine, and Tao. The seventh Soul House also connects with higher consciousness. When a human being's soul reaches this Soul House, it has reached the highest soul standing for a human being.

Apply the Four Power Techniques to self-clear soul mind body blockages from the seventh Soul House and develop the seventh Soul House.

Body Power. Sit up straight. Put the tip of your tongue as close as you can to the roof of your mouth without touching. Males, sit on your left palm facing the Hui Yin area. Females, sit on your right palm facing the Hui Yin area. Place the other palm over the bottom of your lower abdomen and pubic area. Alternatively, you can put both palms on your lower abdomen below your navel or one palm over the other below your navel.

Soul Power. Say *hello:*

> *Dear Divine,*
> *Dear Tao,*

Dear Heaven, Mother Earth, and countless planets, stars, galaxies, and universes,

Dear all saints, including Tao saints, holy saints, and all other saints, buddhas, bodhisattvas, healing angels, archangels, ascended masters, lamas, gurus, kahunas, and all spiritual fathers and mothers on Mother Earth and in all layers of Heaven,

Dear my ancestors,

Dear Tao Song,

I love you, honor you, and appreciate you.

When I sing the Tao Song mantras for the seventh Soul House, please clear soul mind body blockages in my seventh Soul House and develop my seventh Soul House.

I am very grateful.

Thank you. Thank you. Thank you.

Mind Power. Focus your mind on your *first* Soul House. Visualize a golden light ball or a rainbow light ball rotating counterclockwise in that area. If your Third Eye is open, observe whatever images you receive.

Sound Power. Chant or sing silently or aloud:

Weng Ya You Tao (pronounced *wung yah yoe dow*)
Weng Ya You Tao
Weng Ya You Tao
Weng Ya You Tao
Weng Ya You Tao

Weng Ya You Tao
Weng Ya You Tao

Weng Ya You Tao
Weng Ya You Tao
Weng Ya You Tao

Weng Ya You Tao
Weng Ya You Tao
Weng Ya You Tao
Weng Ya You Tao
Weng Ya You Tao

Weng Ya You Tao
Weng Ya You Tao
Weng Ya You Tao
Weng Ya You Tao
Weng Ya You Tao . . .

Let us continue by chanting the second sacred Tao Song mantra for the seventh Soul House.

Chant or sing silently or aloud:

Weng Ya You Zhong (pronounced *wung yah yoe jawng*)
Weng Ya You Zhong
Weng Ya You Zhong
Weng Ya You Zhong
Weng Ya You Zhong

Weng Ya You Zhong
Weng Ya You Zhong
Weng Ya You Zhong
Weng Ya You Zhong
Weng Ya You Zhong

Weng Ya You Zhong
Weng Ya You Zhong
Weng Ya You Zhong
Weng Ya You Zhong
Weng Ya You Zhong

Weng Ya You Zhong
Weng Ya You Zhong
Weng Ya You Zhong
Weng Ya You Zhong
Weng Ya You Zhong . . .

Continue to self-clear soul mind body blockages from the seventh Soul House and develop the seventh Soul House with the third, fourth, and fifth sacred Tao Song mantras:

Weng Ya You Ling (pronounced *wung yah yoe ling*)
Weng Ya You Ling
Weng Ya You Ling
Weng Ya You Ling
Weng Ya You Ling

Weng Ya You Ling
Weng Ya You Ling
Weng Ya You Ling
Weng Ya You Ling
Weng Ya You Ling

Weng Ya You Ling
Weng Ya You Ling
Weng Ya You Ling

Weng Ya You Ling
Weng Ya You Ling

Weng Ya You Ling
Weng Ya You Ling
Weng Ya You Ling
Weng Ya You Ling
Weng Ya You Ling . . .

Weng Ya You Xu (pronounced *wung yah yoe shü*)
Weng Ya You Xu
Weng Ya You Xu
Weng Ya You Xu
Weng Ya You Xu

Weng Ya You Xu
Weng Ya You Xu
Weng Ya You Xu
Weng Ya You Xu
Weng Ya You Xu

Weng Ya You Xu
Weng Ya You Xu
Weng Ya You Xu
Weng Ya You Xu
Weng Ya You Xu

Weng Ya You Xu
Weng Ya You Xu
Weng Ya You Xu
Weng Ya You Xu
Weng Ya You Xu . . .

Weng Ya You Kong (pronounced *wung yah yoe*
   kawng)
Weng Ya You Kong
Weng Ya You Kong
Weng Ya You Kong
Weng Ya You Kong

Weng Ya You Kong
Weng Ya You Kong
Weng Ya You Kong
Weng Ya You Kong
Weng Ya You Kong

Weng Ya You Kong
Weng Ya You Kong
Weng Ya You Kong
Weng Ya You Kong
Weng Ya You Kong

Weng Ya You Kong
Weng Ya You Kong
Weng Ya You Kong
Weng Ya You Kong
Weng Ya You Kong . . .

Chant or sing for three to five minutes now. There is no time limit for this. The longer you chant and the more you chant, the better.

The seventh Soul House represents the highest soul standing for a human being. Very few human beings on Mother Earth can reach this Soul House. Practicing the Tao Song for this

Soul House connects you with Heaven and Tao. Higher consciousness from Heaven and Tao will bless you. When your soul reaches this Soul House, the benefits for your Tao journey are unlimited. Your soul will have the freedom to travel to a special place in Heaven where Tao will guide your soul. If your Third Eye is open, you may see a person whose body soul sits in the seventh Soul House. You will know that this person has reached a very high spiritual standing in Heaven. This person deserves your greatest respect and honor.

DIVINE KARMA CLEANSING FOR THE SEVEN SOUL HOUSES

There are two ways to receive karma cleansing from the Divine. The first way is to receive a Divine Order for Karma Cleansing sent by a divine channel with this authority. The second way is to apply permanent divine treasures, such as Divine Soul Mind Body Transplants, to clear one's own bad karma with the help of divine frequency and vibration with divine love, forgiveness, compassion, and light. The second way takes time. The first way is much faster.

How does the first way, a Divine Order for Karma Cleansing, work? When I or one of my Worldwide Representatives, who are also divine servants, vehicles, and channels, send a Divine Order for Karma Cleansing to someone, Heaven's generals and soldiers and the leaders and workers of the Akashic Records clear the bad karma carried by the recipient's soul.

As I explained earlier in this chapter, there are many kinds of bad karma and many kinds of mind blockages. There are also body blockages, which are energy and matter blockages. A divine servant, vehicle, and channel is given divine authority to remove soul mind body blockages through Divine Karma Cleansing.

Divine Karma Cleansing is the divine way to remove karma accrued over many lifetimes. Divine Karma Cleansing includes divine mind blockage removal, which is the divine way to remove mind blockages, which include negative mind-sets, negative beliefs, negative attitudes, ego, attachments, and more. Divine Karma Cleansing also includes divine body blockage removal, which is the divine way to remove energy blockages and matter blockages.

The second way to receive karma cleansing from the Divine is to apply permanent divine treasures to self-clear bad karma. This will clear bad karma little by little. After receiving permanent divine treasures, one must spend time to practice with them in order to clear bad karma. The first way, Divine Karma Cleansing, is different. Heaven's generals and soldiers and the leaders and workers of the Akashic Records are on duty to clear dark souls from one's systems, organs, cells, DNA, and RNA, or spaces.

Now I will offer permanent Tao treasures that you can apply to self-clear karma in the seven Soul Houses. The power and significance of these permanent Tao treaures is beyond comprehension and imagination. I want every reader and all of humanity to know that chanting or singing Tao Song itself can clear bad karma. Applying Tao Song and permanent divine or Tao treasures to remove bad karma requires dedicated practice.

Prepare. Sit up straight. Put the tip of your tongue as close as you can to the roof of your mouth without touching. Put both palms on your lower abdomen. As you read "Transmission!," the stated permanent treasures will come to your soul.

Tao Order: Tao Golden Light Ball and Golden Liquid Spring of Tao Love Soul Mind Body Transplants

Transmission!

Tao Order: Join Tao Love
Soul Mind Body Transplants as one.

The Tao Love Soul Transplant is the soul of Tao Love.

The Tao Love Mind Transplant is the consciousness of Tao Love.

The Tao Love Body Transplant is the energy and tiny matter of Tao Love.

Each one is a huge golden light being.

Tao Love Soul Mind Body Transplants are the shen qi jing (soul energy matter) of Tao Love.

Congratulations! Each of these three treasures is more than one thousand feet high and more than two hundred feet wide. It usually takes them two to three days to shrink to adapt to your body. After shrinking, their permanent size is still two to three times bigger than your body. You are extremely blessed. Every reader is extremely blessed. Humanity is extremely blessed.

This is my third book to offer permanent Tao treasures. (The previous two are *Tao I* and *Tao II*.) I cannot bow down enough for this honor and authority from Tao to offer this service to every reader.

Apply the Four Power Techniques to self-clear soul mind body blockages from the seven Soul Houses and develop the seven Soul Houses together.

Body Power. Sit up straight. Put the tip of your tongue as close as you can to the roof of your mouth without touching. Males, sit on your left palm facing the Hui Yin area. Females, sit on your right palm facing the Hui Yin area. Place the other palm over the bottom of your lower abdomen and pubic area. Alternatively, you can put both palms on your lower abdomen below your navel or one palm over the other below your navel.

Soul Power. Say *hello:*

> *Dear Divine,*
> *Dear Tao,*
> *Dear Heaven, Mother Earth, and countless planets,*
>   *stars, galaxies, and universes,*
> *Dear all saints, including Tao saints, holy saints, and*
>   *all other saints, buddhas, bodhisattvas, healing*
>   *angels, archangels, ascended masters, lamas, gurus,*
>   *kahunas, and all spiritual fathers and mothers on*
>   *Mother Earth and in all layers of Heaven,*
> *Dear my ancestors,*
> *Dear Tao Song,*
> *I love you, honor you, and appreciate you.*
> *When I chant* Tao Love, *please clear soul mind body*
>   *blockages in my seven Soul Houses and develop all*
>   *of them.*
> *I am very grateful.*
> *Thank you. Thank you. Thank you.*

Mind Power. As usual, focus on your *first* Soul House. Visualize a golden light ball or a rainbow light ball rotating counterclockwise in that area. If your Third Eye is open, observe whatever images you receive.

Sound Power. Chant silently or aloud:

Tao Love
Tao Love
Tao Love
Tao Love
Tao Love
Tao Love
Tao Love . . .

Chant for three to five minutes now. There is no time limit for this chanting. The longer you chant and the more you chant, the better.

To chant *Tao Love* is extremely powerful. Tao Love is love from the Source. You have just received permanent treasures of Tao Love Soul Mind Body Transplants. Continue to chant *Tao Love* to activate these treasures. You could receive remarkable self-cleansing of soul mind body blockages in the seven Soul Houses and remarkable development of the power of your seven Soul Houses.

The seven Soul Houses connect with all systems and organs. They also connect with all kinds of emotions. To chant *Tao Love* is to heal all kinds of sickness in the spiritual, mental, emotional, and physical bodies. I offer the teaching at every opportunity: *Divine and Tao love melt all blockages and transform all life.*

Practice more and more. There is no time limit.

WAI JIAO

As I shared in chapter 2, the Wai Jiao is the biggest space inside the body. It is located in front of the spinal column and back ribs, and includes the chest cavity and abdominal cavity. It also includes the skull cavity.

Remove Soul Mind Body Blockages in the Wai Jiao

The Wai Jiao is like the sea. San Jiao (pronounced *sahn jee-yow*) is like three rivers. Rivers flow to the sea. Therefore, San Jiao connects with the Wai Jiao.

I emphasize again the teaching I offered in chapter 2 about San Jiao. The Upper Jiao is the space above the diaphragm. It includes the heart, lungs, and brain. If there are soul mind body blockages in these major organs, the blockages will move toward the upper part of the Wai Jiao.

The Middle Jiao is the space between the diaphragm and the level of the navel. It includes the liver, gallbladder, stomach, spleen, and pancreas. Soul mind body blockages in these major organs will move toward the middle part of the Wai Jiao.

The Lower Jiao is the space below the level of the navel down to the genital area. It includes the small and large intestines, kidneys, urinary bladder, reproductive organs, and sexual organs. Soul mind body blockages in these organs will move to the lower part of the Wai Jiao.

To clear soul mind body blockages in the Wai Jiao is to serve all the systems and organs in the whole body. This has huge significance.

To sing Tao Song is to self-clear soul mind body blockages in the Wai Jiao. This will benefit San Jiao. It will benefit all systems and all organs.

Sacred Tao Song Mantras to Self-clear Soul Mind Body Blockages in the Wai Jiao

Apply the Four Power Techniques to self-clear soul mind body blockages from the Wai Jiao and develop the power of the Wai Jiao.

Body Power. Sit up straight. Put the tip of your tongue as close as you can to the roof of your mouth without touching. Males, sit on your left palm facing the Hui Yin area. Females, sit on your right palm facing the Hui Yin area. Place the other palm over the bottom of your lower abdomen and pubic area. Alternatively, you can put both palms on your lower abdomen below your navel or one palm over the other below your navel.

Soul Power. Say *hello:*

> *Dear Divine,*
> *Dear Tao,*
> *Dear Heaven, Mother Earth, and countless planets,*
>   *stars, galaxies, and universes,*
> *Dear all saints, including Tao saints, holy saints, and*
>   *all other saints, buddhas, bodhisattvas, healing*
>   *angels, archangels, ascended masters, lamas, gurus,*
>   *kahunas, and all spiritual fathers and mothers on*
>   *Mother Earth and in all layers of Heaven,*
> *Dear my ancestors,*
> *Dear Tao Song,*
> *I love you, honor you, and appreciate you.*
> *When I sing the Tao Song mantras for the Wai Jiao,*

please clear soul mind body blockages in my Wai
Jiao and develop my Wai Jiao.
I am very grateful.
Thank you. Thank you. Thank you.

Mind Power. Focus on your *first* Soul House. Visualize a golden light ball or a rainbow light ball rotating counterclockwise in that area. If your Third Eye is open, observe whatever images you receive.

Sound Power. Chant or sing silently or aloud:

You Ya You Tao (pronounced *yoe yah yoe dow*)
You Ya You Tao
You Ya You Tao
You Ya You Tao
You Ya You Tao

You Ya You Tao
You Ya You Tao
You Ya You Tao
You Ya You Tao
You Ya You Tao

You Ya You Tao
You Ya You Tao
You Ya You Tao
You Ya You Tao
You Ya You Tao

You Ya You Tao
You Ya You Tao
You Ya You Tao
You Ya You Tao
You Ya You Tao . . .

Let us continue by chanting the second sacred Tao Song mantra for the Wai Jiao.

Chant or sing silently or aloud:

You Ya You Zhong (pronounced *yoe yah yoe jawng*)
You Ya You Zhong
You Ya You Zhong
You Ya You Zhong
You Ya You Zhong

You Ya You Zhong
You Ya You Zhong
You Ya You Zhong
You Ya You Zhong
You Ya You Zhong

You Ya You Zhong
You Ya You Zhong
You Ya You Zhong
You Ya You Zhong
You Ya You Zhong

You Ya You Zhong
You Ya You Zhong

You Ya You Zhong
You Ya You Zhong
You Ya You Zhong . . .

Continue to self-clear soul mind body blockages from the Wai Jiao and develop the Wai Jiao with the third, fourth, and fifth sacred Tao Song mantras:

You Ya You Ling (pronounced *yoe yah yoe ling*)
You Ya You Ling
You Ya You Ling
You Ya You Ling
You Ya You Ling

You Ya You Ling
You Ya You Ling
You Ya You Ling
You Ya You Ling
You Ya You Ling

You Ya You Ling
You Ya You Ling
You Ya You Ling
You Ya You Ling
You Ya You Ling

You Ya You Ling
You Ya You Ling
You Ya You Ling
You Ya You Ling
You Ya You Ling . . .

You Ya You Xu (pronounced *yoe yah yoe shü*)
You Ya You Xu
You Ya You Xu
You Ya You Xu
You Ya You Xu

You Ya You Xu
You Ya You Xu
You Ya You Xu
You Ya You Xu
You Ya You Xu

You Ya You Xu
You Ya You Xu
You Ya You Xu
You Ya You Xu
You Ya You Xu

You Ya You Xu
You Ya You Xu
You Ya You Xu
You Ya You Xu
You Ya You Xu . . .

You Ya You Kong (pronounced *yoe yah yoe kawng)*
You Ya You Kong
You Ya You Kong
You Ya You Kong
You Ya You Kong

You Ya You Kong
You Ya You Kong
You Ya You Kong
You Ya You Kong
You Ya You Kong

You Ya You Kong
You Ya You Kong
You Ya You Kong
You Ya You Kong
You Ya You Kong

You Ya You Kong
You Ya You Kong
You Ya You Kong
You Ya You Kong
You Ya You Kong . . .

Chant or sing for three to five minutes now. There is no time limit for this. The longer you chant and the more you chant, the better.

Wai Jiao is the biggest space in the body. Therefore, removing soul mind body blockages from the Wai Jiao is vital for healing the spiritual, mental, emotional, and physical bodies. If you practice only the sacred Tao Song mantras for the Wai Jiao a lot, the benefits for healing, fan lao huan tong, longevity, and immortality would be priceless.

Self-clear Soul Mind Body Blockages in the Wai Jiao with Tao Treasures

Now I will offer permanent Tao treasures that you can apply to self-clear soul mind body blockages in the Wai Jiao.

Prepare. Sit up straight. Put the tip of your tongue as close as you can to the roof of your mouth without touching. Put both palms on your lower abdomen.

As you read "Transmission!," the stated permanent treasures will come to your soul.

Tao Order: Tao Golden Light Ball and Golden Liquid Spring of Tao Forgiveness Soul Mind Body Transplants

Transmission!

Tao Order: Join Tao Forgiveness Soul Mind Body Transplants as one.

The Tao Forgiveness Soul Transplant is the soul of Tao Forgiveness.

The Tao Forgiveness Mind Transplant is the consciousness of Tao Forgiveness.

The Tao Forgiveness Body Transplant is the energy and tiny matter of Tao Forgiveness.

Each one is a huge golden light being.

Tao Forgiveness Soul Mind Body Transplants are the shen qi jing (soul energy matter) of Tao Forgiveness.

Congratulations! Each of these three treasures is also more than one thousand feet high and more than two hundred feet wide. It usually takes them two to three days to shrink to adapt to your body. After shrinking, their permanent size is still two to three times bigger than your body. You are extremely blessed. Every reader is extremely blessed. Humanity is extremely blessed.

This is my third book to offer permanent Tao treasures. I cannot bow down enough for this honor and authority from Tao to offer this service to every reader.

Apply Tao Forgiveness Soul Mind Body Transplants and the Four Power Techniques to self-clear soul mind body blockages in the Wai Jiao and develop the Wai Jiao.

Body Power. Sit up straight. Put the tip of your tongue as close as you can to the roof of your mouth without touching. Males, sit on your left palm facing the Hui Yin area. Females, sit on your right palm facing the Hui Yin area. Place the other palm over the bottom of your lower abdomen and pubic area. Alternatively, you can put both palms on your lower abdomen below your navel or one palm over the other below your navel.

Soul Power. Say *hello:*

> *Dear Divine,*
> *Dear Tao,*
> *Dear Heaven, Mother Earth, and countless planets,*
> *stars, galaxies, and universes,*
> *Dear all saints, including Tao saints, holy saints, and*
> *all other saints, buddhas, bodhisattvas, healing*
> *angels, archangels, ascended masters, lamas, gurus,*
> *kahunas, and all spiritual fathers and mothers on*
> *Mother Earth and in all layers of Heaven,*

Dear my ancestors,
Dear Tao Song,
Dear Tao Forgiveness Soul Mind Body Transplants,
I love you, honor you, and appreciate you.
When I chant Tao Forgiveness, *please clear soul mind*
body blockages in my Wai Jiao and develop my Wai
Jiao.
I am very grateful.
Thank you. Thank you. Thank you.

Mind Power. Focus on your *first* Soul House. Visualize a golden light ball or a rainbow light ball rotating counterclockwise in that area. If your Third Eye is open, observe whatever images you receive.

Sound Power. Chant silently or aloud:

Tao Forgiveness
Tao Forgiveness
Tao Forgiveness
Tao Forgiveness
Tao Forgiveness
Tao Forgiveness
Tao Forgiveness . . .

Chant for three to five minutes now. There is no time limit for this chanting. The longer you chant and the more you chant, the better.

Tao Forgiveness brings inner joy and inner peace. You can apply Tao Forgiveness to self-heal your spiritual, mental, emotional, and physical bodies, as well as to transform your relationships, finances, and every aspect of your life. There is no time limit. Chant more. Then you will understand the power of Tao Forgiveness Soul Mind Body Transplants.

TAO SONG CHANNEL

As I shared in chapter 2, the Tao Song Channel starts from the Hui Yin acupuncture point (between the genitals and anus), flows up through the seven Soul Houses in the center of the body to the Bai Hui acupuncture point at the top of head, then flows down through the Wai Jiao and ends at the Hui Yin acupuncture point.

To heal the Tao Song Channel is to heal all sickness in the spiritual, mental, emotional, and physical bodies. The Tao Song Channel is the secret Tao temple inside the body. It gathers the jing qi shen (matter energy soul) of Tao in order to transform a human being's jing qi shen to Tao jing qi shen. To transform your Tao Song Channel is to transform health, relationships, finances, intelligence, and more, and bring success to every aspect of your life.

Remove Soul Mind Body Blockages in the Tao Song Channel

Removing soul mind body blockages from the Tao Song Channel is vital for transforming all life. How do you remove soul mind body blockages from the Tao Song Channel? Tao has given me sacred Tao Song mantras that you can chant or sing to self-clear soul mind body blockages in the Tao Song Channel and to develop the power of the Tao Song Channel.

Sacred Tao Song Mantras to Self-clear Soul Mind Body Blockages in the Tao Song Channel

Apply the Four Power Techniques to self-clear soul mind body blockages from the Tao Song Channel and develop the power of the Tao Song Channel.

Body Power. Sit up straight. Put the tip of your tongue as close as you can to the roof of your mouth without touching. Males, sit on your left palm facing the Hui Yin area. Females, sit on your right palm facing the Hui Yin area. Place the other palm over the bottom of your lower abdomen and pubic area. Alternatively, you can put both palms on your lower abdomen below your navel or one palm over the other below your navel.

Soul Power. Say *hello:*

> *Dear Divine,*
> *Dear Tao,*
> *Dear Heaven, Mother Earth, and countless planets,*
>   *stars, galaxies, and universes,*
> *Dear all saints, including Tao saints, holy saints, and*
>   *all other saints, buddhas, bodhisattvas, healing*
>   *angels, archangels, ascended masters, lamas, gurus,*
>   *kahunas, and all spiritual fathers and mothers on*
>   *Mother Earth and in all layers of Heaven,*
> *Dear my ancestors,*
> *Dear Tao Song,*
> *I love you, honor you, and appreciate you.*
> *When I sing the Tao Song mantras for the Tao Song*
>   *Channel, please clear soul mind body blockages in*

> *my Tao Song Channel and develop my Tao Song*
> *Channel.*
> *I am very grateful.*
> *Thank you. Thank you. Thank you.*

Mind Power. Focus on your *first* Soul House. Visualize a golden light ball or a rainbow light ball rotating counterclockwise in that area. If your Third Eye is open, observe whatever images you receive.

Sound Power. Chant or sing silently or aloud:

> *Xi You You Tao* (pronounced *shee yoe yoe dow*)
> *Xi You You Tao*
> *Xi You You Tao*
> *Xi You You Tao*
> *Xi You You Tao*
>
> *Xi You You Tao*
> *Xi You You Tao*
> *Xi You You Tao*
> *Xi You You Tao*
> *Xi You You Tao*
>
> *Xi You You Tao*
> *Xi You You Tao*
> *Xi You You Tao*
> *Xi You You Tao*
> *Xi You You Tao*

Xi You You Tao
Xi You You Tao
Xi You You Tao
Xi You You Tao
Xi You You Tao . . .

Let us continue by chanting the second sacred Tao Song mantra for the Tao Song Channel.

Chant or sing silently or aloud:

Xi You You Zhong (pronounced *shee yoe yoe jawng*)
Xi You You Zhong
Xi You You Zhong
Xi You You Zhong
Xi You You Zhong

Xi You You Zhong
Xi You You Zhong
Xi You You Zhong
Xi You You Zhong
Xi You You Zhong

Xi You You Zhong
Xi You You Zhong
Xi You You Zhong
Xi You You Zhong
Xi You You Zhong

Xi You You Zhong
Xi You You Zhong

Xi You You Zhong
Xi You You Zhong
Xi You You Zhong . . .

Continue to self-clear soul mind body blockages from the
Tao Song Channel and develop the Tao Song Channel with the
third, fourth, and fifth sacred Tao Song mantras:

Xi You You Ling (pronounced *shee yoe yoe ling*)
Xi You You Ling
Xi You You Ling
Xi You You Ling
Xi You You Ling

Xi You You Ling
Xi You You Ling
Xi You You Ling
Xi You You Ling
Xi You You Ling

Xi You You Ling
Xi You You Ling
Xi You You Ling
Xi You You Ling
Xi You You Ling

Xi You You Ling
Xi You You Ling
Xi You You Ling
Xi You You Ling
Xi You You Ling . . .

Xi You You Xu (pronounced *shee yoe yoe shü*)
Xi You You Xu
Xi You You Xu
Xi You You Xu
Xi You You Xu

Xi You You Xu
Xi You You Xu
Xi You You Xu
Xi You You Xu
Xi You You Xu

Xi You You Xu
Xi You You Xu
Xi You You Xu
Xi You You Xu
Xi You You Xu

Xi You You Xu
Xi You You Xu
Xi You You Xu
Xi You You Xu
Xi You You Xu . . .

Xi You You Kong (pronounced *shee yoe yoe kawng)*
Xi You You Kong
Xi You You Kong
Xi You You Kong
Xi You You Kong

Xi You You Kong
Xi You You Kong
Xi You You Kong
Xi You You Kong
Xi You You Kong

Xi You You Kong
Xi You You Kong
Xi You You Kong
Xi You You Kong
Xi You You Kong

Xi You You Kong
Xi You You Kong
Xi You You Kong
Xi You You Kong
Xi You You Kong . . .

Chant or sing for three to five minutes now. There is no time limit for this. The more you chant, the better.

The Tao Song Channel is the most important channel for healing all types of sickness, as well as for rejuvenation, longevity, and immortality. The more you chant the Tao Song mantras of the Tao Song Channel, the more benefits you receive for transforming every aspect of your life. Tao Song practice is so simple. The power cannot be explained in words. As I have taught in all of my books and in all of my workshops and retreats, you have to do the practices in order to feel and understand the power of Tao Song and to experience transformation.

Practice more and more. Benefit more and more.

Self-clear Soul Mind Body Blockages in the Tao Song Channel with Tao Treasures

Now I will offer permanent Tao treasures that you can apply to self-clear soul mind body blockages in the Tao Song Channel.

Prepare. Sit up straight. Put the tip of your tongue as close as you can to the roof of your mouth without touching. Put both palms on your lower abdomen.

As you read "Transmission!," the stated permanent treasures will come to your soul.

Tao Order: Tao Golden Light Ball and Golden Liquid Spring of Tao Compassion Soul Mind Body Transplants

Transmission!

Tao Order: Join Tao Compassion Soul Mind Body Transplants as one.

Congratulations! You are very blessed to receive another three priceless Tao treasures. Tao Compassion Soul Mind Body Transplants boost energy, stamina, vitality, and immunity, as well as transform every aspect of life.

Apply Tao Compassion Soul Mind Body Transplants and the Four Power Techniques to self-clear soul mind body blockages in the Tao Song Channel and to develop the Tao Song Channel.

Body Power. Sit up straight. Put the tip of your tongue as close as you can to the roof of your mouth without touching. Males, sit on your left palm facing the Hui Yin area. Females, sit on your right palm facing the Hui Yin area. Place the other palm over the bottom of your lower abdomen and pubic area. Alternatively, you can put both palms on your lower abdomen below your navel or one palm over the other below your navel.

Soul Power. Say *hello:*

> *Dear Divine,*
> *Dear Tao,*
> *Dear Heaven, Mother Earth, and countless planets,*
>   *stars, galaxies, and universes,*
> *Dear all saints, including Tao saints, holy saints, and*
>   *all other saints, buddhas, bodhisattvas, healing*
>   *angels, archangels, ascended masters, lamas, gurus,*
>   *kahunas, and all spiritual fathers and mothers on*
>   *Mother Earth and in all layers of Heaven,*
> *Dear my ancestors,*
> *Dear Tao Song,*
> *Dear Tao Compassion Soul Mind Body Transplants,*
> *I love you, honor you, and appreciate you.*
> *When I chant* Tao Compassion, *please clear soul*
>   *mind body blockages in my Tao Song Channel*
>   *and develop my Tao Song Channel.*
> *I am very grateful.*
> *Thank you. Thank you. Thank you.*

Mind Power. Focus on your first Soul House. Visualize a golden light ball or a rainbow light ball rotating counterclockwise in that area. If your Third Eye is open, observe whatever images you receive.

Sound Power. Chant silently or aloud:

Tao Compassion
Tao Compassion
Tao Compassion
Tao Compassion
Tao Compassion
Tao Compassion
Tao Compassion . . .

Chant for three to five minutes now. There is no time limit for this chanting. The longer you chant and the more you chant, the better.

When you chant *Tao Compassion,* you *are* Tao Compassion. Tao Compassion has power that cannot be explained by words. You have to chant to experience the power. Tao Compassion can transform every aspect of your life. Practice more. The Tao Compassion Soul Mind Body Transplants are permanent Tao treasures. They are priceless gifts. We cannot honor the Divine and Tao enough. To say *thank you* is not enough.

Practice more and more. The benefits are unlimited.

FIVE ELEMENTS

The Five Elements are Wood, Fire, Earth, Metal, and Water.

Remove Soul Mind Body Blockages in the Five Elements

Let me lead you to remove soul mind body blockages in each of your Five Elements.

SACRED TAO SONG MANTRAS TO SELF-CLEAR
SOUL MIND BODY BLOCKAGES FROM AND TO
HEAL AND REJUVENATE THE WOOD ELEMENT

The Wood element includes the liver, gallbladder, eyes, and tendons in the physical body and connects with anger in the emotional body. Millions of people have soul mind body blockages
in the Wood element.

Apply the Four Power Techniques to self-clear soul mind
body blockages from the Wood element and heal and rejuvenate
the Wood element.

Body Power. Sit up straight. Put the tip of your tongue as close
as you can to the roof of your mouth without touching. Males,
sit on your left palm facing the Hui Yin area. Females, sit on your
right palm facing the Hui Yin area. Place the other palm on the
liver. Alternatively, you can put one palm on the lower abdomen
below the navel and the other palm on the liver.

Soul Power. Say *hello:*

> *Dear Divine,*
> *Dear Tao,*
> *Dear Heaven, Mother Earth, and countless planets,*
>   *stars, galaxies, and universes,*
> *Dear all saints, including Tao saints, holy saints, and*
>   *all other saints, buddhas, bodhisattvas, healing*
>   *angels, archangels, ascended masters, lamas, gurus,*
>   *kahunas, and all spiritual fathers and mothers on*
>   *Mother Earth and in all layers of Heaven,*
> *Dear my ancestors,*

Dear Tao Song,
I love you, honor you, and appreciate you.
When I sing the Tao Song mantras for the Wood
element, please clear soul mind body blockages from
my Wood element and heal and rejuvenate my Wood
element.
I am very grateful.
Thank you. Thank you. Thank you.

Mind Power. Focus on your *first* Soul House. Visualize a golden light ball or a rainbow light ball rotating counterclockwise in that area. If your Third Eye is open, observe whatever images you receive.

Sound Power. Chant or sing silently or aloud:

Jiao Ya You Tao (pronounced *jee-yow yah yoe dow*)
Jiao Ya You Tao
Jiao Ya You Tao
Jiao Ya You Tao
Jiao Ya You Tao

Jiao Ya You Tao
Jiao Ya You Tao
Jiao Ya You Tao
Jiao Ya You Tao
Jiao Ya You Tao

Jiao Ya You Tao
Jiao Ya You Tao
Jiao Ya You Tao

Jiao Ya You Tao
Jiao Ya You Tao

Jiao Ya You Tao
Jiao Ya You Tao
Jiao Ya You Tao
Jiao Ya You Tao
Jiao Ya You Tao . . .

Let us continue by chanting the second sacred Tao Song mantra for the Wood element.

Chant or sing silently or aloud:

Jiao Ya You Zhong (pronounced *jee-yow yah yoe jawng*)
Jiao Ya You Zhong
Jiao Ya You Zhong
Jiao Ya You Zhong
Jiao Ya You Zhong

Jiao Ya You Zhong
Jiao Ya You Zhong
Jiao Ya You Zhong
Jiao Ya You Zhong
Jiao Ya You Zhong

Jiao Ya You Zhong
Jiao Ya You Zhong
Jiao Ya You Zhong
Jiao Ya You Zhong
Jiao Ya You Zhong

Jiao Ya You Zhong
Jiao Ya You Zhong
Jiao Ya You Zhong
Jiao Ya You Zhong
Jiao Ya You Zhong . . .

Continue to self-clear soul mind body blockages from the Wood element and heal and rejuvenate the Wood element with the third, fourth, and fifth sacred Tao Song mantras:

Jiao Ya You Ling (pronounced *jee-yow yah yoe ling*)
Jiao Ya You Ling
Jiao Ya You Ling
Jiao Ya You Ling
Jiao Ya You Ling

Jiao Ya You Ling
Jiao Ya You Ling
Jiao Ya You Ling
Jiao Ya You Ling
Jiao Ya You Ling

Jiao Ya You Ling
Jiao Ya You Ling
Jiao Ya You Ling
Jiao Ya You Ling
Jiao Ya You Ling

Jiao Ya You Ling
Jiao Ya You Ling
Jiao Ya You Ling

Jiao Ya You Ling
Jiao Ya You Ling . . .

Jiao Ya You Xu (pronounced *jee-yow yah yoe shü*)
Jiao Ya You Xu
Jiao Ya You Xu
Jiao Ya You Xu
Jiao Ya You Xu

Jiao Ya You Xu
Jiao Ya You Xu
Jiao Ya You Xu
Jiao Ya You Xu
Jiao Ya You Xu

Jiao Ya You Xu
Jiao Ya You Xu
Jiao Ya You Xu
Jiao Ya You Xu
Jiao Ya You Xu

Jiao Ya You Xu
Jiao Ya You Xu
Jiao Ya You Xu
Jiao Ya You Xu
Jiao Ya You Xu . . .

Jiao Ya You Kong (pronounced *jee-yow yah yoe
    kawng*)
Jiao Ya You Kong
Jiao Ya You Kong

Jiao Ya You Kong
Jiao Ya You Kong

Jiao Ya You Kong
Jiao Ya You Kong
Jiao Ya You Kong
Jiao Ya You Kong
Jiao Ya You Kong

Jiao Ya You Kong
Jiao Ya You Kong
Jiao Ya You Kong
Jiao Ya You Kong
Jiao Ya You Kong

Jiao Ya You Kong
Jiao Ya You Kong
Jiao Ya You Kong
Jiao Ya You Kong
Jiao Ya You Kong . . .

Chant or sing for three to five minutes now. There is no time limit for this. The longer you chant and the more you chant, the better.

SACRED TAO SONG MANTRAS TO SELF-CLEAR
SOUL MIND BODY BLOCKAGES FROM AND TO
HEAL AND REJUVENATE THE FIRE ELEMENT

The Fire element includes the heart, small intestine, tongue, and blood vessels (including arteries, veins, and capillaries) in the physical body and connects with anxiety and depression in the emotional body.

Apply the Four Power Techniques to self-clear soul mind body blockages from the Fire element and heal and rejuvenate the Fire element.

Body Power. Sit up straight. Put the tip of your tongue as close as you can to the roof of your mouth without touching. For males, sit on your left palm facing the Hui Yin area. For females, sit on your right palm facing the Hui Yin area. Place the other palm on the heart. Alternatively, you can put one palm on the lower abdomen below the navel and the other palm on the heart.

Soul Power. Say *hello:*

> *Dear Divine,*
> *Dear Tao,*
> *Dear Heaven, Mother Earth, and countless planets,*
>   *stars, galaxies, and universes,*
> *Dear all saints, including Tao saints, holy saints, and*
>   *all other saints, buddhas, bodhisattvas, healing*
>   *angels, archangels, ascended masters, lamas, gurus,*
>   *kahunas, and all spiritual fathers and mothers on*
>   *Mother Earth and in all layers of Heaven,*
> *Dear my ancestors,*
> *Dear Tao Song,*
> *I love you, honor you, and appreciate you.*
> *When I sing the Tao Song mantras for the Fire element,*
>   *please clear soul mind body blockages from my Fire*
>   *element and heal and rejuvenate my Fire element.*

I am very grateful.
Thank you. Thank you. Thank you.

Mind Power. Focus on your *first* Soul House. Visualize a golden light ball or a rainbow light ball rotating counterclockwise in that area. If your Third Eye is open, observe whatever images you receive.

Sound Power. Chant or sing silently or aloud:

Zhi Ya You Tao (pronounced *jr yah yoe dow*)
Zhi Ya You Tao
Zhi Ya You Tao
Zhi Ya You Tao
Zhi Ya You Tao

Zhi Ya You Tao
Zhi Ya You Tao
Zhi Ya You Tao
Zhi Ya You Tao
Zhi Ya You Tao

Zhi Ya You Tao
Zhi Ya You Tao
Zhi Ya You Tao
Zhi Ya You Tao
Zhi Ya You Tao

Zhi Ya You Tao
Zhi Ya You Tao

Zhi Ya You Tao
Zhi Ya You Tao
Zhi Ya You Tao . . .

Let us continue by chanting the second sacred Tao Song mantra for the Fire element.

Chant or sing silently or aloud:

Zhi Ya You Zhong (pronounced *jr yah yoe jawng*)
Zhi Ya You Zhong
Zhi Ya You Zhong
Zhi Ya You Zhong
Zhi Ya You Zhong

Zhi Ya You Zhong
Zhi Ya You Zhong
Zhi Ya You Zhong
Zhi Ya You Zhong
Zhi Ya You Zhong

Zhi Ya You Zhong
Zhi Ya You Zhong
Zhi Ya You Zhong
Zhi Ya You Zhong
Zhi Ya You Zhong

Zhi Ya You Zhong
Zhi Ya You Zhong
Zhi Ya You Zhong
Zhi Ya You Zhong
Zhi Ya You Zhong . . .

Continue to self-clear soul mind body blockages from the Fire element and heal and rejuvenate the Fire element with the third, fourth, and fifth sacred Tao Song mantras:

Zhi Ya You Ling (pronounced *jr yah yoe ling*)
Zhi Ya You Ling
Zhi Ya You Ling
Zhi Ya You Ling
Zhi Ya You Ling

Zhi Ya You Ling
Zhi Ya You Ling
Zhi Ya You Ling
Zhi Ya You Ling
Zhi Ya You Ling

Zhi Ya You Ling
Zhi Ya You Ling
Zhi Ya You Ling
Zhi Ya You Ling
Zhi Ya You Ling

Zhi Ya You Ling
Zhi Ya You Ling
Zhi Ya You Ling
Zhi Ya You Ling
Zhi Ya You Ling . . .

Zhi Ya You Xu (pronounced *jr yah yoe shü)*
Zhi Ya You Xu
Zhi Ya You Xu

Zhi Ya You Xu
Zhi Ya You Xu

Zhi Ya You Xu
Zhi Ya You Xu
Zhi Ya You Xu
Zhi Ya You Xu
Zhi Ya You Xu

Zhi Ya You Xu
Zhi Ya You Xu
Zhi Ya You Xu
Zhi Ya You Xu
Zhi Ya You Xu

Zhi Ya You Xu
Zhi Ya You Xu
Zhi Ya You Xu
Zhi Ya You Xu
Zhi Ya You Xu . . .

Zhi Ya You Kong (pronounced *jr yah yoe kawng)*
Zhi Ya You Kong
Zhi Ya You Kong
Zhi Ya You Kong
Zhi Ya You Kong

Zhi Ya You Kong
Zhi Ya You Kong
Zhi Ya You Kong

Zhi Ya You Kong
Zhi Ya You Kong

Zhi Ya You Kong
Zhi Ya You Kong
Zhi Ya You Kong
Zhi Ya You Kong
Zhi Ya You Kong

Zhi Ya You Kong
Zhi Ya You Kong
Zhi Ya You Kong
Zhi Ya You Kong
Zhi Ya You Kong . . .

Chant or sing for three to five minutes now. There is no time limit for this. The longer you chant and the more you chant, the better.

SACRED TAO SONG MANTRAS TO SELF-CLEAR
SOUL MIND BODY BLOCKAGES FROM AND TO
HEAL AND REJUVENATE THE EARTH ELEMENT

The Earth element includes the spleen, stomach, mouth and lips, gums and teeth, and muscles in the physical body and connects with worry in the emotional body.

Apply the Four Power Techniques to self-clear soul mind body blockages from the Earth element and heal and rejuvenate the Earth element.

Body Power. Sit up straight. Put the tip of your tongue as close as you can to the roof of your mouth without touching. Males, sit on your left palm facing the Hui Yin area. Females, sit on your right palm facing the Hui Yin area. Place the other palm on the spleen. Alternatively, you can put one palm on the lower abdomen below the navel and the other palm on the spleen.

Soul Power. Say *hello:*

> *Dear Divine,*
> *Dear Tao,*
> *Dear Heaven, Mother Earth, and countless planets,*
>   *stars, galaxies, and universes,*
> *Dear all saints, including Tao saints, holy saints, and*
>   *all other saints, buddhas, bodhisattvas, healing*
>   *angels, archangels, ascended masters, lamas, gurus,*
>   *kahunas, and all spiritual fathers and mothers on*
>   *Mother Earth and in all layers of Heaven,*
> *Dear my ancestors,*
> *Dear Tao Song,*
> *I love you, honor you, and appreciate you.*
> *When I sing the Tao Song mantras for the Earth*
>   *element, please clear soul mind body blockages from*
>   *my Earth element and heal and rejuvenate my*
>   *Earth element.*
> *I am very grateful.*
> *Thank you. Thank you. Thank you.*

Mind Power. Focus on your *first* Soul House. Visualize a golden light ball or a rainbow light ball rotating counterclockwise in that area. If your Third Eye is open, observe whatever images you receive.

Sound Power. Chant or sing silently or aloud:

Gong Ya You Tao (pronounced *gawng yah yoe dow*)
Gong Ya You Tao
Gong Ya You Tao
Gong Ya You Tao
Gong Ya You Tao

Gong Ya You Tao
Gong Ya You Tao
Gong Ya You Tao
Gong Ya You Tao
Gong Ya You Tao

Gong Ya You Tao
Gong Ya You Tao
Gong Ya You Tao
Gong Ya You Tao
Gong Ya You Tao

Gong Ya You Tao
Gong Ya You Tao
Gong Ya You Tao
Gong Ya You Tao
Gong Ya You Tao . . .

Let us continue by chanting the second sacred Tao Song mantra for the Earth element.

Chant or sing silently or aloud:

Gong Ya You Zhong (pronounced *gawng yah yoe*
   jawng)
Gong Ya You Zhong
Gong Ya You Zhong
Gong Ya You Zhong
Gong Ya You Zhong

Gong Ya You Zhong
Gong Ya You Zhong
Gong Ya You Zhong
Gong Ya You Zhong
Gong Ya You Zhong

Gong Ya You Zhong
Gong Ya You Zhong
Gong Ya You Zhong
Gong Ya You Zhong
Gong Ya You Zhong

Gong Ya You Zhong
Gong Ya You Zhong
Gong Ya You Zhong
Gong Ya You Zhong
Gong Ya You Zhong . . .

Continue to self-clear soul mind body blockages from the
Earth element and heal and rejuvenate the Earth element with
the third, fourth, and fifth sacred Tao Song mantras:

Gong Ya You Ling (pronounced *gawng yah yoe ling*)
Gong Ya You Ling
Gong Ya You Ling
Gong Ya You Ling
Gong Ya You Ling

Gong Ya You Ling
Gong Ya You Ling
Gong Ya You Ling
Gong Ya You Ling
Gong Ya You Ling

Gong Ya You Ling
Gong Ya You Ling
Gong Ya You Ling
Gong Ya You Ling
Gong Ya You Ling

Gong Ya You Ling
Gong Ya You Ling
Gong Ya You Ling
Gong Ya You Ling
Gong Ya You Ling . . .

Gong Ya You Xu (pronounced *gawng yah yoe shü*)
Gong Ya You Xu
Gong Ya You Xu
Gong Ya You Xu
Gong Ya You Xu

Gong Ya You Xu
Gong Ya You Xu
Gong Ya You Xu
Gong Ya You Xu
Gong Ya You Xu

Gong Ya You Xu
Gong Ya You Xu
Gong Ya You Xu
Gong Ya You Xu
Gong Ya You Xu

Gong Ya You Xu
Gong Ya You Xu
Gong Ya You Xu
Gong Ya You Xu
Gong Ya You Xu . . .

Gong Ya You Kong (pronounced *gawng yah yoe kawng*)
Gong Ya You Kong
Gong Ya You Kong
Gong Ya You Kong
Gong Ya You Kong

Gong Ya You Kong
Gong Ya You Kong
Gong Ya You Kong
Gong Ya You Kong
Gong Ya You Kong

Gong Ya You Kong
Gong Ya You Kong
Gong Ya You Kong
Gong Ya You Kong
Gong Ya You Kong

Gong Ya You Kong
Gong Ya You Kong
Gong Ya You Kong
Gong Ya You Kong
Gong Ya You Kong . . .

Chant or sing for three to five minutes now. There is no time limit for this. The longer you chant and the more you chant, the better.

SACRED TAO SONG MANTRAS TO SELF-CLEAR
SOUL MIND BODY BLOCKAGES FROM AND TO
HEAL AND REJUVENATE THE METAL ELEMENT

The Metal element includes the lungs, large intestine, nose, and skin in the physical body and connects with grief and sadness in the emotional body.

Now let us apply the Four Power Techniques to self-clear soul mind body blockages from the Metal element and heal and rejuvenate the Metal element.

Body Power. Sit up straight. Put the tip of your tongue as close as you can to the roof of your mouth without touching. Males, sit on your left palm facing the Hui Yin area. Females, sit on your right palm facing the Hui Yin area. Place the other palm on the lungs. Alternatively, you can put one palm on the lower abdomen below the navel and the other palm on the lungs.

Soul Power. Say *hello:*

> *Dear Divine,*
> *Dear Tao,*
> *Dear Heaven, Mother Earth, and countless planets,*
> *   stars, galaxies, and universes,*
> *Dear all saints, including Tao saints, holy saints, and*
> *   all other saints, buddhas, bodhisattvas, healing*
> *   angels, archangels, ascended masters, lamas, gurus,*
> *   kahunas, and all spiritual fathers and mothers on*
> *   Mother Earth and in all layers of Heaven,*
> *Dear my ancestors,*
> *Dear Tao Song,*
> *I love you, honor you, and appreciate you.*
> *When I sing the Tao Song mantras for the Metal*
> *   element, please clear soul mind body blockages from*
> *   my Metal element and heal and rejuvenate my*
> *   Metal element.*
> *I am very grateful.*
> *Thank you. Thank you. Thank you.*

Mind Power. Focus on your *first* Soul House. Visualize a golden light ball or a rainbow light ball rotating counterclockwise in that area. If your Third Eye is open, observe whatever images you receive.

Sound Power. Chant or sing silently or aloud:

Shang Ya You Tao (pronounced *shahng yah yoe dow*)
Shang Ya You Tao
Shang Ya You Tao
Shang Ya You Tao
Shang Ya You Tao

Shang Ya You Tao
Shang Ya You Tao
Shang Ya You Tao
Shang Ya You Tao
Shang Ya You Tao

Shang Ya You Tao
Shang Ya You Tao
Shang Ya You Tao
Shang Ya You Tao
Shang Ya You Tao

Shang Ya You Tao
Shang Ya You Tao
Shang Ya You Tao
Shang Ya You Tao
Shang Ya You Tao . . .

Let us continue by chanting the second sacred Tao Song mantra for the Metal element.

Chant or sing silently or aloud:

Shang Ya You Zhong (pronounced *shahng yah yoe jawng*)
Shang Ya You Zhong

Shang Ya You Zhong
Shang Ya You Zhong
Shang Ya You Zhong

Shang Ya You Zhong
Shang Ya You Zhong
Shang Ya You Zhong
Shang Ya You Zhong
Shang Ya You Zhong

Shang Ya You Zhong
Shang Ya You Zhong
Shang Ya You Zhong
Shang Ya You Zhong
Shang Ya You Zhong

Shang Ya You Zhong
Shang Ya You Zhong
Shang Ya You Zhong
Shang Ya You Zhong
Shang Ya You Zhong . . .

Continue to self-clear soul mind body blockages from the Metal element and heal and rejuvenate the Metal element with the third, fourth, and fifth sacred Tao Song mantras:

Shang Ya You Ling (pronounced *shahng yah yoe ling*)
Shang Ya You Ling
Shang Ya You Ling
Shang Ya You Ling
Shang Ya You Ling

Shang Ya You Ling
Shang Ya You Ling
Shang Ya You Ling
Shang Ya You Ling
Shang Ya You Ling

Shang Ya You Ling
Shang Ya You Ling
Shang Ya You Ling
Shang Ya You Ling
Shang Ya You Ling

Shang Ya You Ling
Shang Ya You Ling
Shang Ya You Ling
Shang Ya You Ling
Shang Ya You Ling . . .

Shang Ya You Xu (pronounced *shahng yah yoe shü*)
Shang Ya You Xu
Shang Ya You Xu
Shang Ya You Xu
Shang Ya You Xu

Shang Ya You Xu
Shang Ya You Xu
Shang Ya You Xu
Shang Ya You Xu
Shang Ya You Xu

Shang Ya You Xu
Shang Ya You Xu
Shang Ya You Xu
Shang Ya You Xu
Shang Ya You Xu

Shang Ya You Xu
Shang Ya You Xu
Shang Ya You Xu
Shang Ya You Xu
Shang Ya You Xu . . .

Shang Ya You Kong (pronounced *shahng yah yoe
    kawng*)
Shang Ya You Kong
Shang Ya You Kong
Shang Ya You Kong
Shang Ya You Kong

Shang Ya You Kong
Shang Ya You Kong
Shang Ya You Kong
Shang Ya You Kong
Shang Ya You Kong

Shang Ya You Kong
Shang Ya You Kong
Shang Ya You Kong
Shang Ya You Kong
Shang Ya You Kong

Shang Ya You Kong
Shang Ya You Kong
Shang Ya You Kong
Shang Ya You Kong
Shang Ya You Kong . . .

Chant or sing for three to five minutes now. There is no time limit for this chanting. The longer you chant and the more you chant, the better.

SACRED TAO SONG MANTRAS TO SELF-CLEAR
SOUL MIND BODY BLOCKAGES FROM AND TO
HEAL AND REJUVENATE THE WATER ELEMENT

The Water element includes the kidneys, urinary bladder, ears, and bones in the physical body and connects with fear in the emotional body.

Now let us apply the Four Power Techniques to self-clear soul mind body blockages from the Water element and heal and rejuvenate the Water element.

Body Power. Sit up straight. Put the tip of your tongue as close as you can to the roof of your mouth without touching. Males, sit on your left palm facing the Hui Yin area. Females, sit on your right palm facing the Hui Yin area. Place the other palm on a kidney. Alternatively, you can put one palm on the lower abdomen below the navel and the other palm on a kidney.

Soul Power. Say *hello:*

Dear Divine,
Dear Tao,
Dear Heaven, Mother Earth, and countless planets,
stars, galaxies, and universes,
Dear all saints, including Tao saints, holy saints, and
all other saints, buddhas, bodhisattvas, healing
angels, archangels, ascended masters, lamas, gurus,
kahunas, and all spiritual fathers and mothers on
Mother Earth and in all layers of Heaven,
Dear my ancestors,
Dear Tao Song,
I love you, honor you, and appreciate you.
When I sing the Tao Song mantras for the Water ele-
ment, please clear soul mind body blockages from
my Water element and heal and rejuvenate my
Water element.
I am very grateful.
Thank you. Thank you. Thank you.

Mind Power. Focus on your *first* Soul House. Visualize a golden light ball or a rainbow light ball rotating counterclockwise in that area. If your Third Eye is open, observe whatever images you receive.

Sound Power. Chant or sing silently or aloud:

Yu Ya You Tao (pronounced *yü yah yoe dow*)
Yu Ya You Tao
Yu Ya You Tao
Yu Ya You Tao
Yu Ya You Tao

Yu Ya You Tao
Yu Ya You Tao
Yu Ya You Tao
Yu Ya You Tao
Yu Ya You Tao

Yu Ya You Tao
Yu Ya You Tao
Yu Ya You Tao
Yu Ya You Tao
Yu Ya You Tao

Yu Ya You Tao
Yu Ya You Tao
Yu Ya You Tao
Yu Ya You Tao
Yu Ya You Tao . . .

Let us continue by chanting the second sacred Tao Song mantra for the Water element.

Chant or sing silently or aloud:

Yu Ya You Zhong (pronounced *yü yah yoe jawng*)
Yu Ya You Zhong
Yu Ya You Zhong
Yu Ya You Zhong
Yu Ya You Zhong

Yu Ya You Zhong
Yu Ya You Zhong
Yu Ya You Zhong

Yu Ya You Zhong
Yu Ya You Zhong

Yu Ya You Zhong
Yu Ya You Zhong
Yu Ya You Zhong
Yu Ya You Zhong
Yu Ya You Zhong

Yu Ya You Zhong
Yu Ya You Zhong
Yu Ya You Zhong
Yu Ya You Zhong
Yu Ya You Zhong . . .

Continue to self-clear soul mind body blockages from the Water element and heal and rejuvenate the Water element with the third, fourth, and fifth sacred Tao Song mantras:

Yu Ya You Ling (pronounced *yü yah yoe ling*)
Yu Ya You Ling
Yu Ya You Ling
Yu Ya You Ling
Yu Ya You Ling

Yu Ya You Ling
Yu Ya You Ling
Yu Ya You Ling
Yu Ya You Ling
Yu Ya You Ling

Yu Ya You Ling
Yu Ya You Ling
Yu Ya You Ling
Yu Ya You Ling
Yu Ya You Ling

Yu Ya You Ling
Yu Ya You Ling
Yu Ya You Ling
Yu Ya You Ling
Yu Ya You Ling . . .

Yu Ya You Xu (pronounced *yü yah yoe shü*)
Yu Ya You Xu
Yu Ya You Xu
Yu Ya You Xu
Yu Ya You Xu

Yu Ya You Xu
Yu Ya You Xu
Yu Ya You Xu
Yu Ya You Xu
Yu Ya You Xu

Yu Ya You Xu
Yu Ya You Xu
Yu Ya You Xu
Yu Ya You Xu
Yu Ya You Xu

Yu Ya You Xu
Yu Ya You Xu
Yu Ya You Xu
Yu Ya You Xu
Yu Ya You Xu . . .

Yu Ya You Kong (pronounced *yü yah yoe kawng*)
Yu Ya You Kong
Yu Ya You Kong
Yu Ya You Kong
Yu Ya You Kong

Yu Ya You Kong
Yu Ya You Kong
Yu Ya You Kong
Yu Ya You Kong
Yu Ya You Kong

Yu Ya You Kong
Yu Ya You Kong
Yu Ya You Kong
Yu Ya You Kong
Yu Ya You Kong

Yu Ya You Kong
Yu Ya You Kong
Yu Ya You Kong
Yu Ya You Kong
Yu Ya You Kong . . .

Chant or sing for three to five minutes now. There is no time limit for this. The longer you chant and the more you chant, the better.

The Five Elements is Da Tao. Tao is The Way. Tao is divided into Da Tao (pronounced *dah dow*) and Xiao Tao (pronounced *shee-yow dow*). Da Tao is the Big Way. Xiao Tao is the Small Way. Da Tao is the Tao of Heaven, Mother Earth, and countless planets, stars, galaxies, and universes. Tao is in every aspect of life. Xiao Tao is the Tao of eating, sleeping, working, and more.

There are major universal laws that belong to Da Tao, including Yin Yang, Five Elements, Shen Qi Jing (Message Energy Matter), and Universal Service (karma).

There are countless planets, stars, galaxies, and universes, but they can all be categorized by the Five Elements. For example, there are Wood planets, Fire planets, Earth planets, Metal planets, and Water planets. There are also Wood stars, galaxies, and universes. There are Fire stars, galaxies, and universes. There are Earth stars, galaxies, and universes. There are Metal stars, galaxies, and universes. There are Water stars, galaxies, and universes.

Tao Song mantras for the Five Elements are Tao treasures to heal, bless, rejuvenate, and empower the Five Elements. Tao Song mantras for the Five Elements work for you, your loved ones, your family, pets, humanity, organizations, cities, countries, Mother Earth, and countless planets, stars, galaxies, and universes. You can chant this and all Tao Songs anywhere, any time. You can chant aloud or silently. Every moment you chant, you bring Tao frequency and vibration to transform every aspect of your life.

The most important teaching for everyone is to chant Tao

Songs nonstop. Chant twenty-four hours a day. At bedtime, chant until you fall asleep. Ask the souls of your body's systems, organs, and cells to chant while you sleep. The moment you wake up, chant Tao Song. When you drive, cook, walk, and perform your daily tasks, chant Tao Song silently or aloud. Chant all the time. Make it your intention to chant twenty-four/seven. One day you will be able to achieve this constant practice. If you can do this, you can self-clear your bad karma and transform your health, relationships, finances, intelligence, and more. You can self-heal your spiritual body, mental body, emotional body, and physical body. You can rejuvenate your soul, heart, mind, and body. You can prolong your life. You can move toward immortality. The benefits are immeasurable.

Self-clear Soul Mind Body Blockages
from the Five Elements with Tao Treasures

I will offer permanent Tao treasures that you can apply to self-clear soul mind body blockages from the Five Elements and heal and rejuvenate the Five Elements.

Prepare.

Sit up straight. Put the tip of your tongue as close as you can to the roof of your mouth without touching. Put both palms on your lower abdomen. As you read "Transmission!," the stated permanent treasures will come to your soul.

Tao Order: Tao Golden Light Ball and Golden Liquid Spring of Tao Light Soul Mind Body Transplants

Transmission!

Tao Order: Join Tao Light
Soul Mind Body Transplants as one.

Congratulations! You are extremely blessed. Every reader is extremely blessed. Humanity is extremely blessed.

Let us apply Tao Light Soul Mind Body Transplants and the Four Power Techniques to self-clear soul mind body blockages from the Five Elements and heal and rejuvenate the Five Elements.

Body Power. Sit up straight. Put the tip of your tongue as close as you can to the roof of your mouth without touching. Males, sit on your left palm facing the Hui Yin area. Females, sit on your right palm facing the Hui Yin area. Place the other palm over the bottom of your lower abdomen and pubic area. Alternatively, you can put both palms on your lower abdomen below your navel or one palm over the other below your navel.

Soul Power. Say *hello:*

> *Dear Divine,*
> *Dear Tao,*
> *Dear Heaven, Mother Earth, and countless planets,*
> *stars, galaxies, and universes,*
> *Dear all saints, including Tao saints, holy saints, and*
> *all other saints, buddhas, bodhisattvas, healing*
> *angels, archangels, ascended masters, lamas, gurus,*
> *kahunas, and all spiritual fathers and mothers on*
> *Mother Earth and in all layers of Heaven,*
> *Dear my ancestors,*

Dear Tao Song,
Dear Tao Light Soul Mind Body Transplants,
I love you, honor you, and appreciate you.
Please clear soul mind body blockages from my Five
  Elements and heal and rejuvenate my Five
  Elements.
I am very grateful.
Thank you. Thank you. Thank you.

Mind Power. Focus on your *first* Soul House. Visualize a golden light ball or a rainbow light ball rotating counterclockwise in that area. If your Third Eye is open, observe whatever images you receive.

Sound Power. Chant silently or aloud:

Tao Light
Tao Light
Tao Light
Tao Light
Tao Light
Tao Light
Tao Light . . .

Chant for three to five minutes now. There is no time limit for this chanting. The longer you chant and the more you chant, the better.

Tao Light Soul Mind Body Transplants are permanent treasures from Tao. Please realize that you have just received Tao Light Soul Mind Body Transplants from the Source. Pause for a moment and think about what kind of honor we have received. I cannot bow down enough to be a servant of humanity, wan ling, the Divine, and Tao. I was given the honor and authority to transmit permanent divine and Tao treasures to humanity, pets, organizations, cities, countries, Mother Earth, and countless planets, stars, galaxies, and universes. This is the first time that the Divine and Tao have chosen a servant to transmit Divine and Tao Soul Mind Body Transplants, which are permanent treasures, to humanity and wan ling (all souls in countless planets, stars, galaxies, and universes). I am extremely grateful for the honor that I can serve in this unique way. Humanity and wan ling are extremely blessed that the Divine and Tao are creating these permanent treasures to help humanity and Mother Earth to pass through this difficult time in history.

Sacred Tao Song Mantra for Boosting Energy, Stamina, Vitality, and Immunity

At this moment as I am flowing this book, Tao gave me a new sacred Tao Song mantra: Hei Heng You Tao. "Hei" (pronounced *hay*) is the sacred Tao sound for the first Soul House. "Heng" (pronounced *hung*) is the sacred Tao sound for the second Soul House. "You" (pronounced *yoe*) is the sacred Tao sound for the Wai Jiao. The key wisdom is that *You* is also for the tailbone. The ancient Xiu Lian term for this area of the body is *Wei Lü* (pronounced *way lü*). "Tao" is the Source or The Way.

To chant *Hei Heng You Tao* is to form a light ball circle. This light ball circle starts from the Hui Yin acupuncture point, goes up through the first Soul House to the second Soul House, and then turns down to the tailbone (Wei Lü) area. This is the sacred circle of the Tao power house. This is one of the most powerful sacred Tao Song mantras for boosting energy, stamina, vitality, and immunity.

Apply the Four Power Techniques to self-clear soul mind body blockages and boost energy, stamina, vitality, and immunity.

Body Power. Sit up straight. Put the tip of your tongue as close as you can to the roof of your mouth without touching. Males, sit on your left palm facing the Hui Yin area. Females, sit on your right palm facing the Hui Yin area. Place the other palm over the bottom of your lower abdomen and pubic area. Alternatively, you can put both palms on your lower abdomen below your navel or one palm over the other below your navel.

Soul Power. Say *hello:*

> *Dear Divine,*
> *Dear Tao,*
> *Dear Heaven, Mother Earth, and countless planets,*
>   *stars, galaxies, and universes,*
> *Dear all saints, including Tao saints, holy saints, and*
>   *all other saints, buddhas, bodhisattvas, healing*
>   *angels, archangels, ascended masters, lamas, gurus,*
>   *kahunas, and all spiritual fathers and mothers on*
>   *Mother Earth and in all layers of Heaven,*
> *Dear my ancestors,*
> *Dear Tao Song,*
> *I love you, honor you, and appreciate you.*
> *When I sing the Tao Song mantra for boosting energy,*
>   *stamina, vitality, and immunity, please clear soul*
>   *mind body blockages and boost my energy, stamina,*
>   *vitality, and immunity.*
> *I am very grateful.*
> *Thank you. Thank you. Thank you.*

Mind Power. Focus on your *first* Soul House. Visualize a golden light ball or a rainbow light ball rotating counterclockwise in that area. If your Third Eye is open, observe whatever images you receive.

Sound Power. Chant or sing silently or aloud:

> *Hei Heng You Tao* (pronounced *hay hung yoe dow*)
> *Hei Heng You Tao*
> *Hei Heng You Tao*
> *Hei Heng You Tao*
> *Hei Heng You Tao*
>
> *Hei Heng You Tao*
> *Hei Heng You Tao*
> *Hei Heng You Tao*
> *Hei Heng You Tao*
> *Hei Heng You Tao*
>
> *Hei Heng You Tao*
> *Hei Heng You Tao*
> *Hei Heng You Tao*
> *Hei Heng You Tao*
> *Hei Heng You Tao*
>
> *Hei Heng You Tao*
> *Hei Heng You Tao*
> *Hei Heng You Tao*
> *Hei Heng You Tao*
> *Hei Heng You Tao* . . .

This sacred Tao Song mantra is one of the most powerful sacred Tao mantras to create a Jin Dan. "Jin" (pronounced *jeen*) means *gold*. "Dan" (pronounced *dahn*) means *light ball*. Jin Dan is the Tao power source in the body. The Jin Dan journey is the Tao journey. Jin Dan has the highest power for healing your physical, emotional, mental, and spiritual bodies. Jin Dan is the key to preventing sickness in your physical, emotional, mental, and spiritual bodies. Jin Dan is the highest treasure for purifying your soul, heart, mind, and body. Jin Dan has the highest abilities for rejuvenating your soul, heart, mind, and body.

A human being is not born with a Jin Dan. One must do special Tao practices to form a Jin Dan. An entire chapter of my book *Tao I: The Way of All Life* is dedicated to the Jin Dan. You can learn more about the Jin Dan there. In my book *Tao II: The Way of Healing, Rejuvenation, Longevity, and Immortality,* there is a Jin Dan Da Tao chapter in which I share further teaching about the Jin Dan. Jin Dan is the highest treasure in the Tao journey.

Sacred Tao Song Mantra for Healing, Preventing Sickness, and Blessing Relationships and Finances

The most powerful Tao Song mantra for healing, preventing sickness, and blessing relationships and finances is the Tao Song mantra for the Tao Song Channel. This Tao Song mantra that I shared earlier in this chapter needs to be brought out again to emphasize its power. Remember, this is the sacred Tao Song mantra for healing all sicknesses in the spiritual body, mental body, emotional body, and physical body, as well as for preventing sickness and blessing relationships and finances. Apply this Tao Song mantra to self-clear soul mind body blockages for all sicknesses, relationships, and finances. The benefits of chanting this Tao Song mantra cannot be comprehended enough. The sacred mantra is:

Xi You You Tao

"Xi" (pronounced *shee*) removes soul mind body blockages from the Hui Yin acupuncture point up through the seven Soul Houses to the Bai Hui acupuncture point at the top of the head. "You" (pronounced *yoe*) removes soul mind body blockages in the Wai Jiao. The second "You" means *has*. Tao is The Way. "Xi You You Tao" means *Xi You has the way to transform all life, including health, relationships, finances, intelligence, and more, and to bring success to every aspect of life*. Xi You carries Tao frequency and vibration, with Tao love, forgiveness, compassion, and light. Remember Xi You in your soul, heart, mind, and body all of the time. Xi You is Da Tao. Da Tao Zhi Jian (pronounced *dah dao jr jyen*), *the Big Way is extremely simple*.

Apply the Four Power Techniques to self-clear soul mind body blockages for all sicknesses, relationships, and finances.

Body Power. Sit up straight. Put the tip of your tongue as close as you can to the roof of your mouth without touching. Males, sit on your left palm facing the Hui Yin area. Females, sit on your right palm facing the Hui Yin area. Place the other palm over the bottom of your lower abdomen and pubic area. Alternatively, you can put both palms on your lower abdomen below your navel or one palm over the other below your navel.

Soul Power. Say *hello:*

Dear Divine,
Dear Tao,
Dear Heaven, Mother Earth, and countless planets,
  stars, galaxies, and universes,
Dear all saints, including Tao saints, holy saints, and
  all other saints, buddhas, bodhisattvas, healing
  angels, archangels, ascended masters, lamas, gurus,
  kahunas, and all spiritual fathers and mothers on
  Mother Earth and in all layers of Heaven,
Dear my ancestors,
Dear Tao Song,
I love you, honor you, and appreciate you.
When I sing the Tao Song mantra for healing,
  preventing sickness, and blessing relationships and
  finances, please heal and prevent sickness, and bless
  my relationships and finances.
I am very grateful.
Thank you. Thank you. Thank you.

Mind Power. Focus on your *first* Soul House. Visualize a golden light ball or a rainbow light ball rotating counterclockwise in that area. If your Third Eye is open, observe whatever images you receive.

Sound Power. Chant or sing silently or aloud:

Xi You You Tao (pronounced *shee yoe yoe dow*)
Xi You You Tao
Xi You You Tao
Xi You You Tao
Xi You You Tao

Xi You You Tao
Xi You You Tao
Xi You You Tao
Xi You You Tao
Xi You You Tao

Xi You You Tao
Xi You You Tao
Xi You You Tao
Xi You You Tao
Xi You You Tao

Xi You You Tao
Xi You You Tao
Xi You You Tao
Xi You You Tao
Xi You You Tao . . .

Chant or sing for three to five minutes now. There is no time limit for this. The longer you chant and the more you chant, the better.

Remember Xi You You Tao from the bottom of your heart. These four sacred Tao sounds and this sacred Tao Song mantra have power beyond, beyond our minds' comprehension and imagination. Chant or sing this Tao Song mantra and unlimited blessings for healing and transforming of relationships and finances will come to you.

How does Xi You You Tao work? The root blockages of sickness and challenges in relationships and finances are bad karma. Xi You You Tao is one of the highest sacred Tao mantras. It carries Tao frequency and vibration with Tao love, forgiveness, compassion, and light. Bad karma is spiritual debt. Chanting *Xi You You Tao* offers you Tao virtue to pay your spiritual debts in order to be forgiven for your mistakes in this lifetime and previous lifetimes. This is a top secret.

It takes time to totally self-clear your bad karma through chanting sacred Tao mantras. Self-clearing karma is different from receiving a Divine or Tao Order for Karma Cleansing. Divine and Tao Orders for Karma Cleansing direct Heaven's generals and soldiers and the leaders and workers of the Akashic Records to remove bad karma from your book in the Akashic Records and to fully open Heaven's virtue bank to pay your spiritual debt for the karma cleansing service that you receive. Chanting Tao Song mantras clears bad karma through your personal effort, but you have to chant a lot in order to self-clear all bad karma.

This one of the top sacred Tao mantras can be summarized in one sentence:

**Xi You You Tao is the sacred Tao Song
mantra for Tao normal creation.**

The process of normal creation is:

**Tao creates One. One creates Two.
Two creates Three. Three creates all things.**

**Tao ➔ One ➔ Two ➔ Three ➔ all things
creates**

If you are sick in the spiritual, mental, emotional, or physical body or have a blockage in relationships or finances, the process of Tao normal creation is blocked. To chant or sing *Xi You You Tao* is to remove soul mind body blockages for your health, relationships, and finances. In fact, it removes soul mind body blockages in your process of Tao normal creation.

Sacred Tao Song Mantra for Rejuvenation, Longevity, and Immortality

Another most important sacred Tao mantra is for rejuvenation, longevity, and immortality. I am releasing another highest sacred Tao mantra now:

You Xi You Tao

"You" removes soul mind body blockages from the Wai Jiao and the spinal cord. "Xi" removes soul mind body blockages from the Bai Hui acupuncture point down through the seven Soul Houses to the Hui Yin acupuncture point. The second "You" means *has*. Tao is The Way. You Xi You Tao (pronounced *yoe shee yoe dow*) means *You Xi has Tao*. You Xi You Tao is one of the most sacred Tao mantras for rejuvenation, longevity, and immortality. This one of the highest sacred Tao mantras can be summarized in one sentence:

You Xi You Tao is the sacred Tao Song mantra for Tao reverse creation.

The process of reverse creation is:

All things return to Three. Three returns to Two. Two returns to One. One returns to Tao.

all things → Three → Two → One → Tao
return to

To first reach fan lao huan tong (transform old age to the health and purity of the baby state) and then achieve longevity and attain immortality is the process of Tao reverse creation.

Let us apply the sacred Tao Song mantra You Xi You Tao for Tao reverse creation and the Four Power Techniques for rejuvenation, fan lao huan tong, longevity, and immortality.

Body Power. Sit up straight. Put the tip of your tongue as close as you can to the roof of your mouth without touching. Males, sit on your left palm facing the Hui Yin area. Females, sit on your right palm facing the Hui Yin area. Place the other palm over the bottom of your lower abdomen and pubic area. Alternatively, you can put both palms on your lower abdomen below your navel or one palm over the other below your navel.

Soul Power. Say *hello:*

> *Dear Divine,*
> *Dear Tao,*
> *Dear Heaven, Mother Earth, and countless planets,*
>   *stars, galaxies, and universes,*
> *Dear all saints, including Tao saints, holy saints, and*
>   *all other saints, buddhas, bodhisattvas, healing*
>   *angels, archangels, ascended masters, lamas, gurus,*
>   *kahunas, and all spiritual fathers and mothers on*
>   *Mother Earth and in all layers of Heaven,*
> *Dear my ancestors,*
> *Dear Tao Song,*
> *I love you, honor you, and appreciate you.*
> *When I sing the Tao Song mantra for rejuvenation,*
>   *longevity, and immortality, please remove soul mind*

body blockages for rejuvenation, longevity, and
immortality.
I am very grateful.
Thank you. Thank you. Thank you.

Mind Power. Focus on your first Soul House. Visualize a golden light ball or a rainbow light ball rotating counterclockwise in that area. If your Third Eye is open, observe whatever images you receive.

Sound Power. Chant or sing silently or aloud:

You Xi You Tao (pronounced *yoe shee yoe dow*)
You Xi You Tao
You Xi You Tao
You Xi You Tao
You Xi You Tao

You Xi You Tao
You Xi You Tao
You Xi You Tao
You Xi You Tao
You Xi You Tao

You Xi You Tao
You Xi You Tao
You Xi You Tao
You Xi You Tao
You Xi You Tao

You Xi You Tao
You Xi You Tao
You Xi You Tao
You Xi You Tao
You Xi You Tao . . .

Chant or sing for three to five minutes now. There is no time limit for this. The longer you chant and the more you chant, the better.

In the Tao journey there are five steps:

- **Shen Sheng Jing**—"Shen" means *kidneys*. "Sheng" means *produce*. "Jing" means *matter*. "Shen sheng jing" (肾生精, pronounced *shun shung jing*) means *kidneys produce jing*.
- **Lian Jing Hua Qi**—"Lian" means *cook*. "Jing" means *matter*. "Hua" means *transform*. "Qi" means *vital energy or life force*. Qi, in fact, is tiny matter. "Lian jing hua qi" (炼精化气, pronounced *lyen jing hwah chee*) is the process of jing (created by the kidneys) moving down in front of the spinal column to two invisible holes in front of the tailbone and going into the spinal cord.
- **Lian Qi Hua Shen**—"Lian" means *cook*. "Qi" means *vital energy or life force*. "Hua" means *transform*. "Shen" means *soul or message*. Shen is even tinier matter than qi. "Lian qi hua shen" (炼气化神, pronounced *lyen chee hwah shun*) is the process of moving *qi from the spinal cord to the brain*.

- **Lian Shen Huan Xu**—"Lian" means *cook*. "Shen" means *soul or message*. "Huan" means *transform*. "Xu" means *purity and emptiness*. Lian shen huan xu (炼神还虚, pronounced *lyen shun hwahn shü*) means *energy flows from the brain to the heart to purify the heart more and more*.
- **Lian Xu Huan Tao**—"Lian" means *cook*. "Xu" means *purity and emptiness*. "Huan" means *transform*. Tao is the Source. "Lian xu huan Tao" (炼虚还道, pronounced *lyen shü hwahn dow*) means *the heart reaches total purity and melds with Tao*.

You Xi You Tao includes these five steps. This is the most powerful sacred Tao Song mantra for rejuvenation, fan lao huan tong, longevity, and immortality. This is a lifetime practice. There is no time limit to how long you should chant. The more you chant and the longer you chant, the better.

Millions of people have health challenges in the spiritual, mental, emotional, and physical bodies. Millions of people are searching for rejuvenation, fan lao huan tong, longevity, and immortality. I am releasing one of the most powerful practical techniques to heal and rejuvenate at the same time.

Sacred Tao Song Mantra for Healing, Rejuvenation, Longevity, and Immortality

The sacred Tao Song mantra for Healing, Rejuvenation, Longevity, and Immortality combines the sacred Tao Song mantra for Tao normal creation with the sacred Tao Song mantra for Tao reverse creation.

Let us apply the Sacred Tao Song mantra for Healing, Rejuvenation, Longevity, and Immortality by using the Four Power Techniques.

Body Power. Sit up straight. Put the tip of your tongue as close as you can to the roof of your mouth without touching. Males, sit on your left palm facing the Hui Yin area. Females, sit on your right palm facing the Hui Yin area. Place the other palm over the bottom of your lower abdomen and pubic area. Alternatively, you can put both palms on your lower abdomen below your navel or one palm over the other below your navel.

Soul Power. Say *hello:*

> *Dear Divine,*
> *Dear Tao,*
> *Dear Heaven, Mother Earth, and countless planets,*
>   *stars, galaxies, and universes,*
> *Dear all saints, including Tao saints, holy saints, and*
>   *all other saints, buddhas, bodhisattvas, healing*
>   *angels, archangels, ascended masters, lamas, gurus,*
>   *kahunas, and all spiritual fathers and mothers on*
>   *Mother Earth and in all layers of Heaven,*
> *Dear my ancestors,*
> *Dear Tao Song,*
> *I love you, honor you, and appreciate you.*
> *When I sing the Tao Song mantra for healing,*
>   *rejuvenation, longevity, and immortality, please*
>   *heal, rejuvenate, and prolong my life to reach*
>   *immortality.*
> *I am very grateful.*
> *Thank you. Thank you. Thank you.*

Mind Power. Focus on your *first* Soul House. Visualize a golden light ball or a rainbow light ball rotating counterclockwise in that area. If your Third Eye is open, observe whatever images you receive.

Sound Power. Chant or sing silently or aloud:

Xi You You Tao (pronounced *shee yoe yoe dow*)
Xi You You Tao
Xi You You Tao
Xi You You Tao
Xi You You Tao

You Xi You Tao (pronounced *yoe shee yoe dow*)
You Xi You Tao
You Xi You Tao
You Xi You Tao
You Xi You Tao

Xi You You Tao
Xi You You Tao
Xi You You Tao
Xi You You Tao
Xi You You Tao

You Xi You Tao
You Xi You Tao
You Xi You Tao
You Xi You Tao
You Xi You Tao . . .

Chant for at least three to five minutes. In fact, I strongly suggest that you chant for at least a half-hour. The more you chant and the longer you chant, the better. If you can chant one or two hours per time, that is much better. Combining these two highest sacred Tao Song mantras can transform your health, relationships, finances, intelligence, and more and bring success to every aspect of your life. These two sacred Tao Song mantras can help you rejuvenate, reach fan lao huan tong, prolong life, and reach immortality. This is a daily practice. You can practice anywhere, anytime. You can chant out loud or silently. In fact, if you chant these two sacred Tao Song mantras silently nonstop, every aspect of your life could transform beyond words, comprehension, and imagination.

Complete Sacred Tao Song Mantras for Self-clearing Soul Mind Body Blockages in the Seven Soul Houses, Wai Jiao, Tao Song Channel, and Five Elements; for Boosting Energy, Stamina, Vitality, and Immunity; for Healing, Preventing Sickness, and Blessing Relationships and Finances; and for Rejuvenation, Longevity, and Immortality

After learning all of the new sacred Tao Song mantras in this chapter, we can combine all of them together in one practice. This practice is vital for transforming, enlightening, and bringing success to all aspects of your life, including your health, relationships, finances, intelligence, and more.

Apply the Four Power Techniques to self-clear soul mind body blockages from the Seven Soul Houses, Wai Jiao, Tao Song Channel, and Five Elements; to boost energy, stamina, vitality, and immunity; to heal, prevent sickness, and to bless relationships and finances; and to rejuvenate, prolong life, and to move to immortality.

Body Power. Apply the same Body Power as with most of the other practices in this book. Sit up straight. Put the tip of your tongue as close as you can to the roof of your mouth without touching. Males, sit on your left palm facing the Hui Yin area. Females, sit on your right palm facing the Hui Yin area. Place the other palm over the bottom of your lower abdomen and pubic area. Alternatively, you can put both palms on your lower abdomen below your navel or one palm over the other below your navel.

Soul Power. Say *hello:*

> *Dear Divine,*
> *Dear Tao,*
> *Dear Heaven, Mother Earth, and countless planets,*
>   *stars, galaxies, and universes,*
> *Dear all saints, including Tao saints, holy saints, and*
>   *all other saints, buddhas, bodhisattvas, healing*
>   *angels, archangels, ascended masters, lamas, gurus,*
>   *kahunas, and all spiritual fathers and mothers on*
>   *Mother Earth and in all layers of Heaven,*
> *Dear my ancestors,*
> *Dear Tao Song,*
> *I love you, honor you, and appreciate you.*
> *When I sing the complete sacred Tao Song mantras,*
>   *please transform, enlighten, and bring success to*
>   *every aspect of my life, including my health,*
>   *relationships, finances, intelligence, and more.*

I am very grateful.
Thank you. Thank you. Thank you.

Mind Power. Focus on your *first* Soul House. Visualize a golden light ball or a rainbow light ball rotating counterclockwise in that area. If your Third Eye is open, observe whatever images you receive.

Sound Power. Chant or sing silently or aloud:

FIRST SOUL HOUSE

Hei Ya You Tao (pronounced *hay yah yoe dow*)
Hei Ya You Tao
Hei Ya You Tao
Hei Ya You Tao
Hei Ya You Tao

Hei Ya You Zhong (pronounced *hay yah yoe jawng*)
Hei Ya You Zhong
Hei Ya You Zhong
Hei Ya You Zhong
Hei Ya You Zhong

Hei Ya You Ling (pronounced *hay yah yoe ling*)
Hei Ya You Ling
Hei Ya You Ling
Hei Ya You Ling
Hei Ya You Ling

Hei Ya You Xu (pronounced *hay yah yoe shü*)
Hei Ya You Xu
Hei Ya You Xu
Hei Ya You Xu
Hei Ya You Xu

Hei Ya You Kong (pronounced *hay yah yoe kawng*)
Hei Ya You Kong
Hei Ya You Kong
Hei Ya You Kong
Hei Ya You Kong

SECOND SOUL HOUSE

Heng Ya You Tao (pronounced *hung yah yoe dow*)
Heng Ya You Tao
Heng Ya You Tao
Heng Ya You Tao
Heng Ya You Tao

Heng Ya You Zhong (pronounced *hung yah yoe jawng)*
Heng Ya You Zhong
Heng Ya You Zhong
Heng Ya You Zhong
Heng Ya You Zhong

Heng Ya You Ling (pronounced *hung yah yoe ling*)
Heng Ya You Ling
Heng Ya You Ling

Heng Ya You Ling
Heng Ya You Ling

Heng Ya You Xu (pronounced *hung yah yoe shü*)
Heng Ya You Xu
Heng Ya You Xu
Heng Ya You Xu
Heng Ya You Xu

Heng Ya You Kong (pronounced *hung yah yoe kawng*)
Heng Ya You Kong
Heng Ya You Kong
Heng Ya You Kong
Heng Ya You Kong

THIRD SOUL HOUSE

Hong Ya You Tao (pronounced *hawng yah yoe dow*)
Hong Ya You Tao
Hong Ya You Tao
Hong Ya You Tao
Hong Ya You Tao

Hong Ya You Zhong (pronounced *hawng yah yoe jawng*)
Hong Ya You Zhong
Hong Ya You Zhong
Hong Ya You Zhong
Hong Ya You Zhong

Hong Ya You Ling (pronounced *hawng yah yoe ling*)
Hong Ya You Ling
Hong Ya You Ling
Hong Ya You Ling
Hong Ya You Ling

Hong Ya You Xu (pronounced *hawng yah yoe shü*)
Hong Ya You Xu
Hong Ya You Xu
Hong Ya You Xu
Hong Ya You Xu

Hong Ya You Kong (pronounced *hawng yah yoe
   kawng*)
Hong Ya You Kong
Hong Ya You Kong
Hong Ya You Kong
Hong Ya You Kong

FOURTH SOUL HOUSE

Ah Ya You Tao (pronounced *ah yah yoe dow*)
Ah Ya You Tao
Ah Ya You Tao
Ah Ya You Tao
Ah Ya You Tao

Ah Ya You Zhong (pronounced *ah yah yoe jawng*)
Ah Ya You Zhong

Ah Ya You Zhong
Ah Ya You Zhong
Ah Ya You Zhong

Ah Ya You Ling (pronounced *ah yah yoe ling*)
Ah Ya You Ling
Ah Ya You Ling
Ah Ya You Ling
Ah Ya You Ling

Ah Ya You Xu (pronounced *ah yah yoe shü*)
Ah Ya You Xu
Ah Ya You Xu
Ah Ya You Xu
Ah Ya You Xu

Ah Ya You Kong (pronounced *ah yah yoe kawng*)
Ah Ya You Kong
Ah Ya You Kong
Ah Ya You Kong
Ah Ya You Kong

FIFTH SOUL HOUSE

Xi Ya You Tao (pronounced *shee yah yoe dow*)
Xi Ya You Tao
Xi Ya You Tao
Xi Ya You Tao
Xi Ya You Tao

Xi Ya You Zhong (pronounced *shee yah yoe jawng*)
Xi Ya You Zhong
Xi Ya You Zhong
Xi Ya You Zhong
Xi Ya You Zhong

Xi Ya You Ling (pronounced *shee yah yoe ling*)
Xi Ya You Ling
Xi Ya You Ling
Xi Ya You Ling
Xi Ya You Ling

Xi Ya You Xu (pronounced *shee yah yoe shü*)
Xi Ya You Xu
Xi Ya You Xu
Xi Ya You Xu
Xi Ya You Xu

Xi Ya You Kong (pronounced *shee yah yoe kawng*)
Xi Ya You Kong
Xi Ya You Kong
Xi Ya You Kong
Xi Ya You Kong

SIXTH SOUL HOUSE

Yi Ya You Tao (pronounced *yee yah yoe dow*)
Yi Ya You Tao
Yi Ya You Tao
Yi Ya You Tao
Yi Ya You Tao

Yi Ya You Zhong (pronounced *yee yah yoe jawng*)
Yi Ya You Zhong
Yi Ya You Zhong
Yi Ya You Zhong
Yi Ya You Zhong

Yi Ya You Ling (pronounced *yee yah yoe ling*)
Yi Ya You Ling
Yi Ya You Ling
Yi Ya You Ling
Yi Ya You Ling

Yi Ya You Xu (pronounced *yee yah yoe shü*)
Yi Ya You Xu
Yi Ya You Xu
Yi Ya You Xu
Yi Ya You Xu

Yi Ya You Kong (pronounced *yee yah yoe kawng*)
Yi Ya You Kong
Yi Ya You Kong
Yi Ya You Kong
Yi Ya You Kong

SEVENTH SOUL HOUSE

Weng Ya You Tao (pronounced *wung yah yoe dow*)
Weng Ya You Tao
Weng Ya You Tao
Weng Ya You Tao
Weng Ya You Tao

Weng Ya You Zhong (pronounced *wung yah yoe jawng*)
Weng Ya You Zhong
Weng Ya You Zhong
Weng Ya You Zhong
Weng Ya You Zhong

Weng Ya You Ling (pronounced *wung yah yoe ling*)
Weng Ya You Ling
Weng Ya You Ling
Weng Ya You Ling
Weng Ya You Ling

Weng Ya You Xu (pronounced *wung yah yoe shü*)
Weng Ya You Xu
Weng Ya You Xu
Weng Ya You Xu
Weng Ya You Xu

Weng Ya You Kong (pronounced *wung yah yoe kawng*)
Weng Ya You Kong
Weng Ya You Kong
Weng Ya You Kong
Weng Ya You Kong

WAI JIAO

You Ya You Tao (pronounced *yoe yah yoe dow*)
You Ya You Tao
You Ya You Tao

You Ya You Tao
You Ya You Tao

You Ya You Zhong (pronounced *yoe yah yoe jawng*)
You Ya You Zhong
You Ya You Zhong
You Ya You Zhong
You Ya You Zhong

You Ya You Ling (pronounced *yoe yah yoe ling*)
You Ya You Ling
You Ya You Ling
You Ya You Ling
You Ya You Ling

You Ya You Xu (pronounced *yoe yah yoe shü*)
You Ya You Xu
You Ya You Xu
You Ya You Xu
You Ya You Xu

You Ya You Kong (pronounced *yoe yah yoe kawng*)
You Ya You Kong
You Ya You Kong
You Ya You Kong
You Ya You Kong

TAO SONG CHANNEL

Xi You You Tao (pronounced *shee yoe yoe dow*)
Xi You You Tao

Xi You You Tao
Xi You You Tao
Xi You You Tao

Xi You You Zhong (pronounced *shee yoe yoe jawng*)
Xi You You Zhong
Xi You You Zhong
Xi You You Zhong
Xi You You Zhong

Xi You You Ling (pronounced *shee yoe yoe ling*)
Xi You You Ling
Xi You You Ling
Xi You You Ling
Xi You You Ling

Xi You You Xu (pronounced *shee yoe yoe shü*)
Xi You You Xu
Xi You You Xu
Xi You You Xu
Xi You You Xu

Xi You You Kong (pronounced *shee yoe yoe kawng*)
Xi You You Kong
Xi You You Kong
Xi You You Kong
Xi You You Kong

WOOD ELEMENT

Jiao Ya You Tao (pronounced *jee-yow yah yoe dow*)
Jiao Ya You Tao

Jiao Ya You Tao
Jiao Ya You Tao
Jiao Ya You Tao

Jiao Ya You Zhong (pronounced *jee-yow yah yoe*
    jawng)
Jiao Ya You Zhong
Jiao Ya You Zhong
Jiao Ya You Zhong
Jiao Ya You Zhong

Jiao Ya You Ling (pronounced *jee-yow yah yoe ling*)
Jiao Ya You Ling
Jiao Ya You Ling
Jiao Ya You Ling
Jiao Ya You Ling

Jiao Ya You Xu (pronounced *jee-yow yah yoe shü*)
Jiao Ya You Xu
Jiao Ya You Xu
Jiao Ya You Xu
Jiao Ya You Xu

Jiao Ya You Kong (pronounced *jee-yow yah yoe*
    kawng)
Jiao Ya You Kong
Jiao Ya You Kong
Jiao Ya You Kong
Jiao Ya You Kong

FIRE ELEMENT

Zhi Ya You Tao (pronounced *jr yah yoe dow*)
Zhi Ya You Tao
Zhi Ya You Tao
Zhi Ya You Tao
Zhi Ya You Tao

Zhi Ya You Zhong (pronounced *jr yah yoe jawng*)
Zhi Ya You Zhong
Zhi Ya You Zhong
Zhi Ya You Zhong
Zhi Ya You Zhong

Zhi Ya You Ling (pronounced *jr yah yoe ling*)
Zhi Ya You Ling
Zhi Ya You Ling
Zhi Ya You Ling
Zhi Ya You Ling

Zhi Ya You Xu (pronounced *jr yah yoe shü*)
Zhi Ya You Xu
Zhi Ya You Xu
Zhi Ya You Xu
Zhi Ya You Xu

Zhi Ya You Kong (pronounced *jr yah yoe kawng*)
Zhi Ya You Kong
Zhi Ya You Kong
Zhi Ya You Kong
Zhi Ya You Kong

EARTH ELEMENT

Gong Ya You Tao (pronounced *gawng yah yoe dow*)
Gong Ya You Tao
Gong Ya You Tao
Gong Ya You Tao
Gong Ya You Tao

Gong Ya You Zhong (pronounced *gawng yah yoe
   jawng*)
Gong Ya You Zhong
Gong Ya You Zhong
Gong Ya You Zhong
Gong Ya You Zhong

Gong Ya You Ling (pronounced *gawng yah yoe ling*)
Gong Ya You Ling
Gong Ya You Ling
Gong Ya You Ling
Gong Ya You Ling

Gong Ya You Xu (pronounced *gawng yah yoe shü*)
Gong Ya You Xu
Gong Ya You Xu
Gong Ya You Xu
Gong Ya You Xu

Gong Ya You Kong (pronounced *gawng yah yoe
   kawng*)
Gong Ya You Kong

Gong Ya You Kong
Gong Ya You Kong
Gong Ya You Kong

METAL ELEMENT

Shang Ya You Tao (pronounced *shahng yah yoe dow*)
Shang Ya You Tao
Shang Ya You Tao
Shang Ya You Tao
Shang Ya You Tao

Shang Ya You Zhong (pronounced *shahng yah yoe jawng*)
Shang Ya You Zhong
Shang Ya You Zhong
Shang Ya You Zhong
Shang Ya You Zhong

Shang Ya You Ling (pronounced *shahng yah yoe ling*)
Shang Ya You Ling
Shang Ya You Ling
Shang Ya You Ling
Shang Ya You Ling

Shang Ya You Xu (pronounced *shahng yah yoe shü*)
Shang Ya You Xu
Shang Ya You Xu
Shang Ya You Xu
Shang Ya You Xu

Shang Ya You Kong (pronounced *shahng yah yoe*
  kawng)
Shang Ya You Kong
Shang Ya You Kong
Shang Ya You Kong
Shang Ya You Kong

WATER ELEMENT

Yu Ya You Tao (pronounced *yü yah yoe dow*)
Yu Ya You Tao
Yu Ya You Tao
Yu Ya You Tao
Yu Ya You Tao

Yu Ya You Zhong (pronounced *yü yah yoe jawng*)
Yu Ya You Zhong
Yu Ya You Zhong
Yu Ya You Zhong
Yu Ya You Zhong

Yu Ya You Ling (pronounced *yü yah yoe ling*)
Yu Ya You Ling
Yu Ya You Ling
Yu Ya You Ling
Yu Ya You Ling

Yu Ya You Xu (pronounced *yü yah yoe shü*)
Yu Ya You Xu
Yu Ya You Xu

Yu Ya You Xu
Yu Ya You Xu

Yu Ya You Kong (pronounced *yü yah yoe kawng*)
Yu Ya You Kong
Yu Ya You Kong
Yu Ya You Kong
Yu Ya You Kong

BOOST ENERGY, STAMINA, VITALITY, AND IMMUNITY

Hei Heng You Tao (pronounced *hay hung yoe dow*)
Hei Heng You Tao
Hei Heng You Tao
Hei Heng You Tao
Hei Heng You Tao

Hei Heng You Tao
Hei Heng You Tao
Hei Heng You Tao
Hei Heng You Tao
Hei Heng You Tao

Hei Heng You Tao
Hei Heng You Tao
Hei Heng You Tao
Hei Heng You Tao
Hei Heng You Tao

Hei Heng You Tao
Hei Heng You Tao

Hei Heng You Tao
Hei Heng You Tao
Hei Heng You Tao

Hei Heng You Tao
Hei Heng You Tao
Hei Heng You Tao
Hei Heng You Tao
Hei Heng You Tao

HEALING AND PREVENTING ALL SICKNESS IN THE
SPIRITUAL, MENTAL, EMOTIONAL, AND PHYSICAL
BODIES; BLESSING RELATIONSHIPS AND FINANCES

Xi You You Tao (pronounced *shee yoe yoe dow*)
Xi You You Tao
Xi You You Tao
Xi You You Tao
Xi You You Tao

Xi You You Tao
Xi You You Tao
Xi You You Tao
Xi You You Tao
Xi You You Tao

Xi You You Tao
Xi You You Tao
Xi You You Tao
Xi You You Tao
Xi You You Tao

Xi You You Tao
Xi You You Tao
Xi You You Tao
Xi You You Tao
Xi You You Tao

Xi You You Tao
Xi You You Tao
Xi You You Tao
Xi You You Tao
Xi You You Tao

REJUVENATION, FAN LAO HUAN TONG, LONGEVITY, AND IMMORTALITY

You Xi You Tao (pronounced *yoe shee yoe dow*)
You Xi You Tao
You Xi You Tao
You Xi You Tao
You Xi You Tao

You Xi You Tao
You Xi You Tao
You Xi You Tao
You Xi You Tao
You Xi You Tao

You Xi You Tao
You Xi You Tao
You Xi You Tao
You Xi You Tao
You Xi You Tao

You Xi You Tao
You Xi You Tao
You Xi You Tao
You Xi You Tao
You Xi You Tao

You Xi You Tao
You Xi You Tao
You Xi You Tao
You Xi You Tao
You Xi You Tao

This practice is the complete chanting of this book. As with all practices, the more you chant and the longer you chant, the better the results you could achieve.

Practice more and more.

Remove soul mind body blockages from your seven Soul Houses, Wai Jiao, Tao Song Channel, Five Elements, relationships, finances, and every aspect of life.

Boost your energy, stamina, vitality, and immunity.

Heal and prevent all sickness.

Bless your relationships and finances.

Rejuvenate, prolong life, and move toward immortality.

Tao Song is song from the Source.

Tao Song carries Tao frequency and vibration that can transform the frequency and vibration of every aspect of life, including health, relationships, finances, intelligence, and more.

Tao Song carries Tao love, which melts all blockages and transforms all life.

Tao Song carries Tao forgiveness, which brings inner joy and inner peace.

Tao Song carries Tao compassion, which boosts energy, stamina, vitality, and immunity.

Tao Song carries Tao light, which heals, prevents sickness, purifies and rejuvenates soul, heart, mind, and body, as well as transforms relationships, finances, and every aspect of life.

Thank you to the Source who has passed sacred Tao Song mantras to me so that I can share them with humanity and wan ling (all souls). I am honored and humbled to be a servant of you, humanity, Mother Earth, all souls, the Divine, and Tao.

> *Chanting Chanting Chanting*
> *Tao chanting is healing*
> *Chanting Chanting Chanting*
> *Tao chanting is rejuvenating*
>
> *Singing Singing Singing*
> *Tao singing is transforming*
> *Singing Singing Singing*
> *Tao singing is enlightening*
>
> *Humanity is waiting for Tao chanting*
> *All souls are waiting for Tao singing*
> *Tao chanting removes all blockages*
> *Tao singing brings inner joy*
>
> *Tao is chanting and singing*
> *Humanity and all souls are nourishing*
> *Humanity and all souls are chanting and singing*
>
> *World love, peace and harmony are coming*
> *World love, peace and harmony are coming*
> *World love, peace and harmony are coming*

How to Increase the Power of Your Tao Song

*T*HE DIVINE AND Tao have trained me directly how to sing Soul Song, Divine Soul Song, and Tao Song. They have given me sacred and secret wisdom, knowledge, and practical techniques. I have never received any professional voice coaching or training. How did the Divine and Tao train me? How can you use these secrets to increase the power of *your* Soul Song, Divine Soul Song, and Tao Song singing? I will give you the answers in this chapter.

The Most Important Secrets for Increasing the Power of Your Tao Song Singing

The Divine and Tao taught me the most important secret for singing Tao Song. In one sentence:

When you sing Tao Song, put your mind on the first Soul House, which is the energy source for singing.

Let me explain further.

HUI YIN ACUPUNCTURE POINT AND FIRST SOUL HOUSE

I have explained the location, significance, benefits, and power of the Hui Yin acupuncture point and the first Soul House in chapters 2 and 3. The key wisdom and major secret is to put your mind on the first Soul House, which includes the Hui Yin acupuncture point, when you sing. Do not think of anything else. Put your mind completely on the first Soul House.

It is especially important to avoid thinking that your voice is flowing from your mouth or vocal cords, which is what people commonly think. To explain the true source of our Tao Song, the Divine and Tao gave me a one-sentence secret:

Tao Song radiates from the Tao Song Channel in every direction, three hundred sixty degrees.

In fact, the Divine and Tao told me not to think about the source of my sound. Just put the mind on the first Soul House, and the sound will radiate out from the Tao Song Channel naturally. This is significant because the Tao Song Channel is the Tao temple and Tao source inside the body. I will now review and emphasize the most important aspects of the earlier teaching in this book on the Tao Song Channel.

The Tao Song Channel starts at the Hui Yin acupuncture point located between the genitals and anus, flows up through the seven Soul Houses in the center of the body to the Bai Hui acupuncture point at the top of the head, and then flows down in front of the spinal column through the Wai Jiao, returning to the Hui Yin acupuncture point. The Tao Song Channel has unlimited significance, benefits, and power. The major teachings are:

- The Hui Yin acupuncture point gathers the jing qi shen (matter energy soul) of the entire body's yin and connects with Mother Earth.
- The Bai Hui acupuncture point gathers the jing qi shen of the entire body's yang and connects with Heaven.
- The seven Soul Houses connect with the Five Elements, which include every system, every organ, and every cell.
- The Wai Jiao is the biggest space in the body. It is the seat of one's soul, mind, and body. The shen qi jing of the entire body flows to and through the Wai Jiao.
- The Tao Song Channel is a sacred Tao temple that connects with Tao.
- The Tao Song Channel gathers the jing qi shen of Heaven, Mother Earth, and countless planets, stars, galaxies, and universes. It also gathers the jing qi shen of Tao, which can transform your jing qi shen to Tao jing qi shen.
- Tao Song radiates from the Tao Song Channel in every direction, three hundred sixty degrees.
- The Tao Song Channel is a sacred Tao temple for purifying one's soul, heart, mind, and body and for

transforming the frequency and vibration of one's soul, heart, mind, and body to Tao frequency and vibration.

- The Tao Song Channel is the most important sacred Tao temple for increasing one's power for healing, rejuvenation, longevity, and immortality.
- The Tao Song Channel is the key for the Tao journey.

SELF-CLEAR SOUL MIND BODY BLOCKAGES IN THE SEVEN SOUL HOUSES, WAI JIAO, AND TAO SONG CHANNEL

In chapter 3 of this book I taught and led everyone to practice the sacred Tao Song mantras for the seven Soul Houses, Wai Jiao, and Tao Song Channel. If you cannot sing Tao Songs well, the reason can be summarized in one sentence:

Soul mind body blockages in the seven Soul Houses, Wai Jiao, and Tao Song Channel prevent one from singing Tao Song well.

Therefore:

Remove soul mind body blockages in the seven Soul Houses, Wai Jiao, and Tao Song Channel in order to sing Tao Song well.

In order to self-clear soul mind body blockages in the seven Soul Houses, Wai Jiao, and Tao Song channel, chant the Tao Song mantras for the seven Soul Houses, Wai Jiao, and Tao Song Channel. Chant a lot. Chant the Complete Sacred Tao Mantras for Self-clearing Soul Mind Body Blockages in the Seven Soul

Houses, Wai Jiao, Tao Song Channel, and Five Elements; for Boosting Energy, Stamina, Vitality, and Immunity; for Healing, Preventing Sickness, and Blessing Relationships and Finances; and for Rejuvenation, Longevity, and Immortality (pages 218–239) again and again. This is a vital practice for improving your Tao Song singing. There is no time limit for this chanting. There are no other requirements. Just sing or chant these Tao Song mantras again and again and your Tao Song will improve automatically.

When you sing or chant any Tao Song, always apply the most important secret: put your mind on the first Soul House. Your Tao Song Channel is like a bicycle tire. It needs to be inflated and expanded with air, which is pumped in through a valve. Your first Soul House is the valve for the Tao Song Channel. When you focus on your first Soul House, the Hui Yin point and other energy sources there will pump energy into the Tao Song Channel, filling it with power.

Sacred Process to Transform Your Soul Song to Tao Song

In chapter 1, you learned how to bring out your own Soul Song. First, chant 3396815 (San San Jiu Liu Ba Yao Wu), pronounced *sahn sahn jeo leo bah yow woo,* as fast as you can to bring out your Soul Language.

Your Soul Language carries your soul frequency and vibration. Because your soul is the boss of your mind and body, your soul frequency and vibration can transform the frequency and vibration of your mind and body.

Your Soul Language carries soul love, which can melt all blockages, including your mind blockages and body blockages.

Your Soul Language carries soul forgiveness, which brings inner joy and inner peace.

Your Soul Language carries soul compassion, which boosts energy, stamina, vitality, and immunity.

Your Soul Language carries soul light, which heals, prevents sickness, purifies and rejuvenates soul, heart, mind, and body, transforms relationships, finances, intelligence, and more, and brings success to every aspect of life.

After you bring out your Soul Language, transform your Soul Language to Soul Song as I taught you in chapter 2. Soul Song has a higher frequency and vibration than Soul Language.

In chapter 3 you learned the Tao Song mantras for self-clearing soul mind body blockages in the Seven Soul Houses, Wai Jiao, and Tao Song Channel. Those are standard Tao Songs created by the Source.

How do you bring out your own Tao Song? In one sentence:

To bring out your own Tao Song, receive Tao Song Soul Mind Body Transplants.

Tao Song Soul Mind Body Transplants transform your Soul Song to Tao Song automatically because Tao Song Soul Mind Body Transplants carry Tao frequency and vibration with Tao love, forgiveness, compassion, and light. After receiving Tao Song Soul Mind Body Transplants, the power and abilities of your Tao Song are beyond words, comprehension, and imagination.

Tao Song Soul Mind Body Transplants—Permanent Treasures to Increase the Power of Your Tao Song

The Divine and Tao are creators and manifesters. In July 2003 the Divine chose me as a servant of humanity and the Divine to transmit permanent divine treasures to humanity and wan ling (all souls). These treasures are Divine Soul Mind Body Transplants and more. In 2008 Tao chose me as servant of humanity and Tao to transmit permanent Tao frequency treasures to humanity and wan ling. These treasures are Tao Soul Mind Body Transplants and more.

If a person's kidneys fail, conventional modern medicine offers dialysis. If dialysis is not sufficient, a kidney transplant may be necessary. Conventional modern medicine offers kidney transplants, liver transplants, heart transplants, and transplants of other physical organs.

The Divine chose me to offer Divine Soul Transplants for systems (for example, cardiovascular system or digestive system), for organs, for parts of the body, and for cells. A Divine Soul Transplant is a light being created by the Divine to replace the original soul of a system, organ, part of the body, or cells with a divine soul. This soul is karma-free and eager to serve with its divine frequency and vibration.

Everything has a soul, a mind (consciousness), and a body (energy and matter). In 2008 the Divine gave me the honor to offer Divine Mind Transplants. A Divine Mind Transplant is another light being created by the Divine to replace the consciousness of a system, organ, part of the body, or cells with divine consciousness.

The Divine also asked me to offer Divine Body Transplants. A Divine Body Transplant is another light being created by the Divine to replace the energy and tiny matter of a system, organ, part of the body, or cells with divine energy and tiny matter.

Divine Soul Mind Body Transplants are three light beings created in the heart of the Divine. When I offer a Divine Order for Divine Soul Mind Body Transplants and say *Transmission!*, the Divine transmits Soul Mind Body Transplants to the recipient to replace the soul, mind, and body of the requested system, organ, part of the body, or cells.

The Divine has also shown me how to offer Soul Mind Body Transplants of divine qualities such as Divine Love Soul Mind Body Transplants, Divine Forgiveness Soul Mind Body Transplants, Divine Compassion Soul Mind Body Transplants, and Divine Light Soul Mind Body Transplants. A Divine Love Soul Transplant is a light being created by the Divine. A Divine Love Mind Transplant is another light being created by the Divine that carries divine consciousness. A Divine Love Body Transplant is also a light being created by the Divine that carries divine energy and divine tiny matter.

Divine Love Soul Mind Body Transplants are new divine treasures that the Divine creates instantly in his heart and sends to the recipient's body. Divine treasures are generally downloaded to a human being's lower abdomen.

Divine Soul Mind Body Transplants are permanent treasures that will accompany the recipient forever. Everyone has parents, loved ones, friends, and colleagues. They are your *yang* companions. When you receive Divine Soul Mind Body Transplants, they become your divine *yin* companions. After your physical life ends, these treasures will continue to accompany your soul for all your future lifetimes. Therefore, Divine Soul Mind Body Transplants are permanent divine treasures.

Tao Soul Mind Body Transplants come from the Source. Similar to Divine Soul Mind Body Transplants, the Source can create Tao Soul Mind Body Transplants for a system, organ, part of the body, and cells or for a particular quality, such as Tao love or Tao compassion. The Source can create anything. Whatever you can imagine, the Source can create. Whatever you cannot imagine, the Source can also create.

Tao Soul Mind Body Transplants carry Tao frequency and vibration, which transforms the frequency and vibration of all life in countless planets, stars, galaxies, and universes.

Tao Soul Mind Body Transplants carry Tao love, which melts all blockages and transforms all life.

Tao Soul Mind Body Transplants carry Tao forgiveness, which brings inner joy and inner peace.

Tao Soul Mind Body Transplants carry Tao compassion, which boosts energy, stamina, vitality, and immunity.

Tao Soul Mind Body Transplants carry Tao light, which heals, prevents sickness, purifies and rejuvenates soul, heart, mind, and body, transforms relationships, finances, intelligence, and more, and brings success to every aspect of life.

Why do I repeat the teaching in these last five sentences again and again in my books? Because they are a mantra. Do not read through these phrases quickly. Read this mantra from your heart. Remember the one-sentence reading secret I shared with you and humanity earlier in this book:

What you read is what you become.

Why do I repeat the teachings about Tao frequency and vibration, Tao love, Tao forgiveness, Tao compassion, and Tao light? Because every time you read *Tao frequency and vibration*, you are invoking Tao frequency and vibration. When you read *Tao love*, open your heart and soul to connect with Tao love. When you read *Tao forgiveness*, you *are* Tao forgiveness. When you read *Tao compas-*

sion, you are offering Tao compassion. When you read *Tao light,* you are fulfilled with Tao light. Therefore, do not quickly go through these important sentences. In fact, I suggest that you repeat these sentences out loud when you read them. Even better, stop reading now and spend ten minutes just repeating these phrases. Each one carries the frequency, vibration, and message of the particular quality. The benefits that you can receive by repeating these sentences are beyond words, comprehension, and imagination.

In order to emphasize the power of these five sacred Tao sentences, I will repeat them one more time. Read from the bottom of your heart. Feel the power. Feel the frequency. Receive the benefits.

Tao Soul Mind Body Transplants carry Tao frequency and vibration, which transform the frequency and vibration of all life.

Tao Soul Mind Body Transplants carry Tao love, which melts all blockages and transforms all life.

Tao Soul Mind Body Transplants carry Tao forgiveness, which brings inner joy and inner peace.

Tao Soul Mind Body Transplants carry Tao compassion, which boosts energy, stamina, vitality, and immunity.

Tao Soul Mind Body Transplants carry Tao light, which heals, prevents sickness, purifies and rejuvenates soul, heart, mind, and body, and transforms relationships, finances, intelligence, and more, and brings success to every aspect of life.

Thank you. Thank you. Thank you.

We deeply appreciate Tao Soul Mind Body Transplants.

We cannot honor Tao Soul Mind Body Transplants enough.

We are extremely grateful for this honor.

Words are not enough to express our greatest honor.

Thoughts are not enough to express our greatest gratitude.

Now I am ready to offer permanent Tao treasures to you.

Prepare. Sit up straight. Place the tip of your tongue as close as you can to the roof of your mouth without touching. Put both palms on your lower abdomen. As you read "Transmission!," the stated permanent treasures will come to your soul.

Tao Order: Tao Golden Light Ball and Golden Liquid Spring of Tao Song of Tao Love, Peace, and Harmony Soul Mind Body Transplants

Transmission!

Tao Order: Join Tao Song of Tao Love, Peace, and Harmony Soul Mind Body Transplants as one.

You are extremely blessed. Humanity is blessed.

You have received Source Soul Mind Body Transplants of Tao Song of Tao Love, Peace, and Harmony, three huge golden light beings that are the soul, consciousness, energy, and tiny matter of this Tao Song.

Activate your Tao Song of Tao Love, Peace, and Harmony Soul Mind Body Transplants by asking them to bless your Tao Song singing. Your Soul Song has been instantly transformed to Tao Song by these Tao Soul Mind Body Transplants. Your Soul Song carries your soul frequency. Tao Song of Tao Love, Peace, and Harmony Soul Mind Body Transplants carry *Source* frequency. This itself is deeply transformational. This is how blessed you are.

Now prepare to sing your Soul Song, which is already Tao Song because of the Tao treasures you have received. This is the value of Tao Song of Tao Love, Peace, and Harmony Soul Mind Body Transplants. Are you honored and blessed?

Sing your own Tao Song now for one minute.

At this moment, I am holding a Tao Song Tao Dance Workshop in Markham, Ontario, Canada. About fifty students are on site, with many more participating via live webcast. Let me ask the students here, "How many people feel that your Tao Song is better after receiving the Tao Song of Tao Love, Peace, and Harmony Soul Mind Body Transplants?"

Nancy Elyze Brier said, "Master Sha, with every class I hear something different in my voice. It has helped me immensely. My voice gets richer every time."

Nancy sang her Tao Song.

I asked people to comment on Nancy's singing. The feedback included "powerful," "rich," "soulful."

Marilyn Smith said, "After the amazing download, I felt there was more of a connection throughout the whole Tao Song Channel."

Marilyn sang her Tao Song.

Comments about Marilyn's Tao Song included "soothing," "profound," "simply love."

Next I offered Tao Song of Tao Love, Forgiveness, Compassion, and Light Soul Mind Body Transplants to Marzena Preis as a demo.

First Marzena sang her Tao Song before receiving the downloads. Comments from participants included "gentle," "passionate," "loving."

Tao Order: Tao Song of Tao Love, Forgiveness, Compassion, and Light Soul Mind Body Transplants to Marzena Preis

Transmission!

Tao Order: Join Tao Song of Tao Love, Forgiveness, Compassion, and Light Soul Mind Body Transplants as one.

Marzena sang again after receiving Tao Song of Tao Love, Forgiveness, Compassion, and Light Soul Mind Body Transplants. Comments from workshop participants included "more compassion," "fuller," "more strength."

Carmen Badoi sang a Tao Song before receiving the Tao Song of Tao Love, Forgiveness, Compassion, and Light Soul Mind Body Transplants.

Comments: "sweet," "pleasant," "gentle."

Tao Order: Tao Song of Tao Love, Forgiveness, Compassion, and Light Soul Mind Body Transplants to Carmen Badoi

Transmission!

Tao Order: Join Tao Song of Tao Love, Forgiveness, Compassion, and Light Soul Mind Body Transplants as one.

Carmen sang again after receiving the downloads.

Participants' comments: "more clarity and resonance," "it was like she was more open," "her Soul Song felt more playful."

Carmen said that when she received the Tao Song of Tao Love, Forgiveness, Compassion, and Light Soul Mind Body Transplants, there was a clearing in her throat as though a frog had been removed.

Now I will offer Tao Song of Tao Love, Forgiveness, Compassion, and Light Soul Mind Body Transplants to you.

Prepare. Put the tip of your tongue as close as you can to the roof of your mouth without touching. Put both palms on your lower abdomen. Focus your mind on your lower abdomen. Relax to receive these priceless Tao treasures. As you read "Transmission!," the stated permanent treasures will come to your soul.

Tao Order: Tao Song of Tao Love, Forgiveness, Compassion, and Light Soul Mind Body Transplants

Transmission!

Tao Order: Join Tao Song of Tao Love, Forgiveness, Compassion, and Light Soul Mind Body Transplants as one.

You are extremely blessed. Humanity is blessed.

All Tao Song teaching and singing is to touch people's hearts. The totality of the spiritual journey can be summarized in one word: *purification.* Purify the heart and everything will follow. Ming xin jian xing (pronounced *ming sheen jyen shing*), *enlighten your heart to see your true self, which is your soul.* Then you will touch and open the hearts of others. This is key for accomplishing the goal of the Soul Light Era: wan ling rong he (all souls joining as one, pronounced *wahn ling rawng huh*).

Important Principles for Your Tao Song Singing

To be a powerful Tao Song Singer, you need to master the following:

- When you sing Tao Song, go into the hero condition to shine Tao love, forgiveness, compassion, and light. You are a Tao temple. You are Tao presence.
- Alternate yin and yang in your Tao Song. Yin yang balance is vital for every aspect of life. When you sing, sing softly at times and sing loudly at other times. Sing some high notes and sing some low notes. Sing fast and sing slow. Variety is the key.
- Follow nature's way when you sing Tao Song. Do not use your mind to guide you. Tao will guide you.
- Feel great honor that you are serving when you sing Tao Song. You are a servant of Tao to give love, care, and compassion to humanity and wan ling.
- Have Tao confidence. Every part of your body, especially the seven Soul Houses, Wai Jiao, Tao Song Channel, abdominal, chest, and skull cavities, diaphragm, and vocal cords, join as one to bring out your singing.
- The Tao Song Channel is a Tao temple. Your Tao Song frequency and vibration radiate out from your Tao Song Channel in every direction, three hundred sixty degrees. Do not think that the sound comes from your mouth and vocal cords. It comes from the Tao Song Channel as it vibrates.
- Always put your mind on the first Soul House. Never put your mind in any other place. If you cannot sing your Tao Song well, you have soul mind body blockages in your seven Soul Houses, Wai Jiao, Tao Song Channel, abdominal, chest, and skull cavities, diaphragm, and vocal cords. You have to practice Tao Song for these areas to remove soul mind body block-

ages. I taught you how in this book. Sing again and again to remove the blockages gradually. With time and practice, they could be completely removed.

- Sing Tao Song slowly. There is no need to rush. For the beginner, slower is faster. When you sing slowly, you can feel the love, forgiveness, compassion, light, grace, sincerity, honesty, kindness, purity, integrity, generosity, and much more. Sing slowly at first. Then Tao may sometimes guide you to sing faster. Just as with a speaker who speaks too fast, people may find it difficult to be deeply touched and inspired if you sing too quickly. People may find it difficult to receive deep insights. Speak slowly so that people can receive properly and absorb the teaching better. The same is true for Tao Song singing.

- Before you begin singing, remember to say *hello* to the Divine, Tao, Mother Earth, and countless planets, stars, galaxies, and universes. You are a universal servant. You are serving humanity and wan ling, as well as countless planets, stars, galaxies, and universes. Be honored to be a servant. When you are a Total GOLD servant ("G" is gratitude, "O" is obedience, "L" is loyalty, "D" is devotion to the Divine and Tao), you can bring out all kinds of divine and Tao qualities.

- Also say *hello* to every system, organ, and cell of your body to show your gratitude before you sing Tao Song. Say *I am so honored to sing Tao Song. Please help me by coordinating to bring out the best divine and Tao qualities to be a great servant. Thank you.*

- When you sing Tao Song, you are doing service Xiu Lian. Every moment you are singing Tao Song, you are transforming every aspect of your life, including health, relationships, finances, intelligence, and more. At the same time, you are serving the transformation of humanity and wan ling. You are bringing success to every aspect of your life, fulfilling your physical journey and your soul journey.

The Soul Light Era began on August 8, 2003. It will last fifteen thousand years. The final goal of the Soul Light Era is wan ling rong he, *all souls joining as one.* This means all souls will reach Tao Oneness. That is the ultimate goal of this era.

Sing. Sing. Sing.
Serve. Serve. Serve.
Heal. Heal. Heal.
Rejuvenate. Rejuvenate. Rejuvenate.
Transform. Transform. Transform.
Enlighten. Enlighten. Enlighten.
Bring love, peace, and harmony to humanity, Mother Earth, and all universes.
Reach wan ling rong he.
Reach Tao Oneness.
Tao Fa Zi Ran (follow nature's way, pronounced *dow fah dz rahn*)
Tao Fa Zi Ran
Tao Fa Zi Ran

Divine Treasures
Tao Treasures

Heal me
Rejuvenate me

Heal my loved ones
Rejuvenate my loved ones

Heal humanity
Rejuvenate humanity

Heal Mother Earth
Rejuvenate Mother Earth

Heal all souls
Rejuvenate all souls

Bring love, peace, and harmony
Bring love, peace, and harmony
Bring love, peace, and harmony
Bring love, peace, and harmony

Now I will offer Tao Song of Tao Grace Soul Mind Body Transplants to you.

Prepare. Sit up straight. Put the tip of your tongue as close as you can to the roof of your mouth without touching. Put both palms on your lower abdomen. Focus your mind on your lower abdomen. Relax to receive these priceless Tao treasures. As you read "Transmission!," the stated permanent treasures will come to your soul.

Tao Order: Tao Song of Tao Grace
Soul Mind Body Transplants

Transmission!

Tao Order: Join Tao Song of Tao Grace
Soul Mind Body Transplants as one.

Thank, you, Tao. Thank you. Thank you. Thank you. Now I will lead you to practice. Apply the Four Power Techniques.

Body Power. Sit up straight. Put the tip of your tongue as close as you can to the roof of your mouth without touching. Contract your anus slightly. Put both hands on your lower abdomen below your navel in the Yin Yang Palm Hand Position (see figure 3 on page 15).

Soul Power. Say *hello:*

> *Dear soul mind body of Tao Song of Tao Grace Soul*
>   *Mind Body Transplants,*
> *I love you, honor you, and appreciate you.*
> *Please turn on.*
> *Dear all Tao Song treasures I have received from this*
>   *book,*
> *I love you, honor you, and appreciate you.*
> *Please turn on to increase the power of my Tao Song.*
> *Thank you.*

Mind Power. As usual, focus on your first Soul House. Visualize a golden light ball or a rainbow light ball rotating counterclockwise in that area. If your Third Eye is open, observe whatever images you receive.

Sound Power. Sing your Tao Song for one to two minutes.

You have just received permanent Source treasures of Tao Song of Tao Grace Soul Mind Body Transplants. Continue to sing to activate these treasures. The longer you sing and the more you sing, the better. There is no time limit. You could receive remarkable cleansing of soul mind body blockages in the seven Soul Houses, Wai Jiao, and Tao Song Channel.

The more you sing, you more you could notice that your Tao Song is transforming. You received the Tao Song of Tao Grace Soul Mind Body Transplants to ensure that your Tao Song carries Tao Grace. You are extremely blessed. Humanity is blessed. You are a vehicle to bring more Tao presence to humanity and Mother Earth.

Now I will offer more Tao treasures to you: Tao Song of Tao Inspiration Soul Mind Body Transplants.

Prepare. Sit up straight. Put the tip of your tongue as close as you can to the roof of your mouth without touching. Put both palms on your lower abdomen. Focus your mind on your lower abdomen. Relax to receive these priceless Tao treasures. As you read "Transmission!," three huge Tao light beings will come to your soul.

Tao Order: Tao Song of Tao Inspiration Soul Mind Body Transplants

Transmission!

Tao Order: Join Tao Song of Tao Inspiration Soul Mind Body Transplants as one.

Now I will lead you to practice. Apply the Four Power Techniques.

Body Power. Sit up straight. Put the tip of your tongue as close as you can to the roof of your mouth without touching. Contract your anus slightly. Put both hands on your lower abdomen below your navel in the Yin Yang Palm Position (see figure 3).

Soul Power. Say *hello:*

> *Dear soul mind body of Tao Song of Tao Inspiration*
> * Soul Mind Body Transplants,*
> *I love you, honor you, and appreciate you.*
> *Please turn on.*
> *Dear all Tao Song treasures I have received from this*
> * book,*
> *I love you, honor you, and appreciate you.*
> *Please turn on to increase the power of my Tao Song.*
> *Thank you.*

Mind Power. As usual, focus on your first Soul House. Visualize a golden light ball or a rainbow light ball rotating counterclockwise in that area. If your Third Eye is open, observe whatever images you receive.

Sound Power. Sing your Tao Song for one to two minutes.

You have just received permanent Source treasures of Tao Song of Tao Inspiration Soul Mind Body Transplants. Continue to sing to activate these treasures. The longer you sing and the more you sing, the better. You could receive remarkable cleansing of soul mind body blockages in the seven Soul Houses, Wai Jiao, and Tao Song Channel.

The more you sing, the more you could notice that your Tao Song is transforming. You have received the Tao Song of Tao

Inspiration Soul Mind Body Transplants to ensure that your Tao Song carries Tao Inspiration. You are extremely blessed. Humanity is blessed.

I will continue to offer priceless Tao treasures to you.

Prepare. Sit up straight. Put the tip of your tongue as close as you can to the roof of your mouth without touching. Put both palms on your lower abdomen. Focus your mind on your lower abdomen. Relax to receive these priceless Tao treasures. As you read "Transmission!," the stated permanent treasures will come to your soul.

Tao Order: Tao Song of Tao Purity Soul Mind Body Transplants

Transmission!

Tao Order: Join Tao Song of Tao Purity Soul Mind Body Transplants as one.

Now I will lead you to practice. Apply the Four Power Techniques.

Body Power. Sit up straight. Put the tip of your tongue as close as you can to the roof of your mouth without touching. Contract your anus slightly. Put both hands on your lower abdomen below your navel in the Yin Yang Palm Position (see figure 3).

Soul Power. Say *hello:*

> *Dear soul mind body of Tao Song of Tao Purity Soul Mind Body Transplants,*

I love you, honor you, and appreciate you.
Please turn on.
Dear all Tao Song treasures I have received from this
    book,
I love you, honor you, and appreciate you.
Please turn on to increase the power of my Tao Song.
Thank you.

Mind Power. Apply the same Mind Power focus and visualization as in the previous practices in this chapter.

Sound Power. Sing your Tao Song for one to two minutes.

You have just received permanent Source treasures of Tao Song of Tao Purity Soul Mind Body Transplants. Continue to sing to activate these treasures. The longer you sing and the more you sing, the better. Tao Purity could give you remarkable cleansing of soul mind body blockages in the seven Soul Houses, Wai Jiao, and Tao Song Channel.

The more you sing, the more you could notice that your Tao Song is transforming. You received the Tao Song of Tao Purity Soul Mind Body Transplants to ensure that your Tao Song carries Tao Purity. You are extremely blessed. Humanity is blessed.

Purity is very important on the spiritual journey. This treasure could help you to avoid creating new bad karma. Remember the teaching: see no evil, hear no evil, speak no evil, think no evil, which is purity of the eyes, purity of the ears, purity of the mouth, purity of the mind.

Now I will offer you Tao Song of Tao Kindness Soul Mind Body Transplants.

Prepare. Sit up straight. Put the tip of your tongue as close as you can to the roof of your mouth without touching. Put both palms on your lower abdomen. Focus your mind on your lower abdomen. Relax to receive these priceless Tao treasures. As you read "Transmission!," the three priceless permanent treasures will come to your soul.

Tao Order: Tao Song of Tao Kindness Soul Mind Body Transplants

Transmission!

Tao Order: Join Tao Song of Tao Kindness Soul Mind Body Transplants as one.

Now I will lead you to practice. Apply the Four Power Techniques.

Body Power. Sit up straight. Put the tip of your tongue as close as you can to the roof of your mouth without touching. Contract your anus slightly. Put both hands on your lower abdomen below your navel in the Yin Yang Palm Position (see figure 3).

Soul Power. Say *hello:*

> *Dear soul mind body of Tao Song of Tao Kindness*
> *Soul Mind Body Transplants,*
> *I love you, honor you, and appreciate you.*
> *Please turn on.*
> *Dear all Tao Song treasures I have received from this*
> *book,*

I love you, honor you, and appreciate you.
Please turn on to increase the power of my Tao Song.
Thank you.

Mind Power. As usual, focus on your first Soul House. Visualize a golden light ball or a rainbow light ball rotating counterclockwise in that area. If your Third Eye is open, observe whatever images you receive.

Sound Power. Sing your Tao Song for one to two minutes.

You have just received permanent Source treasures of Tao Song of Tao Kindness Soul Mind Body Transplants. Continue to sing to activate these treasures. The longer you sing and the more you sing, the better. You could receive remarkable cleansing of soul mind body blockages in the seven Soul Houses, Wai Jiao, and Tao Song Channel.

The more you sing, the more you could notice that your Tao Song is transforming. You have received the Tao Song of Tao Kindness Soul Mind Body Transplants to ensure that your Tao Song carries Tao Kindness. You are extremely blessed. Humanity is blessed.

Now prepare to receive more priceless Tao treasures in the same way you have done to receive the previous Tao treasures.

Prepare. Sit up straight. Put the tip of your tongue as close as you can to the roof of your mouth without touching. Put both palms on your lower abdomen. Focus your mind on your lower abdomen. Relax to receive these priceless Tao treasures. As you read "Transmission!," the stated permanent treasures will come to your soul.

Tao Order: Tao Song of Tao Sincerity and Honesty Soul Mind Body Transplants

Transmission!

Tao Order: Join Tao Song of Tao Sincerity and Honesty Soul Mind Body Transplants as one.

Now I will lead you to practice. Apply the Four Power Techniques.

Body Power. Use the same Body Power as in the previous practices in this chapter.

Soul Power. Say *hello:*

> *Dear soul mind body of Tao Song of Tao Sincerity and*
>   *Honesty Soul Mind Body Transplants,*
> *I love you, honor you, and appreciate you.*
> *Please turn on.*
> *Dear all Tao Song treasures I have received from this*
>   *book,*
> *I love you, honor you, and appreciate you.*
> *Please turn on to increase the power of my Tao Song.*
> *Thank you.*

Mind Power. As usual, focus on your first Soul House. Visualize a golden light ball or a rainbow light ball rotating counterclockwise in that area. If your Third Eye is open, observe whatever images you receive.

Sound Power. Sing your Tao Song for one to two minutes.

You have just received permanent Source treasures of Tao Song of Tao Sincerity and Honesty Soul Mind Body Transplants. Continue to sing to activate these treasures. The longer you sing and the more you sing, the better. You could receive remarkable cleansing of soul mind body blockages in the seven Soul Houses, Wai Jiao, and Tao Song Channel.

The more you sing, the more you could feel that your Tao Song is transforming. You received the Tao Song of Tao Sincerity and Honesty Soul Mind Body Transplants to ensure that your Tao Song carries Tao Sincerity and Honesty. You are extremely blessed. You carry more and more Tao presence. Humanity is blessed.

I will now offer additional priceless Tao treasures.

Prepare. Sit up straight. Put the tip of your tongue as close as you can to the roof of your mouth without touching. Put both palms on your lower abdomen. Focus your mind on your lower abdomen. Relax to receive these priceless Tao treasures. As you read "Transmission!," the stated permanent treasures will come to your soul.

Tao Order: Tao Song of Tao Inner Joy and Inner Peace Soul Mind Body Transplants

Transmission!

Tao Order: Join Tao Song of Tao Inner Joy and Inner Peace Soul Mind Body Transplants as one.

Now I will lead you to practice. Apply the Four Power Techniques.

Body Power. Sit up straight. Put the tip of your tongue as close as you can to the roof of your mouth without touching. Contract your anus slightly. Put both hands on your lower abdomen below your navel in the Yin Yang Palm Position (see figure 3).

Soul Power. Say *hello:*

> *Dear soul mind body of Tao Song of Tao Inner Joy*
>   *and Inner Peace Soul Mind Body Transplants,*
> *I love you, honor you, and appreciate you.*
> *Please turn on.*
> *Dear all Tao Song treasures I have received from this*
>   *book,*
> *I love you, honor you, and appreciate you.*
> *Please turn on to increase the power of my Tao Song.*
> *Thank you.*

Mind Power. As usual, focus on your first Soul House. Visualize a golden light ball or a rainbow light ball rotating counterclockwise in that area. If your Third Eye is open, observe whatever images you receive.

Sound Power. Sing your Tao Song for one to two minutes.

You have just received permanent Source treasures of Tao Song of Tao Inner Joy and Inner Peace Soul Mind Body Transplants. Continue to sing to activate these treasures. The longer you sing and the more you sing, the better. You could receive remarkable cleansing of soul mind body blockages in the seven Soul Houses, Wai Jiao, and Tao Song Channel.

The more you sing, the more you could feel that your Tao Song is transforming. You received the Tao Song of Tao Inner

Joy and Inner Peace Soul Mind Body Transplants to ensure that your Tao Song carries Tao Inner Joy and Inner Peace. You are extremely blessed. Humanity is blessed.

Thank you Tao and the Source, for the gifts of priceless Tao Song Soul Mind Body Transplants. These are gifts beyond comprehension. Many people have spoken of Heaven coming to Mother Earth. Permanent Divine and Tao treasures are Heaven literally coming to Mother Earth. They are Divine and Tao presence on Mother Earth. They are Divine and Tao presence that resides permanently with your soul. We are so fortunate that Tao and the Source have offered these priceless treasures to you and every reader. I am grateful to be a servant of the Divine and Tao.

Apply these priceless permanent Tao treasures to empower your Tao Song singing and to offer healing, rejuvenation, and life transformation for health, relationships, finances, intelligence, and more, and to bring success to every aspect of your life. Apply these treasures to serve.

You could notice instantly that your singing has been transformed by applying the Tao Song Soul Mind Body Transplants you have received. Tao Song Soul Mind Body Transplants carry power from the Source. They carry Tao frequency and vibration that can transform the frequency and vibration of your Tao Song and of everyone and everything. Some of you may take some time to notice a difference in your Tao Song singing. Continue to practice. Apply the Tao treasures you have received. As you apply the treasures and practice, soul mind body blockages in your Tao singing will be removed little by little. Your Tao Song singing will transform accordingly.

The Tao treasures you have received in this chapter will help you with all kinds of singing, whether you sing in a choir, are a professional singer, or just like to sing for fun. Humanity is extremely blessed and honored that the Source is willing to give these treasures as gifts to every reader. Professional singers know how difficult it is to improve their singing abilities and to increase their power. It could take years of hard work. You have received Tao acceleration. Practice more and more. You are extremely blessed.

Tao Oneness Practice

Tao is the Source and Creator. Tao creates One. Tao *is* One. One is Tao. Now I am ready to release the most important secrets, wisdom, knowledge, and practical techniques to empower your Tao Song; to heal, rejuvenate, and prolong life; and to transform relationships, finances, and every aspect of life. It is named Tao Oneness Practice.

The title of this book is *Tao Song and Tao Dance: Sacred Sound, Movement, and Power from the Source for Healing, Rejuvenation, Longevity, and Transformation of All Life.* Can we create one Tao Song practice that can serve healing, rejuvenation, longevity, transformation of relationships, finances, intelligence, and more, and success in every aspect of life?

Yes, we can.

In my previous book of the Soul Power Series, *Tao II: The Way of Healing, Rejuvenation, Longevity, and Immortality,* I shared the important sacred phrase *Bao yuan shou yi* (抱元守一, pronounced *bao ywen sho yee*). "Bao" means *hold.* "Yuan" means *ball,* which is the Jin Dan in this context. "Shou" means *focus or concentrate.* "Yi" means *one.* "Bao yuan shou yi" means *hold and concentrate only on the golden light ball, which is the Jin Dan.*

Tao is One. One is Tao. The Jin Dan journey is the Tao journey. The Jin Dan gathers jing qi shen (matter energy soul) of Heaven,

Mother Earth, and countless planets, stars, galaxies, and universes. The Jin Dan is Tao. The Jin Dan is formed in the lower abdomen. In this book I have taught you to focus on your first Soul House. *The Jin Dan can be formed in the first Soul House.* This wisdom is the key to developing the power of your first Soul House.

In my *Tao I* and *Tao II* books I shared one of the most important ancient spiritual teachings, *Tian di ren he yi*. "Tian" (pronounced *tyen*) means *Heaven*. "Di" (pronounced *dee*) means *Mother Earth*. "Ren" (pronounced *wren*) means human being. "He" (pronounced *huh*) means *join*. "Yi" (pronounced *yee*) means *one*. "Tian di ren he yi" means *Heaven, Mother Earth, and human being join as one.*

Where do Heaven, Mother Earth, and human being join as one in a human being's body? This teaching can be summarized in one sentence:

The jing qi shen of Heaven, Mother Earth, and human being join as one in the lower abdomen to form the Jin Dan.

I will now formally release the top sacred and secret practice: Tao Oneness Practice.

Tao Oneness Practice is the top healing practice.

Tao Oneness Practice is the top rejuvenation practice.

Tao Oneness Practice is the top practice to reach fan lao huan tong, which is to transform old age to the health and purity of the baby state.

Tao Oneness Practice is the top secret of longevity.

Tao Oneness Practice is the sacred practice of immortality.

Tao Oneness Practice is a forgiveness practice, which is one of the most important spiritual practices for self-clearing karma in order to transform every aspect of life.

Tao Oneness Practice is the sacred practice to transform relationships, finances, intelligence, and more, and to bring success to every aspect of life.

Tao Oneness Practice shares with you and humanity that Tao is in your lower abdomen. Forming and growing the Jin Dan is the process to reach Tao.

In my book *Tao II: The Way of Healing, Rejuvenation, Longevity, and Immortality,* I shared that the Jin Dan journey is the immortal journey. The initial Jin Dan could be 10 percent of the size of a small grain of rice. To grow the Jin Dan is to form Tao ti (pronounced *dow tee*). "Tao ti" means *Tao body.* Once you form your complete Tao body, you have reached the immortal condition. This requires that you grow your Jin Dan to the size of your entire body. With normal methods, it could take a Tao practitioner thousands of lifetimes, even hundreds of thousands of lifetimes to form Tao ti.

Humanity is extremely blessed in the Soul Light Era, which started on August 8, 2003, and will last fifteen thousand years. I was extremely blessed and honored to be a chosen servant to have the authority to offer Divine and Tao Jin Dan Soul Mind Body Transplants to chosen ones. Up to now hundreds of chosen ones have received Divine or Tao Jin Dan Soul Mind Body Transplants. This is the first time in history that the Divine and Tao have offered their Jin Dan's to humanity in this way. The Jin Dan has layers. Just the first layer of Jin Dan download from the Divine and Tao could save a serious spiritual practitioner thousands of lifetimes of personal effort to form the equivalent of Jin Dan. That is how blessed the chosen ones who have received a Divine or Tao Jin Dan are.

I will share one story to explain further how blessed those who are chosen to receive Divine or Tao Jin Dan Soul Mind

Body Transplants are. At the end of 2010 I visited the Wudang Mountains in the northwestern part of Hubei Province in China. The Wudang Mountains are known for many Taoist monasteries, palaces, and temples that together comprise a UNESCO World Heritage Site. The monasteries were historic centers for academic research, teaching, and practice of all kinds of ancient Chinese arts. In traditional Tao the Wudang Mountains are a sacred place because many of the highest Tao saints reached Tao there.

I was honored to meet a top Tao master in the Wudang Mountains. He is a great doctor of traditional Chinese medicine and one of the top professors of the Tao college in the Wudang Mountains. He is an expert on the Jin Dan. He confirmed that accomplishing the Jin Dan journey usually takes thousands of lifetimes.

I communicated with the Divine and Tao. They told me that this Tao master is an old soul who has lived about 1,300 lifetimes as a human being. Most human beings on Mother Earth have lived fewer than 1,000 lifetimes as a human being. This top Tao master has been on the Tao journey for approximately 1,100 lifetimes. His Jin Dan has grown to 74 percent of the size of his fist. This is a great success. The highest saints who have reached Tao have taken hundreds of thousands or millions of lifetimes in their spiritual journeys to grow their Jin Dans to the size of their bodies to reach Tao.

In my book *Tao I: The Way of All Life*, I shared the teaching that no one is born with a Jin Dan. Special Tao practice is required to create a Jin Dan. Now, in this special time of humanity's transition and Mother Earth's purification, the Divine and Tao have decided to offer ten layers of Jin Dan Soul Mind Body Transplants to chosen ones who are on the Tao immortal journey. The first layer of Divine Jin Dan Soul Mind Body Transplants gives the recipient a fist-sized Jin Dan. I have offered the first layer Divine Jin Dan Soul Mind Body Transplants to hundreds of chosen ones. Compare this with the top Wudang master who has been on the Tao journey for 1,100 lifetimes to achieve his Jin Dan that is 74 percent of the size of his fist. We are extremely lucky. We are extremely blessed that the Divine and Tao are offering ten layers of Divine and Tao Jin Dan Soul Mind Body Transplants to humanity.

When I met this Tao master in the Wudang Mountains, he stared at my body for a few minutes and asked, "How have you grown your Jin Dan?" I replied, "I have received all layers of Divine and Tao Downloads and practice with them." Then he asked, "How do you do healing?" I said, "I apply Divine and Tao Downloads to offer healing." He scanned my body intensely again and said, "I have never seen anyone who has the kind of Jin Dan you have. I have never heard about the kind of healing that you just described. You are doing *shen gong*." "Shen" means *saint*. "Gong" means *practice*. "Shen gong" (pronounced *shun gawng*) means *saint practice*. He continued, "You do not need to go through the serious steps of traditional Tao Jin Dan practice. Follow Heaven. Follow the saints. What they have taught you and the treasures downloaded to you are beyond the comprehension of traditional Tao practice."

I asked him another question, "What is the future of Tao teaching?" He paused for a moment, then closed his eyes, and meditated for a while. When he opened his eyes, he replied, "In the future, Tao teaching will be very popular all over the world, but it will not be the traditional Tao teaching."

This story about my meeting with this top Tao master emphasizes that my Tao teaching and the Divine and Tao downloads that are an essential part of my Tao teaching are not traditional Tao. I am not teaching Taoism. I have shared with humanity that the Divine chose me as a servant, vehicle, and channel in July 2003. Tao chose me as a servant, vehicle, and channel in August 2008. I am honored to be this kind of servant to offer Tao teaching directly from the Divine and Tao.

In summary, Tao Oneness Practice is to form and grow the Jin Dan to the size of your body, which is to accomplish your Tao body (Tao ti). If you can grow your Jin Dan to the size of your body, you have reached Tao. Millions of traditional Tao practitioners in history have dreamed of reaching Tao. I share the essence of traditional Tao but I am teaching new secrets, wisdom, knowledge, and practical techniques of Tao directly from the Divine and Tao. I offer Divine and Tao Jin Dan Soul Mind Body Transplants and other permanent divine and Tao treasures to chosen ones in order to speed their Tao journey. I am the servant of humanity, wan ling (all souls), the Divine, and Tao. The Tao journey is to reach Tao. To *reach* Tao is to *meld* with Tao. This means that Tao is you and you are Tao. Tao Oneness Practice is the top practice to reach Tao.

Tao Oneness Practice is to focus your mind on the first Soul House or on the lower abdomen. Everything comes from the first Soul House. Whatever you do, whatever you speak, whatever you hear, whatever you think, whatever you chant, whatever you meditate—all come from the first Soul House. As I shared in my book *Tao II*, "Xing zou zuo wo, bu li zhe ge" (行走坐卧不离这个, pronounced *shing dzoe dzwaw waw boo lee juh guh*), which means *walking, sitting, or lying down, always put your mind on the lower abdomen.* Anytime, anywhere in your whole life, always put your mind on your Jin Dan. This is to form and expand the Jin Dan. This is to connect with Tao.

I learned this ancient wisdom many years ago and tried to follow this great practice. It took me more than five years of serious practice to accomplish this. If you cannot focus your mind on the lower abdomen all of the time, do not be disappointed. It takes time to develop this habit.

Now I will lead you to do Tao Oneness Practice to transform your health, relationships, finances, and every aspect of life, as well as to empower your Tao Song.

Apply the Four Power Techniques.

Body Power. Sit up straight. Put the tip of your tongue as close as you can to the roof of your mouth without touching. Contract your anus slightly. Put your Yin Yang Palm (see figure 3 on page 15) on your lower abdomen below your navel.

Soul Power. Say *hello:*

> *Dear Divine,*
> *Dear Tao,*
> *Dear soul mind body of all spiritual fathers and mothers*
>   *in all layers of Heaven and on Mother Earth,*
> *Dear Heaven,*
> *Dear Mother Earth,*
> *Dear countless planets, stars, galaxies, and universes,*
> *Dear San San Jiu Liu Ba Yao Wu,*
> *Dear my Soul Language,*
> *Dear Sha's Golden Healing Ball,*
> *Dear Divine Love Peace Harmony Rainbow Light*
>   *Ball,*
> *Dear my Tao Song,*
> *Dear Tao Song Soul Mind Body Transplants of Tao*

*Song of Tao Love, Peace, and Harmony; Tao Song
of Tao Love, Forgiveness, Compassion, and Light;
Tao Song of Tao Grace; Tao Song of Tao Inspiration; Tao Song of Tao Purity; Tao Song of Tao
Kindness; Tao Song of Tao Sincerity and Honesty;
and Tao Song of Tao Inner Joy and Inner Peace,*

*Dear all of the people, animals, and environments that
I have ever hurt, harmed, taken advantage of, or
made any kind of mistake against in past lifetimes
and in this lifetime,*

I sincerely apologize.

Please forgive me.

*Dear all souls who have harmed me in past lifetimes
and in this lifetime,*

I forgive you totally.

I love, honor, and appreciate all of you.

*Please turn on all Divine and Tao treasures for healing
and life transformation.*

Please heal my _____ (make a request for healing
your spiritual body, mental body, emotional
body, or physical body).

Please bless my relationships with _____ (name the
persons with whom you request a relationship
blessing).

Please bless my finances.

Please bless my intelligence.

Please bless my success.

Please bless _____ (make a request for any part of
your life).

*Please increase the power of my Tao Song so that I can
become a better servant for humanity and wan ling.*

I am extremely grateful.
Thank you. Thank you. Thank you.

Mind Power. Focus on your *first* Soul House. Visualize a golden light ball or a rainbow light ball rotating counterclockwise in that area. If your Third Eye is open, observe whatever images you receive.

Sound Power. Sing your Tao Song.

Sing your Tao Song for at least three to five minutes, three to five times per day. The longer you sing and more often you sing, the better. There is no time limit. For chronic or life-threatening conditions, or for serious blockages in relationships and other aspects of life, sing Tao Song for two hours or more per day. Add up all of the time that you sing throughout the day to total two hours or more.

This is one example of a Tao Oneness Practice. In fact, Tao Oneness Practice is a daily practice. It is within every aspect of your life. When you eat, think about the power accumulating in your Jin Dan every time you swallow. When you drink, think about your Jin Dan. When you speak, your Jin Dan radiates power and wisdom because the Jin Dan is a Tao treasure. The Jin Dan carries Tao secrets, wisdom, knowledge, and practical techniques for health, relationships, finances, and intelligence, as well as success in every aspect of life. The Jin Dan blesses every aspect of your life. The Jin Dan is Tao. If you understand this, you will understand the power of Tao Oneness Practice better.

In one sentence:

What you do, what you speak, what you see, what you hear, and what you think is Tao Oneness Practice.

Tao is the father and mother of countless planets, stars, galaxies, and universes. Tao creates all. Tao serves all. Tao Oneness Practice serves all. The purpose of life is to serve. Service Xiu Lian is the highest Xiu Lian.

Tao Song Tao Dance Healer Training Program

I have thousands of students around the world. I have created more than one thousand Divine Healers worldwide. From August 29 through September 1, 2011, I held my first Tao Song Tao Dance Healer Certification Retreat in Markham, Ontario, Canada. Tao Song Tao Dance Healers are powerful healers who offer healing and blessing through their Tao Song and Tao Dance. Their healing blessings carry Tao frequency and vibration with Tao love, forgiveness, compassion, and light.

To become a Tao Song Tao Dance Healer, one must:

- Complete teleclass training and homework
- Receive Divine Jin Dan Soul Mind Body Transplants
- Receive Divine and Tao Karma Cleansing for the seven Soul Houses, Wai Jiao, and Tao Song Channel
- Receive Tao Rainbow Light Ball and Rainbow Liquid Spring of Tao Song Tao Dance Healer Soul Mind Body Transplants
- Apply Tao Song Tao Dance Soul Mind Body Transplants, one's Divine Jin Dan, and other treasures to offer healing and blessing for yourself and others in order to transform health, relationships, finances, intelligence, and more, and to bring success in every aspect of life.

I will train and certify thousands and thousands of Tao Song and Tao Dance Healers to serve humanity. Everyone enrolled in my Tao Song Tao Dance Healer Training Program receives Tao Rainbow Light Ball and Rainbow Liquid Spring of Tao Song Tao Dance Healer Soul Mind Body Transplants and must complete the above requirements to fully empower their Tao Song and Tao Dance and receive certification. These Source treasures are extremely powerful and will serve humanity very well for healing, rejuvenation, and transformation of all aspects of life.

Approximately fifty students completed the first Tao Song Tao Dance Healer Certification Retreat. After the retreat, one participant sent me the following email, which this one is delighted to share:

> *Dear Master Sha,*
>
> *I would like to share something with you. For the first time, I am able and would be happy to give up my life, family, money, and the human experience to serve you and your mission to serve all humanity.*
>
> *In my life I was blessed with good health, good parents, good family, good friends, and an unbelievably interesting life that I never dreamed of having. I knew I had nothing to do with it. Why?*
>
> *I was also blessed with no particular talent, skills, or good memory to make a living. I did listen well. I did not trust how I could ever make a living without skills, and I was terrified of the world. Money was my insurance and protection in the physical world, no matter what I believed in spiritually.*

From the age of seven I would save roughly 50 percent of all my income and gifts of money given to me by my father and mother.

I did not trust anyone or myself with investing and making a profit. I was so paranoid; I only wanted to know how much I could lose. I also knew I had to make my income through investing because no one would hire me for my skills and memory. As I said, my main talent is listening.

My investing policy was based on fear: how much could I lose, not how much I could make. It worked.

Then at 45 years of age I met Sathya Sai Baba, called "the man of miracles," and he changed my life. Over a period of twenty-six years I traveled thirteen times to see him, hoping for a private audience. It never happened. I was disappointed, but I kept going back. Nevertheless, I always learned so much, and one of his teachings was that humans could also do miracles as he did. He never empowered this to happen, but I always remembered the teaching. Jesus also said we could do miracles as he did to help humanity.

I never dreamed that miracles could happen through me until last week [in the Tao Song Tao Dance Healer Certification Retreat]. *There is no way I would ever leave the mission or you. I finally hope that **love** runs my life and not **fear**, even though it seemed to have helped in creating my financial security. It also helped to support the mission.*

These last six days were so wonderful thanks to you and your team.

I am an unconditional servant for the mission.
I love you. I love you. I love you.
Thank you. Thank you. Thank you.

Let me summarize the vital points for increasing the power of your Tao Song:

- Receive Tao Song Soul Mind Body Transplants, including Tao Song of Tao Love, Peace, and Harmony Soul Mind Body Transplants; Tao Song of Tao Love, Forgiveness, Compassion, and Light Soul Mind Body Transplants; Tao Song of Tao Grace Soul Mind Body Transplants; Tao Song of Tao Inspiration Soul Mind Body Transplants; Tao Song of Tao Purity Soul Mind Body Transplants; Tao Song of Tao Kindness Soul Mind Body Transplants; Tao Song of Tao Sincerity and Honesty Soul Mind Body Transplants; and Tao Song of Tao Inner Joy and Inner Peace Soul Mind Body Transplants.

  These Tao treasures have been offered to you in this book. They carry Tao frequency and vibration with Tao love, forgiveness, compassion, and light. As you turn them on, they will transform your Tao Song more and more deeply. The power of your Tao Song will be enhanced further and further. You are extremely blessed. Humanity is blessed.

- Practice the Tao Songs of the Seven Soul Houses, Wai Jiao, and Tao Song Channel. I have introduced and led everyone in many practices in chapter 3.

You can practice with me by listening to the recordings on my YouTube channel, www.youtube.com/zhigangsha. Do these practices every day. The empowerment for your Tao Song cannot be emphasized enough. The transformation for every aspect of your life cannot be emphasized enough.

- Do the Tao Oneness Practice until it becomes automatic as you go about your daily life. Tao is in every aspect of life. Every activity and task can be part of this practice.

- Practice your own Tao Song dedicatedly and persistently. Always remember to put your mind on the first Soul House. The power of your Tao Song will radiate out from your first Soul House and Tao Song Channel in all directions, three hundred sixty degrees. Keep your awareness on your first Soul House at all times.

- Be a Total GOLD servant. Have total gratitude, total obedience, total loyalty, and total devotion to the Divine and Tao. The more you serve, the more power your Tao Song is given by the Divine and Tao.

Select Tao Song Tao Dance Healers will be certified as Tao Song Singers and Tao Dancers. The quality of my Tao Song Singers and Tao Dancers must be very high. To become certified as a Tao Song Singer or Tao Dancer one must perform at a professional level. Each Tao Song Singer must pass the rigorous evaluation of Tao Song Teacher and Tao Song Coach, Helene Ziebarth, and each Tao Dancer must pass the rigorous evaluation of Tao Dance

Teacher, Eli Ho. Finally, one must be approved by Divine and Tao Guidance in order to become certified as a Tao Song Singer or Tao Dancer. This designation is a tremendous honor and gift to humanity.

TAO SONG SINGER

A Tao Song Singer is a new singing professional that the Source asked me to create. I held the first International Soul Song Soul Dance Concert in Neuss (Düsseldorf), Germany, on June 13, 2009. I held the first Tao Song Tao Dance Concert in Berlin, Germany, on June 29, 2011. I held the second Tao Song Tao Dance Concert with newly certified Tao Song Singers and Tao Dancers in Markham, Canada, on September 3, 2011. My certified Tao Song Singers, certified Tao Dancers, and I will continue to offer Tao Song Tao Dance Concerts all over the world. To perform in Tao Song Tao Dance Concerts, singers and dancers must be certified as Tao Song Singers and Tao Dancers, respectively, by the Institute of Tao Song and Tao Dance.

Tao Song Singers receive Source Tao Song Singer Soul Mind Body Transplants. These treasures carry more than three thousand Tao saints from the Source. When Tao Song Singers sing, they offer healing and blessing with Tao frequency and vibration that carry Tao love, forgiveness, compassion, and light.

To become a Tao Song Singer, one may need to receive additional Tao Soul Mind Body Transplants such as Tao Song of Tao Resonance Soul Mind Body Transplants, Tao Song of Tao Overtones Soul Mind Body Transplants, Tao Song of Tao Breathing Channel Soul Mind Body Transplants, Tao Song of Tao Hearing Channel Soul Mind Body Transplants, Tao Song of Tao Presence Soul Mind Body Transplants, and more.

In September 2011 I certified the following initial group of Tao Song Singers at the first Tao Song Tao Dance Healer Certification Retreat in Markham, Ontario, Canada:

Master Marilyn Smith
Master Peter Hudoba
Master Cynthia Marie Deveraux
Master Patricia Smith
Master Sher O'Rourke
Helene Ziebarth
Rick Riecker
Dr. Carol Magda
Ioana Badoi
Marzena Preis
Nancy Elyze Brier
Victoria Swan

I have certified Helene Ziebarth as the first Tao Song Teacher and Tao Song Coach. Helene has been a professional singer, voice teacher, and voice coach for more than forty years. She received a professional music teacher degree and a degree in rhythmical dance in 1969, and received a degree as a voice teacher and classical artistic singer in 1981. Helene has personally taught and coached many world-renowned singers who have sung major leading roles in national opera houses and concert halls internationally. She has been published in several major newspapers in Germany and Norway as a singer and as a voice teacher.

Tao Song Singers will perform in Tao Song Tao Dance Concerts all over the world. Tao Song Tao Dance Concerts are unique. The full name of these concerts is always "Tao Song Tao

Dance Concert for Healing and Rejuvenation" because the Tao saints who accompany the Tao Song Singers and Tao Dancers radiate Tao frequency and vibration with Tao love, forgiveness, compassion, and light. Because of this, the healing and rejuvenation power of a Tao Song Singer (and Tao Dancer) cannot be fully expressed in words.

TAO DANCER

Like Tao Song Singers, Tao Dancers also receive transmissions from the Source. Their Source Tao Dancer Soul Mind Body Transplants carry more than three thousand Tao saints from the Source who accompany the Tao Dancer when he or she offers service. Tao Dancer Soul Mind Body Transplants carry Tao frequency and vibration with Tao love, forgiveness, compassion, and light that can transform health, relationships, finances, intelligence, and more, as well as bring success in every aspect of life. The healing and rejuvenation power of a Tao Dancer cannot be expressed enough.

I certified the following initial group of Tao Dancers at the first Tao Song Tao Dance Healer Certification Retreat on September 1, 2011:

Master Patricia Smith
Eli Ho
Min Lei
Robyn Rice
Henderson Ong
Jason Yoon
Jessica Tobin

Kavita Sarathy

Dr. Linda Brown

I have certified Eli Ho as the first Tao Dance Teacher. She has been a professional dancer and dance teacher for many years, and has received many international awards. Her students have taken part in national and international dance championships, winning the Austrian Open, the European Open, and the World Championship numerous times. Eli won the European Open Choreography Prize in 2006 and was honored with the Josef-Krainer-Heimatpreis, a national hometown award for special achievements in Styria, Austria. Her work has been published in many national and international newspapers and magazines. Since 2010 Eli has been doing Soul Dance and Tao Dance intensively.

In Ramsau, Austria, earlier this year (2011) I met a man who had been blind for nearly ten years. His vision was partially restored after he received my healing. This was an absolute miracle. However, although at times he could see clearly, at other times he could not. He shared with the other retreat participants that when Eli Ho performed a Tao Dance on stage to the music of the *Tao Jing*, he was able to see her Tao Dance very clearly. Eli's Tao Dance helped his vision a lot.

Serve. Serve. Serve.
Practice. Practice. Practice.
More blessings from the Divine and Tao. More blessings from the Divine and Tao. More blessings from the Divine and Tao.
More power in your Tao Song. More power in your Tao Song. More power in your Tao Song.

Serve more. Serve more. Serve more.

Love, peace, and harmony for humanity, Mother Earth, and countless planets, stars, galaxies, and universes. Love, peace, and harmony for humanity, Mother Earth, and countless planets, stars, galaxies, and universes. Love, peace, and harmony for humanity, Mother Earth, and countless planets, stars, galaxies, and universes.

Love you. Love you. Love you.

Thank you. Thank you. Thank you.

Tao Dance

HUMAN BEINGS CAN dance. You may not realize that your beloved soul dances inside your body. Countless saints, healing angels, archangels, lamas, gurus, kahunas, buddhas, bodhisattvas, and all types of spiritual fathers and mothers in soul form also dance in Heaven. Every soul has its dance. Countless souls love to dance.

Dance is movement. Millions of people love to dance. Millions of people love to watch dance. From before recorded history to today, dance has been important for rituals, ceremonies, celebrations, communication, courtship, entertainment, and more.

Dance has been used for social purposes, artistic purposes, spiritual purposes, romantic purposes, storytelling purposes, physical purposes, entertainment purposes, athletic purposes, and more.

Dance is healing. It can move *qi* (vital energy or life force). It can balance soul, heart, mind, and body. It can remove soul mind body blockages.

Dance is service. It can express love, care, compassion, beauty, grace, joy, forgiveness, light, potential, and more. It can stimulate and inspire. It can make oneself and others happier, healthier, wiser, more peaceful, and more.

Countless souls love to dance. Every soul has its dance. Air dances as wind and more. Water dances around obstacles. Many plants dance with the sun and the wind. Bees dance in their hive. Birds dance in flocks. Chimpanzees do a rain dance. Many creatures dance before they mate. Mating itself is dance. The parts of an atom constantly dance. The planets constantly dance in their orbits. Countless souls in countless planets, stars, galaxies, and universes dance. Dance is a universal art and a universal expression.

Tao Dance is unique. It is created by the Source. I am honored to be a servant, vehicle, and channel of Tao to bring Tao Dance to humanity.

What Is Tao Dance?

Tao Dance is Tao-guided dance. Tao Dance is not guided by the mind. A Tao Dancer flows movements guided by Tao, which is the Source. He or she does not follow any choreography, formula, or rules. Tao Dance can go beyond the control of the yin yang world.

Tao Dance carries Tao frequency and vibration, which can transform the frequency and vibration of health, relationships, finances, intelligence, and more, and bring success to every aspect of life.

Tao Dance carries Tao love, which melts all blockages and transforms all life.

Tao Dance carries Tao forgiveness, which brings inner joy and inner peace.

Tao Dance carries Tao compassion, which boosts energy, stamina, vitality, and immunity.

Tao Dance carries Tao light, which heals, prevents sickness, purifies and rejuvenates the soul, heart, mind, and body, prolongs life, and transforms relationships, finances, and every aspect of life.

Significance, Benefits, and Power of Tao Dance

Tao Dance has returned from ancient times to our era, the Soul Light Era that began on August 8, 2003. The unique movements of Tao Dance were last present on Mother Earth during the last Shang Gu ("far ancient") era, which began about forty-five thousand years ago and, like every major era of Mother Earth and the universe, lasted fifteen thousand years.

The Source shared with me that in the last Shang Gu era, the leading healing modality was Tao Song and Tao Dance. In fact, sickness was much less common in that era than it is today. People in that era prevented sickness through Tao Song and Tao Dance. They were very blessed. If one can prevent sickness, then health, vitality, and every aspect of one's life will benefit.

When a Tao Dancer performs Tao Dance, this dance carries Tao frequency and vibration with Tao love, forgiveness, compassion, and light, which could remove soul mind body blockages underlying all sickness in the spiritual, mental, emotional, and physical bodies.

The energy and light that flow through Tao Dance are beyond imagination. You must do Tao Dance yourself to feel and appreciate its power, magnificence, nourishment, and comfort throughout your whole body. When you do Tao Dance, Tao love, forgiveness, compassion, and light radiate from your soul, heart, mind, and body. You could be deeply moved. Others could also be moved and touched. The beauty and attraction of Tao Dance cannot be expressed by words or comprehended by thoughts.

I would like you to experience a Tao Dance by Tao Dance Teacher Eli Ho. Go to my YouTube channel, www.youtube.com/zhigangsha, to watch a video of Eli performing Tao Dance to the Tao Jing, the 75-line "Tao Classic" in my book *Tao I*. Feel the power of Tao Dance. Experience the amazing healing, blessing, nourishment, and beauty of Tao Dance.

As you watch Eli perform Tao Dance of Tao Jing, you could have an "aha!" or "wow!" moment. Her Tao Dance has moved thousands of people all over the world. As a Tao Dancer, she has received more than three thousand Tao saints from the Shang Gu period. As she performs Tao Dance, these Shang Gu saints dance together with her to radiate Tao love, forgiveness, compassion, light, and more. A spiritual being with an advanced Third Eye can see the thousands of Shang Gu saints dancing with Eli.

Every Tao Dancer performs Tao Dance accompanied by thousands of high level saints in soul form. One cannot be appointed as a Tao Dancer through one's own desire and request. A Tao Dancer can receive his or her saint team only through a Tao Order to transmit Source Tao Dancer Soul Mind Body Transplants to the Tao Dancer. I am honored to be the servant, vehicle, and channel of Tao to create Tao Dancers at this time on Mother Earth.

Here is Eli Ho's experience of Tao Dancing in her own words: "Doing Tao Dance brings me to emptiness in my soul, mind, and body. At the same time, I become one with Mother Earth, Heaven, universes, and all of the saints who dance with me. Doing Tao Dance, I feel great joy, love, beauty, forgiveness, compassion, gratitude, humbleness, and light that lift me up above this Earth. I am flying with no boundaries, no restraints. My soul, mind, and body join as one with the music, tempo, and movements. They join as one with time itself—a heavenly feeling beyond words and comprehension."

As you have experienced with Eli Ho's Tao Dance, a single Tao Dancer is powerful. Imagine four, seven, or more Tao Dancers performing Tao Dance together with many thousands of Shang Gu saints supporting the group. A group Tao Dance has power totally beyond comprehension. The significance, benefits, and power of Tao Dance are truly unlimited. This cannot be explained by any words, even words as beautiful and heart-touching as Eli Ho's in the preceding paragraph. One must experience Tao Dance. One must perform Tao Dance. In one sentence:

To experience the power and magnificence of Tao Dance, do it.

Tao Dance Soul Mind Body Transplants—Permanent Treasures to Increase the Power of Your Tao Dance

I am honored to be a servant, vehicle, and channel of Tao to bring permanent Tao Dance Soul Mind Body Transplants to humanity. Tao Dance Soul Mind Body Transplants carry Tao frequency and vibration with Tao love, forgiveness, compassion, and light that can transform all life. As with the Tao Song Soul Mind Body Transplants and any Divine or Tao Soul Mind Body Transplants, they are Heaven coming to Mother Earth.

I will now offer eight sets of Tao Dance Soul Mind Body Transplants as gifts to you.

Prepare. Put the tip of your tongue as close as you can to the roof of your mouth without touching. Put both palms on your lower abdomen. Totally relax. Open your heart and soul. As you read "Transmission!," the stated permanent treasures will come to your soul.

Tao Order: Tao Dance of Tao Love, Peace, and Harmony Soul Mind Body Transplants

Transmission!

Tao Order: Join Tao Dance of Tao Love, Peace, and Harmony Soul Mind Body Transplants as one.

You are extremely blessed.

Tao Order: Tao Dance of Tao Love, Forgiveness, Compassion, and Light Soul Mind Body Transplants

Transmission!

Tao Order: Join Tao Dance of Tao Love, Forgiveness, Compassion, and Light Soul Mind Body Transplants as one.

You are extremely blessed.

Tao Order: Tao Dance of Tao Grace Soul Mind Body Transplants

Transmission!

Tao Order: Join Tao Dance of Tao Grace Soul Mind Body Transplants as one.

You are extremely blessed.

Tao Order: Tao Dance of Tao Inspiration
Soul Mind Body Transplants

Transmission!

Tao Order: Join Tao Dance of Tao Inspiration
Soul Mind Body Transplants as one.

You are extremely blessed.

Tao Order: Tao Dance of Tao Purity
Soul Mind Body Transplants

Transmission!

Tao Order: Join Tao Dance of Tao Purity
Soul Mind Body Transplants as one.

You are extremely blessed.

Tao Order: Tao Dance of Tao Kindness
Soul Mind Body Transplants

Transmission!

Tao Order: Join Tao Dance of Tao Kindness
Soul Mind Body Transplants as one.

You are extremely blessed.

Tao Order: Tao Dance of Tao Sincerity and Honesty Soul Mind Body Transplants

Transmission!

Tao Order: Join Tao Dance of Tao Sincerity and Honesty Soul Mind Body Transplants as one.

You are extremely blessed.

Tao Order: Tao Dance of Tao Inner Joy and Inner Peace Soul Mind Body Transplants

Transmission!

Tao Order: Join Tao Dance of Tao Inner Joy and Inner Peace Soul Mind Body Transplants as one.

You are extremely blessed.

These treasures are priceless permanent treasures from the Source. Now let us apply these treasures to transform all life.

Apply Tao Dance Soul Mind Body Transplants for Healing, Rejuvenation, Longevity, Transformation of Relationships, Finances, Intelligence, and More, and Bringing Success to Every Aspect of Life

Now let me lead you to do Tao Oneness Dancing with Tao Dance Soul Mind Body Transplants for healing, rejuvenation, longevity, transformation of relationships, finances, intelligence, and more, and bringing success to every aspect of life.

Apply the Four Power Techniques.

Body Power. Stand with your feet shoulder-width apart. Put the tip of your tongue as close as you can to the roof of your mouth without touching. Contract your anus slightly for a few seconds.

Soul Power. Say *hello:*

> *Dear Divine,*
> *Dear Tao,*
> *Dear soul mind body of all spiritual fathers and mothers*
>   *in all layers of Heaven and on Mother Earth,*
> *Dear Heaven,*
> *Dear Mother Earth,*
> *Dear countless planets, stars, galaxies, and universes,*
> *Dear San San Jiu Liu Ba Yao Wu,*
> *Dear my Soul Language,*
> *Dear my Tao Song,*
> *Dear Sha's Golden Healing Ball,*
> *Dear Divine Love Peace Harmony Rainbow Light Ball,*
> *Dear my Tao Dance,*
> *Dear Tao Dance Soul Mind Body Transplants of Tao*
>   *Dance of Tao Love, Peace, and Harmony; Tao*
>   *Dance of Tao Love, Forgiveness, Compassion, and*
>   *Light; Tao Dance of Tao Grace; Tao Dance of Tao*
>   *Inspiration; Tao Dance of Tao Purity; Tao Dance*
>   *of Tao Kindness; Tao Dance of Tao Sincerity and*
>   *Honesty; and Tao Dance of Tao Inner Joy and Inner*
>   *Peace,*

Dear all of the people, animals, and environments that
I have ever hurt, harmed, taken advantage of, or
made any kind of mistake against in past lifetimes
and in this lifetime,
I sincerely apologize.
Please forgive me.
Dear all souls who have hurt, harmed, or taken
advantage of me in past lifetimes and in this lifetime,
I forgive you totally.
I love, honor, and appreciate all of you.
Please turn on all my Divine and Tao treasures,
including Tao Dance treasures, for healing and life
transformation.
Please heal my _____ (make a request for healing
of your spiritual body, mental body, emotional
body, or physical body).
Please bless my relationships with _____ (name the
persons for whom you request a relationship
blessing).
Please bless my finances or business _____ (name
your business).
Please bless my intelligence.
Please bless my success.
Please bless _____ (make a request for any part of
your life).
Please increase the power of my Tao Dance so that I
can become a better servant for humanity and
wan ling.
I am extremely grateful.
Thank you. Thank you. Thank you.

Mind Power. Focus your mind on your first Soul House and on any or all of your healing and blessing requests. Visualize bright golden light or bright rainbow light radiating in all of them.

Sound Power. Sing your Tao Song silently or aloud. Singing Tao Song while you dance will add the power of your Tao Song to your Tao Dance.

Start to dance as you focus on your first Soul House. Relax. Connect with Tao and your Tao Dance saint team if you have received one as a certified Tao Dancer. Allow your movement to be guided by Tao. Your Tao Dance movement may be slow and subtle or fast and vigorous. At times your Tao Dance could resemble stretching. Allow the movement, rhythm, and tempo to flow. Whatever way your Tao Dance manifests is totally fine. Everyone's Tao Dance could be unique.

Dance for at least three to five minutes. Dance three to five times per day. The longer you dance and the more you dance, the better. There is no time limit. To self-heal chronic or life-threatening conditions, dance two hours or more per day. You can add up all of the time that you dance throughout the day to total two hours or more.

Tao Dance is Tao Movement on Mother Earth. After you receive the Tao Dance Soul Mind Body Transplants offered in this chapter, your dance automatically transforms to Tao Dance because the Tao Dance treasures carry Tao frequency and vibration with Tao love, forgiveness, compassion, and light. The power of your Tao Dance could transform your health, relationships, finances, intelligence, success, and every aspect of your life beyond your imagination. What you need to do is practice. Apply the Tao treasures and dance.

The Tao Oneness Practice I released in chapter 4 is the most important key for Tao Song and Tao Dance. It is the highest secret and sacred practice for healing, rejuvenation, longevity, immortality, transforming relationships, finances, intelligence, and more, and bringing success to every aspect of life.

Mother Earth is in a transition period. There is much disharmony on Mother Earth in every aspect of life. I have created the Love Peace Harmony Movement[1] with Tao Song and Tao Dance. Imagine thousands or millions of people singing Tao Song or doing Tao Dance. Love, peace, and harmony would be in every heart, every family, every city, every country, and more on Mother Earth.

Sing Tao Song. Sing Tao Song. Sing Tao Song.

Do Tao Dance. Do Tao Dance. Do Tao Dance.

Heal. Heal. Heal.

Rejuvenate. Rejuvenate. Rejuvenate.

Enlighten. Enlighten. Enlighten.

Transform. Transform. Transform.

Prolong life. Prolong life. Prolong life.

Immortality. Immortality. Immortality.

---

1. The Love Peace Harmony Movement was created on December 11, 2010. See www.Love PeaceHarmonyMovement.com and my book *Divine Love Peace Harmony Rainbow Light Ball* (Heaven's Library, 2010).

I love my heart and soul

I love all humanity

Join hearts and souls together

Love, peace and harmony

Love, peace and harmony

Important Principles for Your Tao Dance

To be a powerful Tao Dancer, you need to master the following:

- When you do a Tao Dance, go into the hero condition to shine Tao love, forgiveness, compassion, light, beauty, grace, joy, and more. You are a Tao temple. You are Tao presence.
- Alternate yin and yang in your Tao Dance. Yin yang balance is vital for every aspect of life. When you dance, dance slowly at times and dance quickly at other times.
- When you do a Tao Dance, you could stop and hold a beautiful position for two to three seconds before you start to move again. This is named the space of Tao Dance. Space is important for healing, rejuvenation, and transformation of every aspect of life.
- When you do a Tao Dance, let Tao guide you how to move. Be sure not to use your mind to do Tao Dance.
- Develop your Tao Dance Channel. The Tao Dance Channel is the Tao Song Channel together with the

four extremities. The Tao Dance Channel is a Tao temple. Your Tao Dance frequency and vibration radiate out from your Tao Dance Channel in every direction, three hundred sixty degrees.

- Always put your mind on the first Soul House. Never put your mind in any other place. If you cannot dance your Tao Dance well, you have soul mind body blockages in your Tao Dance Channel. You have to practice Tao Dance to remove soul mind body blockages in your Tao Dance Channel. Dance again and again to remove the blockages gradually. With time and practice, they could be completely removed.

- Dance Tao Dance slowly. There is no need to rush. For the beginner, slower is faster. When you dance slowly, you can better feel the love, forgiveness, compassion, light, grace, beauty, joy, sincerity, honesty, kindness, purity, integrity, generosity, and more. Dance slowly at first. Then Tao may sometimes guide you to dance faster.

- Before you begin dancing, remember to say *hello* to the Divine, Tao, Mother Earth, and countless planets, stars, galaxies, and universes. You are a universal servant. You are serving humanity and wan ling, as well as countless planets, stars, galaxies, and universes. Be honored to be a servant. When you are a Total GOLD servant ("G" is gratitude, "O" is obedience, "L" is loyalty, "D" is devotion to the Divine and Tao), you can bring out all kinds of divine and Tao qualities through your Tao Dance.

- Also say *hello* to every system, organ, and cell of your body to show your gratitude before you do Tao Dance. Say *I am so honored to do Tao Dance. Please help me by coordinating to bring out the best divine and Tao qualities to be a great servant. Thank you.*
- When you dance Tao Dance, you are doing service Xiu Lian. Every moment you are doing Tao Dance, you are transforming every aspect of your life, including health, relationships, finances, intelligence, and more. At the same time, you are serving the transformation of humanity and wan ling. You are bringing success to every aspect of your life, fulfilling your physical journey and your soul journey.

Tao Song and Tao Dance are miraculous and profound. Tao Song Singers and Tao Dancers are extremely blessed. You are blessed. Humanity is blessed. Wan ling is blessed.

Conclusion

*T*AO IS THE Source and Creator.
Tao Song is song from the Source.
Tao Dance is dance from the Source.
Tao Song is Tao yin. Tao Dance is Tao yang.
Tao Oneness Practice is created and released.
Tao is The Way of all life.
Tao is the universal principles and laws.

Tao Song and Tao Dance carry Tao frequency, vibration, and power that transform health, relationships, finances, intelligence, and more, and bring success to every aspect of life.

Tao Song and Tao Dance carry Tao love that melts all blockages for all life.

Tao Song and Tao Dance carry Tao forgiveness that brings inner joy and inner peace to all life.

Tao Song and Tao Dance carry Tao compassion that boosts energy, stamina, vitality, and immunity for all life.

Tao Song and Tao Dance carry Tao light that heals, prevents sickness, purifies and rejuvenates soul, heart, mind, and body, and transforms relationships, finances, and every aspect of all life.

Tao Song and Tao Dance are Tao healing for humanity and wan ling.

Tao Song and Tao Dance are sacred treasures for rejuvenation.

Tao Song and Tao Dance are powerful gifts to transform relationships, finances, intelligence, and every aspect of life.

Tao Song and Tao Dance are the key for longevity.

Tao Song and Tao Dance are the secret pathway to immortality.

Sacred and secret Shang Gu wisdom, treasures, and saints of Tao Song and Tao Dance have been released to humanity and wan ling.

Humanity needs Tao Song and Tao Dance.

Mother Earth needs Tao Song and Tao Dance.

Countless planets, stars, galaxies, and universes need Tao Song and Tao Dance.

Tao Song and Tao Dance join yin and yang as one.

To join yin and yang as one is to return to Tao.

Tao. Tao. Tao.

Tao transforms a human's quality.

Tao transforms every aspect of life.

New evolution of humanity has begun.

New scientific development is coming.

Tao leads us to pass through this difficult time on Mother Earth.

Tao Song. Tao Song. Tao Song.

Tao Dance. Tao Dance. Tao Dance.

Bring love, peace, and harmony.

Bring love, peace, and harmony.

Bring love, peace, and harmony.

Love you. Love you. Love you.

Thank you. Thank you. Thank you.

Acknowledgments

$\mathcal{I}$ CANNOT THANK TAO enough.

I cannot thank the Divine enough.

I cannot thank all of my spiritual fathers and mothers on Mother Earth enough, including Dr. and Master Zhi Chen Guo, Professor Da Jun Liu, Dr. and Master De Hua Liu, and my tai chi, qi gong, kung fu, and *I Ching* masters, as well as the masters who prefer not to have their names released.

I cannot thank my spiritual fathers and mothers in Heaven enough, including Guan Yin and her lineage, Peng Zu and his lineage, Pu Ti Lao Zu, Shi Jia Mo Ni Fo, A Mi Tuo Fo, Medicine Buddha, Maitreya, Jesus, Mary, and many other spiritual fathers and mothers from all realms of Heaven.

I cannot thank my physical father and mother enough.

I cannot thank my Worldwide Representatives enough. My twenty-three Worldwide Representatives at this time are Marilyn Smith, Francisco Quintero, Allan Chuck, Peter Hudoba, Cynthia Marie Deveraux, David Lusch, Petra Herz, Patricia Smith, Lynne Nusyna, Peggy Werner, Roger Givens, Maria Sunukjian,

Hannah Stevens, Shu Chin Hsu, Trevor Allen, Ximena Gavino, Sher O'Rourke, Elaine Ward, Sabine Parlow, Lynda Chaplin, Pam Uyeunten, G. K. Khoe, and Gal Mor.

I cannot thank all layers of Soul Healing Teachers and Healers enough.

I cannot thank Tao Song Tao Dance Healers enough.

I cannot thank Tao Song Singers and Tao Dancers enough.

I cannot thank thousands of Shang Gu saints who accompany Tao Song Singers and Tao Dancers enough.

I cannot thank Tao Song Teacher and Voice Coach Helene Ziebarth and Tao Dance Teacher Eli Ho enough.

I cannot thank my thousands of students all over the world enough.

I cannot thank the hundreds of thousands of readers of my books enough.

I cannot thank all humanity enough for giving me the opportunity to serve.

I cannot thank wan ling enough for giving me the opportunity to serve.

I cannot thank my copublisher, Judith Curr of Atria Books, enough. She and her team and colleagues at Simon & Schuster have offered great support to my Soul Power Series. I thank my editor, Johanna Castillo. I thank Chris Lloreda, Amy Tannenbaum, Lisa Keim, Isolde Sauer, Tom Spain, Dan Vidra, and others whom I may have omitted or whose names I do not know.

I cannot thank my chief editor, Allan Chuck, who is one of my Worldwide Representatives, enough for his great editing and for all of his great contributions to the mission. He has edited all of my books.

I cannot thank my senior editor, Elaine Ward, who is also

one of my Worldwide Representatives, enough for her great editing and for all of her great contributions to the mission.

I cannot thank my assistant, Cynthia Marie Deveraux, who is also one of my Worldwide Representatives, enough for transcribing the original manuscript and for her inspiration for this book, as well as for her great contributions to the mission.

I cannot thank Lynda Chaplin, who is also one of my Worldwide Representatives, enough for the figures in this book and for her great contributions to the mission.

I cannot thank all of my family enough for their unconditional love and support.

Love you. Love you. Love you.

Thank you. Thank you. Thank you.

May this book serve humanity, Mother Earth, and wan ling and help them pass through this difficult period in history.

May this book serve the Soul Light Era to bring love, peace, and harmony to humanity, Mother Earth, and countless planets, stars, galaxies, and universes.

I am extremely honored to be a servant of humanity and wan ling.

I love my heart and soul
I love all humanity
Join hearts and souls together
Love, peace and harmony
Love, peace and harmony

A Special Gift

PRACTICE IS NECESSARY to transform any aspect of your life, including health, relationships, finances, intelligence, and more. Throughout this book, I ask you to stop reading in order to spend three minutes, five minutes, or more doing a practice. Without practice, you cannot receive benefits. Practice each line of sacred Tao Song mantras seriously.

The Tao Song mantras are the most sacred, powerful, and profound practices. Tao Song mantras are simple, powerful tools for self-clearing soul mind body blockages for healing, prevention of sickness, rejuvenation, and longevity, as well as for transforming relationships, finances, and every aspect of life. Tao Song mantras are key to your Tao journey, which is your immortality journey.

As a special gift to you, dear reader, I have included in some printings and editions of this book a DVD with video recordings of me singing the key Tao Song mantras that are the subject of this book. Practice with me to experience their benefits. Also included on the DVD is a video of Eli Ho, Tao Dance Teacher, performing Tao Dance to the Tao Jing, seventy-five sacred phrases that are the subject of my *Tao I* book. Experience the beauty and power of Tao Dance. If this copy of the book does not include a DVD, you can find all of these video recordings on my YouTube channel, www.YouTube.com/zhigangsha.

Every moment you are singing Tao Song or dancing Tao Dance, you are transforming every aspect of your life, including health, relationships, finances, intelligence, and more. You are also serving humanity and all souls. You are fulfilling your physical journey and your soul journey.

Remember the teaching:

> *Tao Song and Tao Dance carry Tao frequency and vibration, which can transform the frequency and vibration of your health, relationships, finances, intelligence, and more.*
> *Tao Song and Tao Dance carry Tao love, which melts all blockages and transforms all life.*
> *Tao Song and Tao Dance carry Tao forgiveness, which brings inner joy and inner peace.*
> *Tao Song and Tao Dance carry Tao compassion, which boosts energy, stamina, vitality, and immunity.*
> *Tao Song and Tao Dance carry Tao light, which heals, prevents sickness, purifies and rejuvenates soul, heart, mind, and body, and transforms relationships, finances, and every aspect of life.*

Apply the Four Power Techniques together with the Tao Soul Mind Body Transplants you have received by reading the appropriate sections in this book. Watch and practice with me using the DVD or my YouTube videos again and again.

I am honored to be a servant of you, humanity, the Divine, and Tao.

Track 1   Sacred Tao Song Mantras for the First Soul House
Track 2   Sacred Tao Song Mantras for the Second Soul House
Track 3   Sacred Tao Song Mantras for the Third Soul House
Track 4   Sacred Tao Song Mantras for the Fourth Soul House
Track 5   Sacred Tao Song Mantras for the Fifth Soul House
Track 6   Sacred Tao Song Mantras for the Sixth Soul House
Track 7   Sacred Tao Song Mantras for the Seventh Soul House
Track 8   Sacred Tao Song Mantras for the Wai Jiao
Track 9   Sacred Tao Song Mantras for the Tao Song Channel for Healing
Track 10   Sacred Tao Song Mantras for the Tao Song Channel for Rejuvenation and Longevity
Track 11   Tao Dance to *Tao Jing* by Eli Ho

You are extremely blessed. Humanity is extremely blessed. We are all extremely blessed.

Practice.
Practice.
Practice.

Benefit.
Benefit.
Benefit.

I wish you great success.

Thank you. Thank you. Thank you.

Index

315

Other Books of the Soul Power Series

Soul Wisdom: Practical Soul Treasures to Transform Your Life (revised trade paperback edition). Heaven's Library/Atria Books, 2008. Also available as an audiobook.

The first book of the Soul Power Series is an important foundation for the entire series. It teaches five of the most important practical soul treasures: Soul Language, Soul Song, Soul Tapping, Soul Movement, and Soul Dance.

Soul Language empowers you to communicate with the Soul World, including your own soul, all spiritual fathers and mothers, souls of nature, and more, to access direct guidance.

Soul Song empowers you to sing your own Soul Song, the song of your Soul Language. Soul Song carries soul frequency and vibration for soul healing, soul rejuvenation, soul prolongation of life, and soul transformation of every aspect of life.

Soul Tapping empowers you to do advanced soul healing for yourself and others effectively and quickly.

Soul Movement empowers you to learn ancient secret wisdom and practices to rejuvenate your soul, mind, and body and prolong life.

Soul Dance empowers you to balance your soul, mind, and body for healing, rejuvenation, and prolonging life.

This book offers two permanent Divine Soul Transplants as gifts to every reader. Includes bonus Soul Song for Healing and Rejuvenation of Brain and Spinal Column MP3 download.

Soul Communication: Opening Your Spiritual Channels for Success and Fulfillment (revised trade paperback edition). Heaven's Library/Atria Books, 2008. Also available as an audiobook.

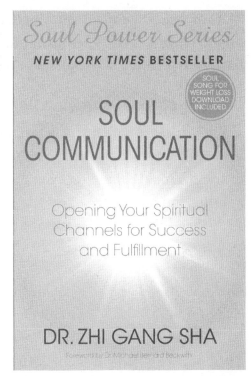

The second book in the Soul Power Series empowers you to open four major spiritual channels: Soul Language Channel, Direct Soul Communication Channel, Third Eye Channel, and Direct Knowing Channel.

The Soul Language Channel empowers you to apply Soul Language to communicate with the Soul World, including your own soul, all kinds of spiritual fathers and mothers, nature, and the Divine. Then, receive teaching, healing, rejuvenation, and prolongation of life from the Soul World.

The Direct Soul Communication Channel empowers you to converse directly with the Divine and the entire Soul World. Receive guidance for every aspect of life directly from the Divine.

The Third Eye Channel empowers you to receive guidance and teaching through spiritual images. It teaches you how to develop the Third Eye and key principles for interpreting Third Eye images.

The Direct Knowing Channel empowers you to gain the highest spiritual abilities. If your heart melds with the Divine's heart or your soul melds with the Divine's soul completely, you do not need to ask for spiritual guidance. You know the truth because your heart and soul are in complete alignment with the Divine.

This book also offers two permanent Divine Soul Transplants as gifts to every reader. Includes bonus Soul Song for Weight Loss MP3 download.

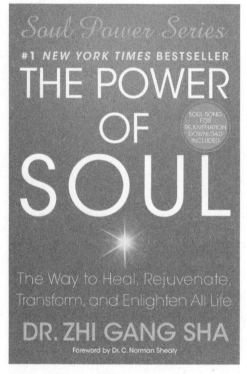

The Power of Soul: The Way to Heal, Rejuvenate, Transform, and Enlighten All Life. Heaven's Library/Atria Books, 2009. Also available as an audiobook and a trade paperback.

The third book of the Soul Power Series is the flagship of the entire series.

The Power of Soul empowers you to understand, develop, and apply the power of soul for healing, prevention of sickness, rejuvenation, transformation of every aspect of life (including relationships and finances), and soul enlightenment. It also empowers you to develop soul wisdom and soul intelligence, and to apply Soul Orders for healing and transformation of every aspect of life.

This book teaches Divine Soul Downloads (specifically, Divine Soul Transplants) for the first time in history. A Divine

Soul Transplant is the divine way to heal, rejuvenate, and transform every aspect of a human being's life and the life of all universes.

This book offers eleven permanent Divine Soul Transplants as a gift to every reader. Includes bonus Soul Song for Rejuvenation MP3 download.

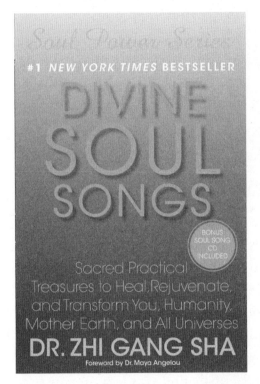

Divine Soul Songs: Sacred Practical Treasures to Heal, Rejuvenate, and Transform You, Humanity, Mother Earth, and All Universes. Heaven's Library/Atria Books, 2009. Also available as an audiobook and a trade paperback.

The fourth book in the Soul Power Series empowers you to apply Divine Soul Songs for healing, rejuvenation, and transformation of every aspect of life, including relationships and finances.

Divine Soul Songs carry divine frequency and vibration, with divine love, forgiveness, compassion, and light, that can transform the frequency and vibration of all aspects of life.

This book offers nineteen Divine Soul Transplants as gifts to every reader. Includes bonus Soul Songs CD with seven samples of the Divine Soul Songs that are the main subjects of this book.

Divine Soul Mind Body Healing and Transmission System: The Divine Way to Heal You, Humanity, Mother Earth, and All Universes. Heaven's Library/Atria Books, 2009. Also available as an audiobook.

The fifth book in the Soul Power Series empowers you to receive Divine Soul Mind Body Transplants and to apply Divine Soul Mind Body Transplants to heal and transform soul, mind, and body. Divine Soul Mind Body Transplants carry divine love, forgiveness, compassion, and light. Divine love melts all blockages and transforms all life. Divine forgiveness brings inner peace and inner joy. Divine compassion boosts energy, stamina, vitality, and immunity. Divine light heals, rejuvenates, and transforms every aspect of life, including relationships and finances.

This book offers forty-six permanent divine treasures, including Divine Soul Transplants, Divine Mind Transplants, and Divine Body Transplants, as a gift to every reader. Includes bonus Soul Symphony of Yin Yang excerpt (MP3 download).

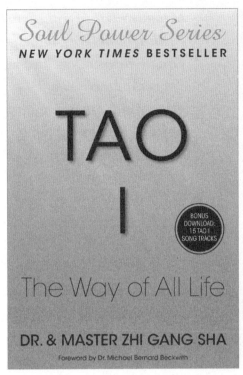

Tao I: The Way of All Life. Heaven's Library/Atria Books, 2010. Also available as an audiobook.

The sixth book of the Soul Power Series shares the essence of ancient Tao teaching and reveals the Tao Jing, a new "Tao Classic" for the twenty-first century. These new divine teachings reveal how Tao is in every aspect of life, from waking to sleeping to eating and more. This book shares advanced soul wisdom and practical approaches for *reaching* Tao. The new sacred teaching in this book is extremely simple, practical, and profound.

Studying and practicing Tao has great benefits, including the ability to heal yourself and others, as well as humanity, Mother Earth, and all universes; return from old age to the health and purity of a baby; prolong life; and more.

This book offers thirty permanent Divine Soul Mind Body Transplants as gifts to every reader and a fifteen-track CD with Master Sha singing the entire Tao Jing and many other major practice mantras.

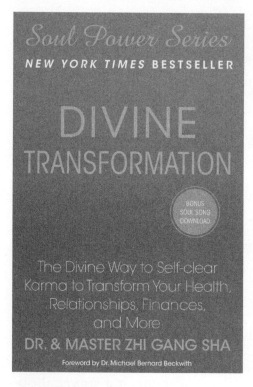

Divine Transformation: The Divine Way to Self-clear Karma to Transform Your Health, Relationships, Finances, and More. Heaven's Library/ Atria Books, 2010. Also available as an audiobook.

The teachings and practical techniques of this seventh book of the Soul Power Series focus on karma and forgiveness. Bad karma is the root cause of any and every major blockage or challenge that you, humanity, and Mother Earth face. True healing is to clear your bad karma, which is to repay or be forgiven your spiritual debts to the souls you or your ancestors have hurt or harmed in all your lifetimes. Forgiveness is a golden key to true healing. Divine self-clearing of bad karma applies divine forgiveness to heal and transform every aspect of your life.

Clear your karma to transform your soul first; then transformation of every aspect of your life will follow.

This book offers thirty rainbow frequency Divine Soul Mind Body Transplants as gifts to every reader and includes four audio tracks of major Divine Soul Songs and practice chants.

Tao II: The Way of Healing, Rejuvenation, Longevity, and Immortality. Heaven's Library/Atria Books, 2010. Also available as an audiobook.

The eighth book of the Soul Power Series is the successor to *Tao I: The Way of All Life. Tao II* reveals the highest secrets and most powerful practical techniques for the Tao journey, which includes one's physical journey and one's spiritual journey.

Tao II gives you the sacred keys for your whole life's practice and shares the Immortal Tao, two hundred and twenty sacred phrases that include not only profound sacred wisdom but also additional simple and practical techniques. *Tao II* explains how to reach *fan lao huan tong*, which means to *transform old age to the health and purity of the baby state*; to prolong life; and to reach immortality to be a better servant for humanity, Mother Earth, and all universes.

This book offers twenty-one Tao Soul Mind Body Transplants as gifts to every reader and includes two audio tracks of major Tao chants for healing, rejuvenation, longevity, and immortality.

"This inspiring documentary has masterfully captured the vital healing work and global mission of Dr. Guo and Dr. Sha."
– Dr. Michael Bernard Beckwith – Founder, Agape International Spiritual Center

This film reveals profound soul secrets and shares the wisdom, knowledge, and practices of Dr. Guo's Body Space Medicine and Dr. Sha's Soul Mind Body Medicine. Millions of people in China have studied with Dr. Guo, who is Dr. Sha's most beloved spiritual father. Dr. Guo is "the master who can cure the incurable." After Dr. Sha heals her ailing father, American filmmaker Sande Zeig accompanies Dr. Sha to China to visit his mentor. At Dr. Guo's clinic, she captures first-ever footage of breakthrough healing practices involving special herbs, unique fire massage, and revolutionary self-healing techniques. These two Soul Masters have a special bond. They are united in their commitment to serve others. As you see them heal and teach, your heart and soul will be touched. Experience the delight, inspiration, wonder, and gratitude that *Soul Masters* brings.

In English and Mandarin with English subtitles. Also in French, German, Japanese, Mandarin and Spanish.

PPV Video Streaming and DVD at
www.soulmastersmovie.com

www.DrSha.com
www.HeavensLibrary.com
HeavensLibrary@DrSha.com
1.888.3396815